THE STATES AND THE NATION SERIES, of which this volume is a part, is designed to assist the American people in a serious look at the ideals they have espoused and the experiences they have undergone in the history of the nation. The content of every volume represents the scholarship, experience, and opinions of its author. The costs of writing and editing were met mainly by grants from the National Endowment for the Humanities, a federal agency. The project was administered by the American Association for State and Local History, a nonprofit learned society, working with an Editorial Board of distinguished editors, authors, and historians, whose names are listed below.

South Carolina

A Bicentennial History

Louis B. Wright

W. W. Norton & Company, Inc.
New York

American Association for State and Local History
Nashville

Published simultaneously in Canada
by George J. McLeod Limited, Toronto

Library of Congress Cataloguing-in-Publication Data

Wright, Louis Booker, 1899–
South Carolina, a bicentennial history.

(States and the Nation)
Bibliography: p.
Includes index.
1. South Carolina—History. I. Title.
II. Series.
F269.W65   975.7   75–19031
ISBN 0   393   05560   4
Printed in the United States of America

1 2 3 4 5 6 7 8 9

For my wife Frances
who has put up with me
for these fifty years

Contents

Illustrations

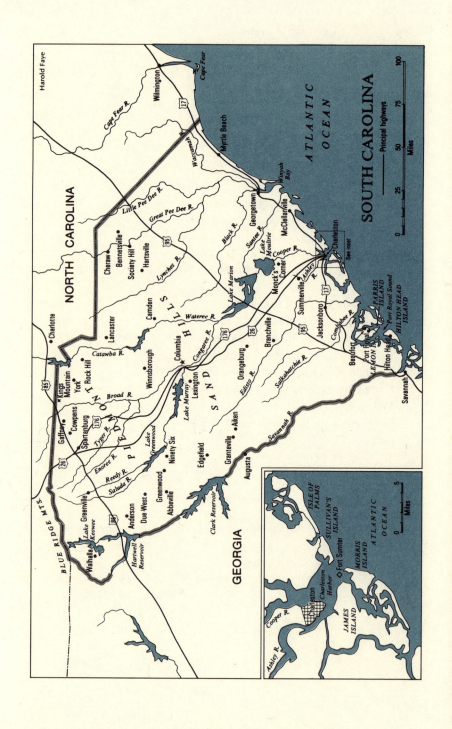

Harold Faye

NORTH CAROLINA

ATLANTIC OCEAN

SOUTH CAROLINA
Principal highways

Miles
0   25   50   75   100

Wilmington
Cape Fear R.
Cape Fear
Myrtle Beach
Waccamaw R.
Little Pee Dee R.
Great Pee Dee R.
Cheraw
Bennettsville
Society Hill
Hartsville
Lynches R.
Black R.
Winyah Bay
Georgetown
McClellanville
Santee R.
Lake Moultrie
Cooper R.
Monck's Corner
Summerville
Jacksonboro
Cooper R.
See inset
Charleston

Charlotte
Lancaster
Camden
Wateree R.
Lake Marion
Congaree R.
Columbia
Winnsborough
Catawba R.
Broad R.
Kings Mountain
York
Rock Hill
Gaffney
Cowpens
Spartanburg
Tyger R.
Enoree R.
Reedy R.
Saluda R.
Lake Murray
Lake Greenwood
Ninety Six
Lexington
Orangeburg
Edisto R.
Aiken
Branchville
Salkahatchie R.
Savannah R.
Edgefield
Graniteville
Augusta
Greenwood
Abbeville
Due West
Anderson
Clark Reservoir
Hartwell Reservoir
Lake Keowee
Walhalla
Greenville
Lake Hartwell

BLUE RIDGE MTS.

P I E D M O N T

S A N D   H I L L S

GEORGIA

Beaufort
Port Royal
LEMON I.
Hilton Head
PARRIS ISLAND
Port Royal Sound
HILTON HEAD ISLAND
Savannah
Combahee R.
Ashley R.

ISLE OF PALMS
SULLIVAN'S ISLAND
Fort Sumter
ATLANTIC OCEAN
Miles
0   5
MORRIS ISLAND
Charleston Harbor
Charleston
Cooper R.
Ashley R.
JAMES ISLAND

Invitation to the Reader

IN 1807, former President John Adams argued that a complete history of the American Revolution could not be written until the history of change in each state was known, because the principles of the Revolution were as various as the states that went through it. Two hundred years after the Declaration of Independence, the American nation has spread over a continent and beyond. The states have grown in number from thirteen to fifty. And democratic principles have been interpreted differently in every one of them.

We therefore invite you to consider that the history of your state may have more to do with the bicentennial review of the American Revolution than does the story of Bunker Hill or Valley Forge. The Revolution has continued as Americans extended liberty and democracy over a vast territory. John Adams was right: the states are part of that story, and the story is incomplete without an account of their diversity.

The Declaration of Independence stressed life, liberty, and the pursuit of happiness; accordingly, it shattered the notion of holding new territories in the subordinate status of colonies. The Northwest Ordinance of 1787 set forth a procedure for new states to enter the Union on an equal footing with the old. The Federal Constitution shortly confirmed this novel means of building a nation out of equal states. The step-by-step process through which territories have achieved self-government and national representation is among the most important of the Founding Fathers' legacies.

The method of state-making reconciled the ancient conflict between liberty and empire, resulting in what Thomas Jefferson called an empire for liberty. The system has worked and remains unaltered, despite enormous changes that have taken

ix

place in the nation. The country's extent and variety now surpass anything the patriots of '76 could likely have imagined. The United States has changed from an agrarian republic into a highly industrial and urban democracy, from a fledgling nation into a major world power. As Oliver Wendell Holmes remarked in 1920, the creators of the nation could not have seen completely how it and its constitution and its states would develop. Any meaningful review in the bicentennial era must consider what the country has become, as well as what it was.

The new nation of equal states took as its motto *E Pluribus Unum*—"out of many, one." But just as many peoples have become Americans without complete loss of ethnic and cultural identities, so have the states retained differences of character. Some have been superficial, expressed in stereotyped images— big, boastful Texas, "sophisticated" New York, "hillbilly" Arkansas. Other differences have been more real, sometimes instructively, sometimes amusingly; democracy has embraced Huey Long's Louisiana, bilingual New Mexico, unicameral Nebraska, and a Texas that once taxed fortunetellers and spawned politicians called "Woodpecker Republicans" and "Skunk Democrats." Some differences have been profound, as when South Carolina secessionists led other states out of the Union in opposition to abolitionists in Massachusetts and Ohio. The result was a bitter Civil War.

The Revolution's first shots may have sounded in Lexington and Concord; but fights over what democracy should mean and who should have independence have erupted from Pennsylvania's Gettysburg to the "Bleeding Kansas" of John Brown, from the Alamo in Texas to the Indian battles at Montana's Little Bighorn. Utah Mormons have known the strain of isolation; Hawaiians at Pearl Harbor, the terror of attack; Georgians during Sherman's march, the sadness of defeat and devastation. Each state's experience differs instructively; each adds understanding to the whole.

The purpose of this series of books is to make that kind of understanding accessible, in a way that will last in value far beyond the bicentennial fireworks. The series offers a volume on every state, plus the District of Columbia—fifty-one, in all.

Each book contains, besides the text, a view of the state through eyes other than the author's—a "photographer's essay," in which a skilled photographer presents his own personal perceptions of the state's contemporary flavor.

We have asked authors not for comprehensive chronicles, nor for research monographs or new data for scholars. Bibliographies and footnotes are minimal. We have asked each author for a summing up—interpretive, sensitive, thoughtful, individual, even personal—of what seems significant about his or her state's history. What distinguishes it? What has mattered about it, to its own people and to the rest of the nation? What has it come to now?

To interpret the states in all their variety, we have sought a variety of backgrounds in authors themselves and have encouraged variety in the approaches they take. They have in common only these things: historical knowledge, writing skill, and strong personal feelings about a particular state. Each has wide latitude for the use of the short space. And if each succeeds, it will be by offering you, in your capacity as a *citizen* of a state *and* of a nation, stimulating insights to test against your own.

James Morton Smith
General Editor

Preface

*T*HE history of South Carolina has been often told by competent historians. Works by David Duncan Wallace, Lewis P. Jones, M. E. Sirmans, E. McPherson Lander, and others provide a wealth of detail that needs no repetition. But the general reader may not have time or inclination for so much instruction. My intention has been to provide a brief description of the development of South Carolina from the earliest times to the present, with such interpretation as seemed to me necessary to explain how we South Carolinians came to be the people we are. I have emphasized the early rather than the later periods, for our origins helped to determine our characteristics as a people. Most of our patterns of behavior and our regional differences developed in the colonial period.

Within the limits prescribed for this volume, it has been impossible even to enumerate many stirring events described in more detailed histories, or to mention all of the heroes—and the villains—who had a part in events of the past. Fortunately, local history has been the preoccupation of scores of writers in the state, and the names of few if any doughty Carolinians in any period have escaped the genealogists. During the Tricentennial celebrations in 1970 the records of the past were ransacked to illuminate the story of South Carolina's development from colony to state. One has only to thumb through Professor Lewis Jones's *Books and Articles on South Carolina History* [1] to see how complete has been the coverage. The magazine, *The Sandlapper,* has been a useful and entertaining medium for the dissemination of information about local history.

---

1. Lewis P. Jones, *Books and Articles on South Carolina History,* Tricentennial Booklet no. 8 (Columbia, S.C.: University of South Carolina Press, 1970).

Some patriotic South Carolinians may feel that I have dwelt overmuch on our shortcomings and have not sufficiently sung our praises. But our virtues ought to be evident without self-praise. We have never been a people to hide our light under a bushel or to shrink from letting the world know of our glories. It has appeared to me more seemly—and more useful—to look at ourselves realistically and to analyze our weaknesses as well as our strengths. If this be heresy, let patriots make the most of it.

I am under great debt to all historians who have preceded me. To my old teacher, Dr. David Duncan Wallace, I owe my initial interest in the history of the state, and I have depended upon his magnificent work for a vast deal of factual information. To later historians my debt is also great, and I have tried to indicate my obligation in relevant places in the text. Any errors and mistakes of interpretation are my own.

I especially appreciate the constant help and encouragement of Mr. Gerald George, Managing Editor of the Bicentennial State Histories, during the preparation of this manuscript. I wish also to express my thanks to Miss Louise Watson and Miss Margaret Watson for valuable suggestions based on their great knowledge of local history. My brother, Major Thomas F. Wright, helped me to renew my acquaintance with many out-of-the-way spots in the Up Country, as did my boyhood friend, Dr. Joseph G. Jenkins. My sister, Miss Margaret Wright, has been diligent in searching out colorful details, and I regret that space does not permit the use of many of them. My greatest debt is to Mrs. Elaine W. Fowler, who has assisted me throughout, in every chapter, in helping to rediscover South Carolina, in typing a tedious manuscript, and in offering useful critical advice.

LOUIS B. WRIGHT

October 9, 1974

South Carolina

Introduction

A Lingering Fragrance

AS a boy brought up in a small town of the South Carolina Up Country in the first two decades of the present century, I contemplated the great world and wondered if I would ever stray beyond the mountains at Caesar's Head or cross the sea from Charleston. Indeed, a journey from my home town of Greenwood to Columbia, the capital, to attend the state fair was an adventure to be remembered and treasured in retrospect. By the time I was eighteen I had had a glimpse of a wider world, for, thanks to World War I, I had been sent to an officers' training camp at Plattsburgh, New York, and during a brief leave had tramped, wide-eyed, over much of the city of New York. Other than that I remained a provincial with an ingrained conviction that South Carolina, or at least a part of it, was especially favored of God. I had no intention of living anywhere else.

Fate, however, decreed otherwise, and I was to wander far before I had time to devote much attention to my native state. For three years after graduation from Wofford College, Spartanburg, it is true, I worked on a South Carolina newspaper, the *Greenwood Index-Journal,* a highly instructive period in my life; but after 1923 I made only sporadic visits to my family in South Carolina. Destiny carried me to every state in the union, to most of Europe, from England to Russia to what used to be called Asia Minor, and to South America—even to the Galapagos Islands.

Always, however, there was the memory of a region of red

3

hills and piney woods; of springtime with green fields, snowy dogwoods, and the soft red of woodbine; of autumn days when damp hickory leaves, kicked up as we hunted for scaly-bark and pig-nuts, gave off a fragrance like spice; of wild grapevines laden with purple muscadines, sweet, juicy, and pungent. It was a good land, filled with happy memories for me, and someday I hoped to return.

So it was a particular pleasure to be asked by the American Association for State and Local History to write a historical account of my native state. I was instructed to give my personal interpretation of the development through more than three centuries of this region, with reference to the role of South Carolina in our national history and to the impact of the nation on South Carolina.

Actually, I had been waiting for more than fifty years for this opportunity, for the chance to answer an essay written by Ludwig Lewisohn and published in *The Nation* on July 12, 1922. Lewisohn called his piece "South Carolina: A Lingering Fragrance." It was supercilious, arrogant, and derogatory—so irritating that for more than half a century I remembered it with distaste. South Carolina had a lingering fragrance for me, but it did not carry the connotation conveyed by Lewisohn's article. I was not the only one irritated by the essay. August Kohn, correspondent at the time for the *Charleston News and Courier,* told me with an appropriate gesture of holding his nose: "There is a fragrance about Lewisohn—the fragrance of a rotten egg."

The repugnant essay began: "A tiny tongue of land extending from Broad Street in Charleston to the beautiful bay formed by the confluence of the Ashley and the Cooper rivers is all of South Carolina that has counted in the past; the memories that cling to the little peninsula are all that count today. More than thirty years have passed since Ben Tillman led the revolt of the agrarians, the 'poor white trash,' and 'wool-hats' of the 'upper country' against the old Charleston aristocracy. He won." And Lewisohn continued in this vein to damn the whole Up Country as a land of ignorant barbarians—red-necks and hoodlums—whose very religion, a strict Protestantism, was a stench in the nostrils of cultivated men. The author of this diatribe, while purporting to praise the ancient cultivation of Charlestonians, contrived also to insult their descendants. He concluded: "A race lived here [Charleston] that loved dignity without ostentation, books and wine and human distinction. Its sins, which were many, fade into the past. They were always less vulgar and ugly than the sins of those who have come after."[1]

Lewisohn's descriptions of both Charleston and the Up Country were libels. As an Up-Countryman myself, I was particularly incensed. Although our shortcomings were manifold, and many of us may have drunk corn liquor from a jug rather than wine from a proper glass, we were neither barbarians nor red-necks—not all of us, at any rate. We did not relish an expatriate ingrate, just because he had made some little literary success in New York, looking down his nose and calling us names.

So after these many years, I hope to answer Lewisohn. This volume will not be a conventional history, for it would be hard to add anything new to the excellent works already in print. The Tricentennial Celebration in 1970 also produced an outpouring of local history and topical narratives. In the space allotted me, I cannot even make a synthesis of all the material available. I shall endeavor, instead, to be selective and report on themes from the first settlement to the present day that seem to me to need emphasis, themes in our early history that may have foreshadowed later events or have had significance in the larger context of our national history. Sometimes I may take the liberty of dwelling on minor affairs when they illustrate comic or serious aspects of our development. Too often, academic histories, it seems to me, discard details of human interest for lack of space—or fear of offending Clio, a stern and stiff-backed muse. For all I care, Clio can go sit beside some abandoned rice field and listen for the ghostly chatter and laughter of people long gone to other and perhaps better fields.

So this volume will include my own observations of the land and my interpretation of its history. It is a country that indeed has for me a lingering fragrance—the fragrance of sweet shrub in the spring, of red clay new-turned by the plow, and of fresh-cut oats and rye. Summer brought the musky perfume of wild roses, the scent of blooming cotton, tasseling corn, and the sweet smell of sorghum cane grown thick in the row, waiting to be cut and hauled to the molasses mill. Autumn and winter had their special aromas, different and more penetrating. Hickory smoke curling from a distant chimney always reminds me of Thanksgiving Day at my grandfather's, for on the way we passed a house where the rich smoke-smell was especially strong. My olfactory memory is keen and brings back vivid scenes peopled with characters who had an impact upon my life in greater or lesser degree. If for Ludwig Lewisohn South Carolina had the lingering fragrance of a vanished civilization, for me it was the opposite. I relished the moment, had faith in the future, and found it a good world.

My affection for the state did not blind me to its faults, then or now, but I have tried to see both our faults and such virtues as we claim in proper perspective. Elsewhere I have done my bit to correct the magnolia-and-moonlight syndrome, the tendency to interpret our past in overripe terms of romanticism. A Carolina versifier, J. Gordon Coogler, known as the "Bard of the Congaree," many years ago observed in what passed for rhyme:

> Alas! for the South, her books have grown fewer—
> She never was much given to literature.[2]

The trouble with too many earlier South Carolinans who turned a hand to literature was that they looked through rose-tinted glasses and glorified the very elements in our culture that carried the seeds of destruction. The state would have fared better in the eyes of the outside world if romantic books had indeed "grown fewer." Saccharine fiction about the clinging-vine beauty and the proud and gallant cavalier ever ready to defend his or her honor in a duel under the live-oaks has given an altogether distorted picture of South Carolina in any period.

2. Irene L. Neuffer, "The Bard of the Congaree," *South Carolina History Illustrated* (Columbia, S.C.: Sandlapper Press, 1970) 1, no. 3: 29–32.

Later, however, another type of fiction, called "realistic" but equally distorted, swung to the opposite extreme and pictured South Carolina as a miasma of bigotry and backwardness—a vast "Tobacco Road." Each genre of literature has been fashionable in its time—and each has been erroneous.

Low Country and Up Country in South Carolina had distinct and separate cultures, the result of topography and of the types of people who settled the different regions. In my youth, before paved highways linked every out-of-the-way town and village, we Up-Country people regarded Charleston and the Low Country as virtually foreign territory. Many a Greenwood citizen had never ventured farther south than Columbia, and we heard stories of the wickedness of Charleston and the leisured indolence of its people.

There was a widespread belief—not without some substance—that Charleston and the Episcopal Church controlled the state. This was a relic of pre-Revolutionary times when South Carolina taxpayers supported the Anglican state church. In the Up Country we were mostly Presbyterians, Methodists, and Baptists. Greenwood had a small Episcopal chapel-of-ease served by a Huguenot minister named Porcher who came up from Charleston once a month to bring a message of solace to the faithful. I was nearly grown before I realized that an Episcopal minister could be anything but a French Huguenot from the Low Country.

During my last year in high school, I made my first visit to Charleston and was astonished at what I saw. It was a hot morning in June, and I observed lawyers and bankers going to their offices in King Street at ten o'clock, the morning half over in my part of the country. Dressed in pristine white linen suits, they strolled leisurely along, stopping now and again to chat with friends and fanning themselves along the way with their Panama hats. Nobody hurried or seemed to regard diligence as a virtue. Such a pace would have scandalized any thrifty businessman in the Up Country. We had been brought up on the maxims of Benjamin Franklin and believed it unchristian not to arise betimes and be up and doing.

My schoolboy observations in Charleston did not, however,

convince me that leisure was wicked. It looked terribly tempt-
ing, though I wondered how a man made a living in slow motion. Upstate it was hardscrabble to keep one's head above
water and stay out of debt.

Later I was to learn of the cultural heritage that the Low
Country had, indeed, bequeathed to the state; of the learning of
its citizens, their contributions to letters and sciences, the
schools and colleges they had founded, their devotion to music,
art, and the theater—in short, of a sophisticated society that
made Charleston one of the most cultivated cities in the American colonies long before we had begun to think of independence
from Great Britain. In spite of devastation in two wars—the
American Revolution and the War Between the States—
Charleston managed to maintain its cultural pre-eminence
through later generations.

The Up Country remained a frontier region until after the
Revolution; and even in the early twentieth century, frontier
conditions persisted in backward areas of the northwest mountain region and isolated pockets in the Sand Hills and the Piedmont. After Eli Whitney's invention of the cotton gin, cotton
became the chief money crop—if that is the word for a commodity that sometimes sold for five cents a pound. By my
boyhood, many farms had been over-planted and were eroded
into yawning red gullies. Tenant farmers and share-croppers,
white and black, lived from hand to mouth. Money was scarce,
but nobody had yet found a way to break from the devastating
one-crop system.

The salvation of the Up Country was industrialization, with
all its attendant ills. Textile mills first brought a modicum of
prosperity to the region. An immense reservoir of cheap labor
was available, and the cotton mills lured men and women from
the hills and from run-down farms. Around each mill the management built clusters of houses, the "mill village," company-
owned and controlled, where most of the employees lived.
Latter-day sociologists have seen nothing but iniquity in such
capitalistic paternalism, but it was a necessary step in the industrial development of South Carolina. Most of the "mill hands"
lived better and had more comforts than they had ever known.

Before the days of motor cars and modern transportation, they had to live within walking distance of their jobs. If the mill owners had not constructed villages, they would have had no employees, for many of these people had migrated from distant localities, and no other housing was available.

The mill workers, most of them poorly educated, in time became almost a separate class. Older townsfolk tended to look down upon people who lived in the mill village. These folk, it is true, were sometimes lawless, sometimes crude and uncouth; they were the "wool-hats" deplored by sophisticates and exploited by demagogic politicians.

But the wool-hats were not the only people in the Up Country. Every community had a body of substantial citizens—landowners, doctors, lawyers, teachers, and professional men of all sorts. Many of them, in other societies, would have been called "landed gentry," but nobody in the Up Country would have dared to use, or even think of, such a hifalutin term. They belonged to what was called the "better element" and were the stabilizing force in the Up Country, opposed to political demagoguery (with which we were too often afflicted), always in the forefront in advocating educational development and civic improvement. Eventually these people, with the aid of the capitalists who developed industry, made the Up Country prosperous, even educated and cultivated. Not everybody, of course, could be thus described, but the region gradually produced an effective body of citizens eager to provide their society with intellectual resources second to none. Probably few read or remembered Lewisohn's indictment, but they had no intention of letting rednecks or obscurantists prevail.

The struggle against demagoguery was long and bitter, because political inequities between the regions had played into the hands of opportunists. The fifty years from 1880 to 1930 were marked by political dissension and violence rarely equalled in even our turbulent history. In this period Benjamin R. Tillman, successively governor and United States senator, led a revolt of Up-Country farmers that wrested control from the Low-Country aristocrats. Although in my own family it was our proud boast that "no Wright ever voted for Ben Tillman," we had to admit that he accomplished some good things; for instance, he succeeded in getting the state to finance schools and colleges in the Piedmont. If we did not approve of his partisan politics, we were not devastated by his victory over the often insolent Charlestonians, ever ready to declare that "no gentleman was ever born above tidewater."

But Tillman was followed by a demagogue without any redeeming virtues, Coleman Blease—"Old Coley," his henchmen affectionately called him. Blease appealed to the worst elements in human nature, to the prejudices of the poor whites, and to bigots eager to invoke white supremacy as an issue. When I was a young reporter in the later years of Blease's career as United States senator, I had the honor of being shot at by some of his followers after a campaign speech in which he had castigated "lying newspapers."

We survived this unhappy period in our political and social development and in time overcame much of the prejudice and bigotry it engendered. Even white supremacy ceased to have its old-time appeal. Integration of the schools came with a minimum of friction, and South Carolina established a far better record than many a more self-righteous state in the North. In the spring of 1974 I drove by an integrated school at Moncks Corner, not one of the more advanced localities in the state, and observed black and white children of various ages playing happily together in the schoolyard with no apparent supervision. A few weeks later, Lander College in Greenwood conferred an honorary degree upon Dr. Benjamin Mays, a distinguished black educator and a native son. The state has taken pride in its modern record of race relations. This development did not come too soon, for South Carolina had much to live down from its earlier days.

The past quarter of a century has seen a remarkable transformation in the ecology and the appearance of South Carolina from the mountains to the sea. Run-down cotton fields no longer exist, nor can one find any eroded "badlands" of red gullies. Years ago, soil erosion specialists began building check dams and planting kudzu, a gargantuan legume that now threatens to envelop some localities.

The arrival of the destructive cotton boll weevil proved a blessing in disguise because it forced farmers to give up a commodity that was increasingly unprofitable and seek other sources of revenue. Farmers are among the most conservative specimens of the human race; only staring calamity will force them to change their ways. The boll weevil proved sufficiently calamitous to turn South Carolina farmers to cattle raising and the growing of fruit, especially peaches. Black Angus steers now graze in green pastures once white with cotton. Spartanburg County is said to produce more peaches than any other county in the nation. Orchards and vineyards also dot the once barren Sand Hills.

The discovery of a means of utilizing pine trees for wood pulp and the building of paper mills also had a profound effect upon the ecology. A loblolly pine will grow to harvesting size in twenty years. Now thousands of acres are growing loblollies neatly planted in rows; they are harvested scientifically in order to keep a crop coming each year. Farmers who once worried about the weather and the price of cotton now sit on their porches, listen happily to cool breezes blowing through their pines, and tot up their increasing profits. Green forests blanket the state, making refuges for game and birds. Wild turkeys, quail (known to us as partridges), and deer have made a phenomenal recovery so that controlled hunting is now permitted in many of the state forests.

Vast areas once consisting of swamps or marginal farms and abandoned plantations are now covered by water—lakes manmade for flood control and electric power. These lakes extend from the far northwest nearly to the coast. The Hartwell Reservoir, on the northern border between South Carolina and Georgia, makes a series of emerald lakes where muddy torrents once washed away the topsoil. Farther down the Savannah, the Clark Hill Reservoir has made a lake of much of what we used to call the Dark Corner of McCormick County. The muddy Saluda River, dammed below Greenwood, has made an important power source and a fishing resort in Lake Greenwood. Lake Murray above Columbia and Lake Marion and Lake Moultrie between Columbia and Charleston are the largest of these power resources. The damming of the Santee River flooded many old rice fields and plantation sites, but it transformed the vast Santee Swamp into a recreation area where fishermen and boating enthusiasts enjoy sports unavailable to earlier generations.

Wildlife devotees are not all pleased by the elimination of swamps and natural breeding places of birds and beasts, but they can still rejoice in the Congaree Swamp and other marsh lands where cottonmouth moccasins, swamp rattlers, the rare and deadly coral snake, turtles and alligators, muskrats, bobcats, foxes, and here and there black bear still flourish, oblivious to the advances of industry.

In my youth South Carolina was a fascinating region, but it is infinitely more attractive today, both economically and scenically. Foreign manufacturers have discovered opportunities in the state and have opened textile, chemical, and other plants. Recently I was amazed to see the West German flag flying alongside our own in front of a textile mill not far from the site of Camp Wadsworth in Spartanburg County, where the Twenty-Seventh Division trained for combat against the Germans in World War I. Spartanburg, for example, now has enclaves of German, Swiss, and Japanese businessmen. Newspapers report negotiations by Kuwaiti Arabs for Kiawah Island off Charleston, which they plan to develop into a resort something like that on the neighboring island of Hilton Head. Verily we may ask what God, Islam, and oil have wrought.

When South Carolina was debating one of its early bond issues for highways—while I was a student at Wofford College—one of my classmates from Charleston was violently opposed to it. "We have one road into Charleston now, and that's enough. We don't want just anybody coming in," he maintained.

This attitude has changed. Outlanders by the thousands have moved into Charleston and its environs. Retired service people, for example, find its atmosphere and amenities to their liking, and generals, admirals, and lesser brass, with their ladies, add glitter to the social life. Charleston society has always welcomed military heroes, especially "officers and gentlemen." Tourism has become an important industry, as word of the glory of ancient Charleston has been spread by brochures describing great town houses, old plantation sites, and the beauty of Magnolia Gardens, Middleton Plantation, and Cypress Gardens, each distinctive in its own way.

Abundant power and deep-water ports have brought industry to the coast as well as to the Up Country. North Charleston, once pre-empted by the Navy Yard (then the main support of Charleston), now is a busy center of varied industries, including important chemical plants. The original Barbadian settlers—the "Goose Creek men"—were Anglicans determined to impose their form of religion upon the whole colony; they must writhe in their tombs at what has happened to this once aristocratic plantation community, now a busy industrial area.

Throughout the state, towns and villages seek to attract tourists by calling attention to handsome gardens, ancient houses, and historic sites. The city of Camden, for example, has restored the scene of one of our less glorious episodes in the Revolutionary War, when General Gates turned tail and ran from the British. But Camden also marks the site of a better battle at Hobkirk Hill. The town lets the visitor know about its gorgeous homes and gardens and its appeal to the horsey set, though it warns riders to stay off the sidewalks.

In the Up Country, the battlefield at Kings Mountain has long been a national park. Recently the battlefield at Cowpens, scene of Tarleton's defeat at the hands of that tough old wagon driver, General Daniel Morgan, has been made a national monument. Less well-known but intensely interesting is Kate Barry's house, Walnut Grove Plantation, a few miles south of Spartanburg. Here one can see the home of a Revolutionary heroine, a scout for the Patriots, with the home-made but ingenious equipment of a frontier plantation in place, as if waiting for the family to return. A bloodstain on a bedroom floor remains to show where a wounded patriot was slaughtered in his bed by the detested Tory, Bloody Bill Cunningham.

Few states demonstrate a greater consciousness of their heritage than South Carolina. A recent journey from the seacoast to the mountains impressed me once again with the natural charm of the respective regions—and the infinite improvement that changing conditions have brought. Frequently we hear only lamentations over the deterioration of the ecology and the corrosive effects of urbanization. Much of this is a yearning for the good old days that never were.

This is not to say that South Carolina has been turned into a garden of delights. Much of it is still ugly, especially the town centers. Years ago, to make way for a paved thoroughfare down its middle, nearly every small town methodically cut down the trees that shaded loafers during long summer afternoons; shabby stores were left glaring in the sun. This was believed to represent progress. There the buildings still squat, nondescript places of business growing uglier and shabbier by the day.

Tumbledown shacks abound on the fringes of towns and sometimes on country roads; nestling in the weeds alongside, rusting farm implements and long-dead automobiles frequently appear. But natural decay—and the high price of scrap metal—will eventually solve this problem. From the first days of settlement we have had shiftlessness, and only the Angel of Death will reform the type of human being scornfully described by my grandmother as "trifling trash, common as pig tracks."

One noticeable improvement is obvious to the motorist. A campaign to discourage littering the highways has been surprisingly effective. Few beer cans clutter the margins of roads, and rarely does one encounter blowing paper or broken Coca-Cola bottles. Either the highway department polices the roads better than formerly or the citizenry have experienced an access of conscience about throwing out rubbish.

April in South Carolina, the time of a recent visit, is a period of contrast as one journeys from southeast to northwest. Along the semi-tropical coast, camellias and azaleas are already fading, though yellow jessamine, with its romantic fragrance, lingers; but as one pushes northward, azaleas of every hue brighten the landscape. Redbud, sometimes called Judas tree (blushing because it permitted Iscariot to expiate his crime from a branch), blooms in profusion. As one reaches the Sand Hills and Piedmont, dogwood makes the country radiant with pink and white.

An easy trip from Spartanburg to Walhalla brings the Blue

Ridge mountains into full view, especially along a new-built section of U.S. 11. So thick are the dogwoods here that they look like patches of snow along the sides of Hogback and Glassy Mountain. The blue-green waters of Lake Jocassee and Lake Keowee recall in their names ancient towns of the Cherokee Nation, once so important to Carolina's economy—and so critical to its security. The waters now supply power to electric turbines and steam from the magic uranium fuel of the Duke Power Company's Keowee-Oconee nuclear plant. There, in the precinct of this new source of energy, visitors are made welcome, instructed in the latest nuclear developments, invited to picnic in beautiful surroundings, and left to ponder the implications of man's ability, at his best, to harness the forces of nature for the benefit of humankind.

The air was clear and crisp, the sky the deepest blue. No hint of pollution tainted the atmosphere. A benison of peace blessed the region. I thought of the One Hundred and Twenty-First Psalm, a favorite of Up-Countrymen: "I will lift up mine eyes unto the hills, from whence cometh my help."

Yet three days before my visit, destructive tornadoes had passed that way. Here and there in mountain coves, pine trees were twisted and snapped. Oaks that had stood a century and more lay on their sides uprooted. Nature, even in the South Carolina Up Country, is not always kind. Nature can be fickle and violent; so can our people.

1

Contentious Commonwealth
Just South of Eden

OUTH Carolinians have always been ready to declare
that their land was only a little less desirable than Eden. A passage in Alexander Ross's epitome of Sir Walter Raleigh's *History of the World* called *The Marrow of History* (1650) asserts
that God placed the earthly paradise on the thirty-fifth parallel
of north latitude, a line running through the northern tier of
South Carolina's present-day counties. This location was said
to guarantee an ideal climate of perpetual spring and summer,
a garden shaded by palm trees described by Raleigh as the greatest blessing and wonder of nature. If no one in the six counties
threaded by the thirty-fifth parallel, from York to Oconee, could
discover one of Raleigh's palms, he might grudgingly concede
that the palmettoes of the Low Country were at least a symbol of paradise—merely misplaced.

Like Biblical Eden, South Carolina from early in its history
was betrayed by a serpent—the serpent of Pride, chief of the
Seven Deadly Sins. Pride led to many collateral faults: overweening individualism, an unwillingness to submit to authority,
every man's conviction of the rightness of his own opinions,
and a thousand contentions that flowed from these characteristics. In the long sweep of history, South Carolina has been one
of the most contentious states of the union.

All sorts and conditions of people, filtering into South Carolina during the colonial period, contributed to a civilization devoid of homogeneity. Like citizens of the city-states of ancient Greece, South Carolinians were always ready to quarrel among themselves, but woe unto the outlander who challenged them either singly or collectively.

Wherever diverse immigrants settled within the colonial province's borders, they developed enclaves of proud and independent citizens. In the Back Country, far from any protective or disciplinary authority, each community for many years was virtually a law unto itself. Everywhere these pioneers developed an extreme individualism that in turn produced an enduring spirit of independence. If at times this independence bordered on anarchy, it nevertheless contributed a quality that made South Carolinians eager to fight any tyranny, real or imagined, foreign or domestic.

Geography and geology have always had an immense influence on people, and the widely differing physical terrain of South Carolina had a lasting impact upon the civilization of the commonwealth. Ultimately, colony and state were divided into Low Country and Up Country, terms that have a special meaning in South Carolina. The inhabitants of the two regions developed widely differing characteristics and concepts of the society they respected or favored. Geological variations in the terrain exerted a profound influence upon regional cultures.

Off the Carolina coast lay a string of low, sandy islands originally covered with marsh grass and scrub, dotted here and there with pines and semi-tropical palmettoes. Such islands provided bases for fortifications to protect early settlements. In a later time a few planters established themselves on ''sea islands,'' where they eventually prospered from the production of a famous long-staple cotton. On many of these islands, notably Hilton Head, scrub and crops have long since disappeared and have been succeeded by glossy real estate developments, golf courses, and fashionable enclaves for the leisured class.

A narrow strip along the shore from the Georgia border at Savannah to the North Carolina line above North Myrtle Beach is characterized by tidal swamps interspersed with rising savannahs of rich alluvial soil. These flatlands along tidewater were the first to be occupied by English settlers.

A short distance inland, the coastal plain, a broad band thirty to fifty miles wide, begins a gradual rise. Though swamps intervene here and there, this area in time became a region of great plantations where the owners grew rich from the cultivation of rice and indigo. Slow-moving rivers and short estuaries sometimes designated as creeks gave access by boat or even oceangoing vessels to these plantations along the water courses. On these streams, occasional high banks, known locally as bluffs, provided ideal sites above the danger of high water for the homes of planters. Some of these bluffs had been occupied since prehistoric times by Indians who here and there left kitchen middens of clam and oyster shells. The bluffs had an additional advantage to both aborigines and later settlers of catching fresh breezes from the sea which helped to disperse dense clouds of mosquitoes from nearby swamps.

A sequence of river systems drains the whole of South Carolina. Beginning with the Savannah (the border between South Carolina and Georgia) the major streams to the northeast include the Salkehatchie-Combahee, the Edisto, the Santee, the Black, the Lynches, the Big and Little Pee Dee, and others. These rivers have many tributaries in the Up Country, all bearing different names. The two rivers which Charlestonians claim ''form the Atlantic Ocean'' are rather short streams, the Ashley on the south side of Charleston and the Cooper on the north. In the early nineteenth century a project to improve navigation from Charleston to the Up Country resulted in the digging of the Santee Canal to connect the Santee River with the Cooper, a venture that failed with the development of the railroads.

The South Carolina Low Country comprises the region between the sea and the fall line: the point where rapids in the rivers hinder navigation. A broad strip below this fall line, stretching from Aiken in the southwest to Cheraw in the northeast, many millions of years ago was the seacoast. As the sea drained away, it left ridges and depressions. This land, infertile and often scrubby, came to be called ''the Sand Hills.'' In the course of time the capital of the state, Columbia, was located in a central section of this sandy region, which includes portions of Aiken, Lexington, Richland, Kershaw, and Chesterfield counties.

In 1791 George Washington, on a journey across the state, asserted that the territory between Camden and Columbia was "the most miserable pine barren" he had ever seen. Other travelers have been equally unkind. As late as the publication in 1941 of the WPA *South Carolina: A Guide to the Palmetto State,* the writer commented: "Stretching to the horizon are sandy troughs and crests, dunes of an ancient beach, overgrown with scrubby blackjacks and pines, scattered with ponds fed by springs or wet weather streams. Unpainted shacks crouch in the hollows for protection against the winds that drive sand through every crevice. Here live the Sand Hillers, who lead a precarious existence and are often victims of pellagra." [1] Satirical commentators sometimes referred to dwellers in this region as "Sandlappers," a designation not generally approved by the natives. But in a later day a popular magazine devoted to South Carolina affairs thought well enough of the term to entitle itself *The Sandlapper.*

One should not make the mistake of believing the Sand Hills are any longer destitute and barren. Experimentation proved this sandy soil good for fruits and melons, and fruit-growing on a commercial scale has brought prosperity to many orchardists. In the spring, acres of peach trees set the landscape aglow with pink. Other growers favor berries, grapes, and small fruits of various sorts. A reforestation program has covered many of the Sand Hills with a blanket of green pines.

Not all of this terrain consists only of sandy ridges. In Aiken County and adjacent territory are rugged red hills, and in Chesterfield County, in the far northeast, hills are high enough to be described as mountains. The High Hills of Santee border the Wateree River to the east before it flows into the Santee. In colonial times these ridges became popular health resorts, which has suggested to some that the term "Santee" in this case does

---

1. *South Carolina: A Guide to the Palmetto State,* Works Progress Administration, American Guide Series (New York: Oxford University Press, 1941), pp. 340–341.

not refer to the river of the same name but to the French word *santé* (meaning health), which Huguenots from the coast may have applied to this hill country when they fled from the plague-stricken lowlands in the summer. The medical profession in the early days believed that contagion came from "the miasma" of the swamps because they had not yet learned about malaria and disease-carrying mosquitoes.

The Sand Hills proved a useful buffer area between Up Country and Low Country. Inhabitants along the fringes of this region might call themselves either Up Countrymen or Low Countrymen, depending upon their individual prejudices. Occasionally some of these people found themselves in a geographical limbo: certain dwellers on the upper Pee Dee disliked being classified as Up Countrymen, but were embarrassed because the Low Country would not claim them.

Beyond the Sand Hills, a vast region of rolling land—almost a third of the state—is called the Piedmont. At its northwest tip, in Oconee, Pickens, Greenville, and Spartanburg counties, the upland rises to mountainous heights. This region was originally forested with both hardwoods and conifers—oak, chestnut, hickory, elm, tulip poplar, and pines. A fertile layer of topsoil, enriched by the humus of rotting leaves, made the region attractive to farmers who penetrated this back country in the eighteenth century. The forest also teemed with deer in incredible numbers, a fact of enormous importance to the commerce of South Carolina in its first century of settlement. Agents from Charleston followed ancient "trading paths" into the back country to barter with Indians for deerskins—an article in great demand in England, where they were used for gloves and other leather commodities.

Not all of the Piedmont was heavily forested. Some areas were covered with dense fields of cane; Long Canes Creek in McCormick County, for instance, commemorates the cane-brakes of that area. But cane growth extended along many other waterways in the Up Country. Vegetation in other unwooded sections included fields of wild pea vines which in primeval times provided forage for deer, elk, and buffalo. After the coming of the white man, herds of cattle, fattened on both cane and pea vines, were driven to markets as far away as Charleston and Philadelphia. The first American cowboys—a tough breed of men—gained their livelihood in the Up Country. The community of Cowpens in Spartanburg County, scene of a famous patriot victory in the Revolutionary War, got its name from this cattle industry.

Much of the Piedmont consists of broad undulating hills with frequent valleys cut by thousands of streams great and small. In South Carolina the smallest streams are called "branches," the equivalent of "runs" in Virginia. Larger streams, smaller than rivers, are "creeks" (but never pronounced "crick," as in some parts of New England). These hills and valleys supported fine timber of many kinds: oak of several varieties (the most valued being the white oak), chestnut (now long since completely destroyed by blight), black walnut (now nearly all cut for furniture and gun stocks), poplar, wild cherry (once popular for furniture), short-leaf pine of several varieties (favored for quick fires, especially as kitchen stove-wood), and many other types of trees and shrubs. Two varieties of hickory provided nuts, the best being the scaly-bark. Black walnuts also supplied Indians and later settlers with food. Chestnuts were so abundant that hogs fattened on them as well as upon bushels of acorns. Smaller shrublike trees called chinquapins bore black nuts about the size of a hazelnut, with a chestnut flavor. Persimmon trees, in the autumn after frost, hung heavy with fruit that candied as the winter wore on until they tasted almost like dates.

Wild plums abounded in the high ground. In lower-lying areas and in the swamps, tangles of blackberry vines, snow-flecked with white blossoms in the early spring, gave promise of a rich harvest of berries in July. In some meadow areas strawberries were so plentiful that travelers reported their horses' legs stained to the knees with juice. In short, all the Piedmont region was clothed in green and was fruitful.

The fertility of the soil ultimately proved its undoing. When the white man destroyed forests and planted his crops in the topsoil, he at first needed no fertilizer. The Indians before him had cleared some ground by girdling the trees with their stone axes and letting them die. Among these gaunt bare sentinels they planted their corn, beans, and pumpkins. In time, storms blew down the decaying trees. But the white man cleared more land and took no thought of erosion. After a few years, the topsoil washed off the hillsides, leaving bare, heavy red clay. Even this clay is fertile—"strong," the farmers call it—if humus is added. But after two centuries of plowing, erosion on these hills often left great gullies which looked in some places like minia-ture badlands of the West. Only in our time has this continuing devastation been checked by reforestation.

The timber resources of South Carolina were enormous. In the coastal region cypress, pine, and live oak supplied lumber valued both at home and abroad. Today old cypresses may still be seen in the swamps with their "knees" protruding above the water. Long avenues of live oaks yet mark the way to vanished plantation houses. On the higher ground grew forests of long-leaf pine (sometimes called yellow pine). These tall, stately trees stood almost free of undergrowth, so that a horseman could ride through the parklike forests. Sap from these pines provided tar, rosin, and turpentine, lucrative commodities known as "ship's stores." Shipwrights favored straight pines for masts for their sailing ships. Heart lumber from these pines was virtually indestructible; not even termites could penetrate their rosin-filled cells. Knots from fallen trees and splinters from the heartwood were called "fat pine" and "lightwood." They burn with a hot, bright, but smoky fire and were much desired as kindling. From a match, a splinter of fat pine would take fire like a candle.

The great forests of long-leaf pine, as well as the cypress, have succumbed to the exploitation of lumber companies, but here and there some trees and a few forests survive, monuments to primeval grandeur. Efforts are being made by the Forestry Service to replant long-leaf pines, but their growth takes much longer than the twenty years needed for loblolly pines now grown for paper mills; a long-leaf will take nearly a lifetime.

The long-leaf pine was indigenous from the uplands of the Low Country to the Sand Hills and beyond. But in most of the Up Country, short-leaf pines were more numerous. Some of these also grew into magnificent trees, the best of which have long since found their way to the sawmills. In the alpine region of the extreme northwest were forests of symmetrical white pines and hemlocks. In this same region, flowering laurel and rhododendron flourished. Throughout the state, in springtime, woods gleamed with white-flowering dogwood and glowed with the pink of Judas trees and the winged red seed of the maple.

Animal and bird life in this land of swamp and forest was varied and abundant. On the coast many kinds of gulls and other sea birds, including pelicans from the tropics, flocked in tidal waters. Swarms of duck of many varieties fed in the shallow swamps; the water must not be too deep, for a duck does not dive for his food but up-ends and grabbles with his beak. Rail and snipe provided game for hunters. On the high ground were coveys of quail and flocks of wild turkey, the most magnificent land bird in America. Woodcock were also numerous. After the white man came, around every house could be found mocking birds, cardinals, and bluebirds. The Up Country had most of the same species.

One bird peculiar to the Low Country, now extinct, was the Carolina parakeet. Another bird, also extinct, was the migratory passenger pigeon which traveled in such flocks that when they roosted at night they frequently broke the limbs of trees. Another migrating bird, known in the North as the bobolink but in the South as the ricebird, was a pest. In the spring these birds on their way North could pull up a great deal of sprouting rice; flying South in the autumn, they landed in the fields in such numbers that planters had to employ "bird minders" to scare them away from the ripening grain—usually to no avail. The fat little birds were a table delicacy that gourmet planters would willingly have done without.

The waterways all teemed with a wide variety of fish. No pollution yet poisoned the streams, and no dams hindered the spawning runs of shad or sturgeon. In the cold waters of the Up Country, trout were plentiful. Many scale fish, no longer seen, have now been supplanted by the ubiquitous catfish.

But nature was also red in tooth and claw in the heavens above and the waters beneath. Alligators haunted the lower reaches of rivers and the swamps, some as long as fourteen feet and more. They preyed on fish and small mammals that ventured near their lairs. Hardly a body of water could be found that did not have a dangerous quota of cottonmouth moccasins. Diamond-back rattlers infested both swamps and uplands. Coral snakes of the cobra kind were not unknown. The uplands also had copperheads, commonly called, in the Up Country, highland moccasins. Slightly less deadly than the rattler and the cottonmouth, they had the unpleasant habit of crawling around human habitations and hiding under doorsteps. Poisonous snakes were so plentiful that it is a marvel that any country child ever grew to maturity; curiously, however, few were ever bitten. The Indians even worshipped the rattler and had herbal remedies that they believed to be antidotes against snakebite.

Birds of prey included eagles and many varieties of hawk. Buzzards kept woods and fields clear of carrion.

Long after the white man had penetrated the back country, panthers, colloquially called catamounts, were common in the forests. They preyed upon deer and later upon calves and sheep. Wildcats were also found both north and south; and black bear roamed the Up Country woods as well as the swamplands. A few bear and wildcat can still be found in the swamps.

Buffalo disappeared soon after explorers and settlers penetrated the back country, but their presence is remembered in the names of numerous Buffalo Creeks. Elk had long since disappeared, though their antlers were occasionally found.

The forests and streams of South Carolina made living relatively easy for the aboriginal inhabitants. Fish and game could be caught easily; as a consequence, the Southern aborigines, unlike Indians in the frigid North, suffered few if any "starving times." The weather was rarely so unfavorable that the capture of game was difficult.

Nobody knows when the aboriginal invaders of this natural paradise arrived. Their ancient origins are subjects for infinite speculation by ethnologists, but the theme is too complex for extended discussion in this brief history. Prehistoric mounds continue to be found by archeologists. Many relics of primitive South Carolinians have been destroyed by the plow, but from time to time ancient burial sites continue to be unearthed as new theories of the origins of man in this region are advanced.

By the time the first white men encountered the Indians of South Carolina they were a mixture of several nations, tribes, and languages. Numerous minor groups were being conquered and absorbed by larger "nations" who would play a prominent part in relations with white settlers later. It is estimated that South Carolina had at that time between twenty-five and thirty different tribal groups. Many are remembered only by names of streams—Edisto, Wateree, Santee, Congaree, Saluda, and others. Historians point out, however, that a name does not necessarily prove that the given tribe of Indians were permanent residents on the stream, because these were wandering folk, constantly at war, pressed by their enemies to seek safer hunting grounds elsewhere. Not even trained ethnologists can untangle the confusion of tribal differentiations, particularly in the coastal areas.

The main linguistic stocks were three: Iroquoian in the northwest, represented by the Cherokees; Siouan occupying all the northeast—more than a third of the state—headed by the Catawbas, especially on the river that bears their name; and the Muskhogean in the southwest consisting of many small groups and tribes, the most dominant being the Cusabos, though included were some scattered villages of Creeks and Chickasaws. A refugee group from Georgia were the Yemassees (also spelled Yamassee). Two other stocks with smaller numbers were the Yuchi and the Algonquian. The Saludas, on the river that bears their name, did not fit into any of these classifications. They soon emigrated to Pennsylvania and were lost to South Carolina history.

For the white settlers, the Cherokees and Catawbas played the most important roles in colonial times. Trade with the Cherokees was of vital commercial importance in the first century of settlement. They were generally friendly, but not always. Their mortal enemies were the Catawbas who, with the exception of one or two episodes, were never hostile to the whites.

The Cherokees, the most advanced of the South Carolina Indians, laid claim to an enormous area in the states of Georgia, Tennessee, South Carolina, and North Carolina. They were a loosely organized confederation of "towns" concentrated in the mountainous region of the north. When the white man first made contact with them, their political organization was so un-defined that they had no paramount chief or central authority. As time went on, they attained greater unity and created a more effective government.

To the southwest of the Cherokees, across the Savannah River, were other powerful nations, the nearest being the Creeks and the Chickasaws. The constant pressure of Creeks upon Cherokees helps to account for their warlike qualities. With the Cherokees, as with other Indians, war was more for sport than for conquest. When a forest diplomat recommended peace between the Cherokees and neighboring tribes, they received the suggestion without enthusiasm, pointing out that, if they had peace, they would no longer have wars, which they enjoyed. The extreme cruelty demonstrated at times by the Cherokees and other Iroquoian Indians stems from this lust for war as a sport.

Despite these aberrations, the Cherokees were a highly intelligent people—one of the nations later to be classified as the Five Civilized Tribes, the others being the Creeks, Chickasaws, Choctaws, and a synthetic conglomerate of various tribes in the Florida Everglades known as the Seminoles.

The Cherokees claimed much of northwest South Carolina as far south as the Saluda River, home of the alien tribe of that name. The Cherokees never made settlements to the south; for them, that portion of the state was merely part of their imperial domain, their hunting ground. By the mid-eighteenth century they had ceded by treaty most of this territory to the whites. A tribal chief called Old Hop was instrumental in legalizing the white occupation of much of what was called Ninety Six District, the region from the Saluda northward to the mountains.

The Catawbas in the northeast prevented the Cherokees from expanding to the coast and forced them to remain a mountain people. A strip of territory along the Catawba River marked the western boundary of these people, who fought the Cherokees for hunting rights between the Catawba and Broad Rivers. At length they agreed that each could hunt in this territory without molestation. The Catawbas were less advanced than the Cherokees. Though they remained friendly with the English, invaders of their country, they eventually succumbed to the white man's diseases and his firewater. Today only a tiny Catawba remnant survives in York County.

The Cherokees, for all their prowess, intelligence, and skills, eventually were driven out of South Carolina. In the 1830s Andrew Jackson removed most of them to the Indian Territory (now Oklahoma) in an exodus called the Trail of Tears, which brought death to many.

A small group of Cherokees whose descendants are now known as the Eastern Band hid in the mountains. Tourists of our time, visiting the North Carolina town of Cherokee in the Great Smokies and a few other localities in that region, frequently encounter these latter-day Cherokees decked out in Sioux war bonnets that their ancestors never knew. The southeastern Indians did not adorn themselves with the elaborate feather headdress of the western tribes. They might attach an eagle feather to their scalp locks or a turkey wing to their cloaks, but that was about all. Americans now expect all Indians to look like Sitting Bull; descendants of a once proud and powerful nation that dominated much of the South Carolina Up Country thus comply with a popular misconception.

The Cherokees, like most other South Carolina Indians, combined agriculture and hunting for subsistence and trade. They cleared fairly large patches for the cultivation of corn, beans, squash, pumpkins, and some tobacco. Much of the work of planting and cultivation was done by the women, though the men girdled the trees and helped to clear fields of undergrowth. Among the Cherokees and other southeastern Indians, women were not regarded as subservient. They "owned" cultivated fields and presided over the harvest, and lineage was traced through the mother rather than the father. A few of the more primitive Indians on the coast lived almost exclusively on fish and game.

These Indians of the southeast lived in various types of huts, but never in tepees characteristic of the Plains Indians. The Cherokees, for example, had substantial houses made of poles and bark. Further south, on the coast, the Indians used marsh grass and palmetto leaves to thatch their huts.

Dress varied from tribe to tribe, but in general was determined by the weather. In the more northerly sections, winter garments were made from animal skins, though the men usually went with their chests bare except in the coldest weather. They customarily wore short skin kilts or tasselled breechclouts. Women wore a skin cloak over their shoulders and a brief skirt, sometimes of skins, sometimes made of feathers and the soft inner bark of the elm. Chiefs occasionally had capes made of irridescent turkey feathers or the plumage of other birds. Powhatan, father of Pocahontas, gave to English visitors a somewhat similar cloak which is still preserved in the Ashmolean Museum at Oxford. Leather moccasins and leggings protected them against rough terrain. In the far south Indians wore very little.

All the Indians used war clubs, sometimes with a sharp rock embedded in the head. Well-shaped stone axes, attached with thongs to a wooden handle, were used as tomahawks. Although the prehistoric aborigines in the southeast apparently had only spears or darts hurled with throwing sticks, by the time the white man arrived they had learned the use of the bow and arrow.

For the capture of small animals, the aborigines made ingenious traps and snares. With nets woven from grass and wood fibers, they seined for fish; they also made fish traps of white-oak withes—a type of trap still used in rural areas. In shallow streams of the Up Country, they built dams to impound fish. Large fish in the coastal region were often taken with fish spears, and the Indians learned early to make bone fishhooks.

The abundance of fish, game, edible roots and plants, nuts, berries, and small fruits added to the variety of food available to the southeastern Indians—an abundance unknown in other regions. This fact may explain why the southeast was invaded from time to time by Iroquois from the Mohawk Valley and by Shawnees from the Ohio.

From the southeastern Indians the white man learned to make an extremely useful means of transportation—the dugout canoe. Great cypress logs in the coastal region made the best canoes. Building fires along the length of a log, primitive artisans charred a short distance into the timber. They then scraped out the charcoal with shells or stone axes and again lighted small fires in the cavity. This procedure continued until they had hollowed out the log to the desired depth. Then they turned it over and scraped the hull smooth. Lashing thwarts with vines across the hollow, they could make seats if needed, or they might sit or kneel in the bottom of the canoe to paddle. Some of these dugouts were large enough to carry a dozen or more men. The white man adopted the dugout and continued to use it to modern times. No bark canoes existed in the South, which had no birch trees. The heavy dugout lacked one advantage of the birch-bark canoe of the North: it was too heavy to be used for long portages.

The southeastern Indians all showed a remarkable capacity to adapt to their environment. They had few of the problems suffered by primitive peoples in less hospitable climates. With relative ease they could feed and clothe themselves. Their existence, it would seem, should have been idyllic, but it lacked security. Everywhere, war was the way of life. From time immemorial, tribe had fought tribe, the strong had slaughtered or enslaved the weak. Long before the white man taught the Indian his ways, slavery was common among them. A tribe might either kill its captives, consign them to hard labor, or adopt them as fellow tribesmen.

Inter-tribal hostility and the inability of the Indians to create or maintain peaceful alliances enabled the white man to play one tribe against another, to divide and rule. South Carolina proved a theater-in-little for this process of destruction and conquest. By the beginning of the nineteenth century this state could show little evidence that the red man had once held sway from the mountains to the sea.

2

Carolina for the English
—and a Few Frenchmen

ONG before Englishmen successfully laid claim to the Carolinas, both Spaniards and Frenchmen had sought their fortunes on these shores, had made settlements that did not survive, and had spilt their blood in contention for the territory.

The first effort to colonize Carolina was made by a Spanish lawyer and government official of Hispaniola (now Santo Domingo and Haiti), a certain Lucas Vásquez de Allyón, who, after sending explorers to investigate the coast, himself led an expedition in 1526 that made a settlement, probably on the Waccamaw River. But Allyón died of malaria, and, after a mutiny and a revolt of the settlement's black slaves (the first blacks introduced into the Carolinas), the remnant of his colony sailed back to Hispaniola. Allyón's efforts had one lasting result, however: his explorers had discovered Hilton Head and Saint Helena Sound, and their reports of the goodness of the land and the fine harbor kept alive Spanish interest in that region.

An Italian navigator in the employ of France, Giovanni da Verrazano, sent out to explore the new land by King Francis I, in 1524 sailed along the Carolina coast, missed Charleston harbor, anchored off the Outer Banks, and in the ship's boat entered what was probably Pamlico Sound, which he took to be the Pacific Ocean. His report helped stir French interest in Carolina.

The first to explore the interior, however, was another Spaniard, Hernando de Soto, who had been with Pizarro in Peru. Lured ever onward in a quest for gold he never found, de Soto wandered across South Carolina in 1540—from the vicinity of Augusta, where he crossed the Savannah, through present-day Edgefield, Greenwood, and Anderson counties until he reached the mountains near Walhalla. Other Spaniards continued to explore the Carolina coast, and attempts were made to establish settlements.

Religion now entered into the rivalry of Spain and France for New World territory. Protestants called Huguenots were especially strong in the French maritime provinces. Their leader was Gaspard de Coligny, Admiral of France. He was responsible, in 1562, for organizing an expedition to settle on the Atlantic coast north of the Spanish possessions. Leading the voyage was Jean Ribaut (sometimes spelled Ribault), a daring and experienced Norman mariner as well as a devout Huguenot. Hoping to establish in the New World a refuge for his fellow Protestants, he recruited 150 men, mostly Huguenot, who sailed from Le Havre in February 1562 in three vessels. Ribaut's second in command was René de Laudonnière.

They made their first landfall near the site of St. Augustine on May 1 and sailed up the St. Johns River which, in honor of the day, they called "the River of May." Thinking this region too close to Spanish territory, Ribaut sailed north and was pleased to find a "mighty river," which he entered. He found the Spanish harbor of Santa Elena (Saint Helena), which he renamed Port Royal. Ribaut and his soldiers went ashore and liked the land, with its aromatic herbs, partridges, wild turkey, and other game. Landing on Lemon Island, Ribaut put up a stone pillar engraved with the arms of the king of France in token of possession. Friendly natives supplied them with food and invited them to stay. Pleased with the hospitality and fruitfulness of the land, Ribaut called for volunteers to remain while he returned to France for supplies and more settlers. Twenty-six men elected to stay and began work on a fort on what is now Parris Island, site of a major U.S. Marine base. To command in his absence, Ribaut appointed Albert de la Pierra, an unfortunate choice. Ribaut sailed for France in June 1562. The little settlement was named Charlesfort in honor of the French king, Charles IX.

It is a curious fact that most of the earliest settlements in North America, whether Spanish, French, or English, were improvident, frequently wracked by mutinies, and poorly managed. The little French enclave at Charlesfort was no exception. The Frenchmen planted no crops and made little effort to hunt or fish. Had it not been for friendly Indians, they would have starved. Pierra, impatient with his subordinates, was severe and cruel in his attempts at discipline. As punishment, he marooned one man—named La Chère—on a barren island and left him to starve. Soon the little band rebelled, murdered Pierra, and rescued La Chère.

Miserable, hungry, and hopeless—for the Indians had now exhausted their own supplies—the men built a rickety vessel and set sail for France. Without navigational instruments or skill, they made slow progress. When all their food was gone and they had even chewed up the leather of their jerkins and shoes, they cast lots to choose one of their number for slaughter. La Chère was the loser, and they ate him. Eventually an English ship picked up the survivors, but few of them ever returned home.

On his return from Charlesfort to France, Ribaut found his country in the throes of religious war and was unable to organize immediately a rescue mission for his colony. Hoping to obtain aid in England, he went to London and appealed to Queen Elizabeth. He apparently offered to claim land for England and establish a settlement of English as well as of French Protestants. Either because the Queen doubted Ribaut's proffered loyalty to English interests or was still unwilling to antagonize Spain, she vacillated and ultimately threw him into prison.

While Ribaut languished in England, the Spanish ambassador in Paris kept Philip II informed of French efforts to establish a base in "Florida." Philip sent orders to the governor of Cuba to investigate. For this purpose, in the spring of 1564, Hernando de Manrique de Rojas sailed up the Atlantic coast, poking into various inlets and inquiring of the Indians about alien white men. At last he reached Port Royal Sound, where he took on board a French youth, Guillaume Rufin, a survivor of Ribaut's little colony at Charlesfort who had refused to join his comrades in their tragic effort to sail home. Rufin had been assimilated into a local Indian tribe, had taken a wife, and apparently was not unhappy with his condition. He readily gave Manrique information about Charlesfort and guided him to the site. The Spaniards burned the small shacks that the Frenchmen had left and dug up and took away from Lemon Island the stone column claiming the territory for France. That done, the expedition returned to Cuba, satisfied that any French presence had been eliminated.

The Spaniards, however, reckoned without the persistent hope of Admiral Coligny to colonize a portion of the New World. Because Ribaut was still in England, Coligny in 1564 appointed René de Laudonnière, a veteran of Ribaut's first venture at Charlesfort, to lead a second expedition to the new land. This group returned to the site on the St. Johns River in Florida that Ribaut had previously discovered but rejected as being too near the Spaniards. There they built a fortification named Fort Caroline, again in honor of King Charles IX.

Laudonnière's companions, unruly, improvident, and contentious, busied themselves looking for treasure instead of planting crops and, like their predecessors, they were soon out of food and eager to go home. They received some slight encouragement a year after their arrival when a famous English buccaneer and slave trader, John Hawkins, homeward bound from contraband trading with Spanish settlements in the Caribbean, anchored his fleet offshore. He gave the French colonists a small store of supplies and traded them a captured ship for a few brass cannon. The colonists would have done well to keep their cannon.

But they were already planning to desert Fort Caroline. As they prepared to sail for home in their newly acquired ship in August 1565, Jean Ribaut, who had obtained his release from the English, arrived off the bar at the mouth of the river with a fleet of seven vessels. The three smallest craft sailed up to the fort, put ashore new colonists, and landed supplies.

At the very time that Ribaut was replenishing Fort Caroline, a Spanish expeditionary force led by Pedro Menéndez de Avilés had touched Cape Canaveral and, on August 28, 1565—the same day Ribaut cast anchor off Fort Caroline—had established a base below Fort Caroline which he named St. Augustín (St. Augustine). St. Augustine, which became the first permanent white settlement in North America, would in time become a threat to the security of the English in South Carolina.

Both Ribaut and Menéndez tried to destroy each other from the sea. Menéndez could not get his ships across the bar at the mouth of the St. Johns River; when Ribaut sailed south to attack Menéndez at St. Augustine, a hurricane beached and wrecked his fleet near modern Daytona. Some 500 survivors, including most of the able-bodied men from Fort Caroline, struggled northward in an effort to get back to their base. In their absence, learning that Fort Caroline was thinly manned, Menéndez marched overland through swamp and jungle to surprise Fort Caroline at dawn on September 20, 1565. He captured the base with the loss of only one man and slaughtered the occupants, including a few women and children. Some of the men he hanged; an inscription over them read: "I do this, not as to Frenchmen, but as to Lutherans."

Restoring the fortifications of Fort Caroline, Menéndez left it garrisoned and changed its name to San Mateo. Learning of Ribaut's shipwrecked mariners, Menéndez then marched south with a small body of troops to Matanzas Inlet, where he rounded them up in two groups. Tricking them into surrender with a promise of such mercy as God might direct, he slaughtered them all, including Ribaut, in cold blood.

Laudonnière and a few of his men escaped the massacre at Fort Caroline and got back to France in the three small ships that escaped the hurricane by being anchored within the bar. Among the survivors was Jacques Le Moyne, a skilled artist, who landed in England and reproduced from memory vivid pictures of Florida scenes. They and John White's watercolors of life on the Carolina coast, painted while White was a member of Raleigh's Roanoke colony, are the earliest authentic pictures of life in North America.

News of the massacre at Fort Caroline, reported by Laudonnière, aroused widespread indignation. In 1568 a French shipowner, Dominique de Gourgues, sailed to St. Johns River, captured and burned San Mateo, and saved as many prisoners as possible in order to hang them at the site of Menéndez's executions. Over the victims he hung an inscription reading: "I do this, not as to Spaniards, nor as to mariners, but as to traitors, robbers, and murderers."

The death of Ribaut was a tragic setback to French hopes of establishing a permanent settlement in Carolina or the region to the south. Had Ribaut lived, the story of French success in the South Atlantic might have been different. Menéndez reported to Philip II: "I think it great good fortune that this man be dead, for the King of France could accomplish more with him and fifty thousand ducats than with other men and five hundred thousand ducats; and he could do more in one year than another in ten." [1]

No successful intrusion into territory claimed by Spain from Cape Canaveral to Virginia occurred for years to come. Some evidence exists that, late in the 1570s, the French built a fort—soon abandoned—near the mouth of the Edisto River. Both French and English corsairs cruised along the south Atlantic coast, hoping to seize Spanish treasure ships. In 1586 Sir Francis Drake, after a raid on Spanish ports in the Caribbean, burned St. Augustine; on his way home he rescued Raleigh's first group of colonists on Roanoke Island.

The Spaniards were still determined to maintain bases in South Carolina and to exclude all invaders. In the spring of 1566 Menéndez landed on Parris Island and, not far from the site of Ribaut's Charlesfort, built a fortification which he named Fort San Felipe. From that base, in the autumn of the same year, Menéndez sent some 150 men to explore the interior of

---

1. Charles E. Bennett, *Laudonniere and Fort Caroline* (Gainesville, Fla.: University of Florida Press, 1964), p. 43.

South Carolina. They were led by a certain Juan Pardo, with instructions to establish bases along the route, roughly that followed earlier by de Soto. Leaving minor garrisons at several sites, Pardo finally reached the mountains by early winter and found himself blocked by snow. He ultimately doubled back and built a blockhouse at a place difficult to locate, called Guatari (Wateree). Some of his subordinates attacked the Indians and aroused their continuing enmity. Although Pardo made a second expedition through the interior, none of his garrisons survived.

Cruelty to the Indians ultimately led to the Spaniards' destruction. In the end, Fort San Felipe itself was surrounded and burned. Even yet, the Spaniards did not give up hope of settling South Carolina. In 1577 once more they built a fort on Parris Island, in sight of the ruins of San Felipe. This time they chose a stronger saint to sponsor their fortification, calling it San Marcos. Even so, it too eventually fell. The year after Drake's raid on St. Augustine, the Spaniards abandoned San Marcos and moved the remnant of their garrison back to Florida to rebuild and strengthen St. Augustine. Although Spanish missionaries made sporadic efforts to establish missions in South Carolina, they made little headway with the Indians. Spain had lost its chance of ever making a permanent settlement east of the Savannah River. Success would finally come to late contenders for the territory, the English.

For all of Spain's experience in colonial enterprise, she never realized the necessity of placating the indigenous inhabitants. Although her sovereigns issued numerous decrees requiring the conquerors to deal justly with the Indians, royal authority lay a long way across the Atlantic, and local governors frequently proved either incompetent or rapacious or both.

French efforts to occupy Carolina territory during these early years also failed because of the greater strength of the Spaniards, the religious wars in France, and the poor support of efforts to colonize. Eventually a considerable body of French refugees would find homes in Carolina, but they would live under the protection of England.

The shortcomings of colonial enterprise illustrated in these ef-

forts of Spain and France were characteristic of most early settlements by Europeans, the English included. But by the later
years of the seventeenth century, the English had gained more
experience and were ready to contend with Spain for dominance
on the South Atlantic coast. During the last years of Cromwell's
regime, the English took Jamaica from Spain. Already they had
occupied Barbados, which quickly became a populous island
where planters grew rich from the production of sugar. Jamaica
also attracted many English planters who soon prospered from
sugar. English pirates, sometimes masquerading as honest privateers, made Jamaica a favorite base for depredations against
Spanish shipping—and sometimes against any other luckless
vessels they encountered.

The conquest of Jamaica and the forays of the Jamaican
pirates illustrated the weakness of the Spanish empire in the Caribbean and is one explanation of England's daring to push its
claims to what the Spanish still believed to be the upper reaches
of Florida.

In 1629 Charles I of England granted to one of his favorites,
Sir Robert Heath, then serving as Attorney General, all the territory from 31 degrees to 36 degrees north latitude and extending
to the Great South Sea (Pacific Ocean). The king, of course,
had no notion of the vast extent of this terrain, for Europeans
still believed North America to be a relatively narrow land bar-
rier in the way of a direct sea route to the riches of China and
India. Heath gave this territory the name Carolana in honor of
King Charles I.

Civil strife between king and parliament prevented Heath
from developing his grant, though emigrants were eager to go.
French Huguenots in London, for example, hoping to settle in
Carolana, vigorously encouraged the enterprise—to no avail.
They had to wait for another generation before finding a refuge
in that region.

The failure of Heath's Carolana project left the land unoccupied. Three years after the restoration of Charles II to the
throne, eight land-hungry promoters and courtiers—men who
had some claim upon the new king for helping him regain the
crown—scented gain overseas and petitioned Charles for a grant

of territory south of Virginia. Because it cost the King nothing to give away unoccupied territory in America, he gave to the eight applicants the land awarded by his father to Heath and extinguished the latter's title on the ground that he had not developed the grant. A new charter was issued on March 24, 1663, creating the eight as Lords Proprietors of Carolina, the name they chose to honor the second Charles, merely altering the spelling of the old "Carolana" by one letter.

The Lords Proprietors included some of the most prominent noblemen of the times: George Monck, Duke of Albemarle, who had been instrumental in bringing Charles back from exile; Anthony Ashley Cooper, created first Earl of Shaftesbury in 1672 (and henceforth referred to as Shaftesbury); Edward Hyde, Earl of Clarendon, Lord Chancellor, whose daughter Anne married James II and became the mother of Queen Mary and Queen Anne; William, Earl of Craven; Lord John Berkeley, influential in naval affairs; his brother, Sir William Berkeley, previously governor of Virginia and soon to be reappointed; Sir George Carteret, treasurer of the navy; and Sir John Colleton, planter, of Barbados.

Colleton apparently was the prime mover in the enterprise. Experienced, ambitious, and unscrupulous, he got himself appointed to the Council for Foreign Plantations and was soon a member of the Royal African Company headed by the Duke of York, later James II. The Royal African Company was primarily interested in the African slave trade and in pushing the sale of slaves to English colonists in America. Colleton had learned the value of African slaves in the sugar plantations on Barbados and saw an opportunity of exploiting slave labor in the region south of Virginia. Six of the Proprietors were members of the Royal African Company and of Hudson's Bay Company and were well aware of the potential wealth of overseas enterprise. Their interest in Carolina was profit for themselves.

Two years after the first grant to the Proprietors, the king enlarged their territory under a new charter, extending it from 29 to 36 degrees, 30 minutes north latitude. The southern boundary, therefore, encroached upon legitimate Spanish territory, 100 miles south of the modern border between Georgia and Florida. But because the Proprietors did not attempt settlements beyond the Savannah River, overt conflict with Spain was temporarily averted. Carolina would remain for many years, however, England's southern outpost of empire on this continent, always threatened by Spain from the south and by France from the southwest. For some years to come, no formal distinction would be made between North and South Carolina.

Settlement of Carolina was slow; it was nearly seven years after the first charter before a permanent colony was established in what is now South Carolina. Meantime, the Proprietors were exploring and advertising their land, making tentative efforts to induce immigrants to come from other colonies, and drawing up a system of land tenure and government.

By this time Virginians had drifted down below the Dismal Swamp into the Albemarle Sound region, now claimed by the Proprietors. Governor Berkeley was instructed to set up some sort of government for these pioneers. A few New Englanders had tried to establish a colony at the mouth of the Cape Fear River, but they soon sailed away, damning the country in a "writing" left nailed to a post. Hogs and cattle left behind multiplied and supplied food for later settlers. In 1665 the Proprietors granted sole right to settle the Cape Fear country to a company of Barbadians, who fared little better than the New Englanders: two years later they abandoned their village, "Charles Town"—a name soon to be attached to a permanent settlement to the south.

To stimulate the colonial enterprise, Shaftesbury soon became the driving force. Colleton had died, the Duke of Albemarle had dropped out of public life, Clarendon was in disgrace, and one or two of the other Proprietors were no longer active. In 1669 Shaftesbury, with the aid of his secretary and personal physician, John Locke, drew up a plan of government for Carolina which he called the Fundamental Constitutions, one of the more curious documents of the seventeenth century. The respective responsibilities of Locke and Shaftesbury for its authorship have never been determined, but recent scholarship is inclined to attribute the main ideas to Shaftesbury.

The Fundamental Constitutions, frequently tinkered with and

revised, never actually became an instrument of government in the colony, but the document was often invoked by the Proprietors. Shaftesbury apparently never thought it could be put into effect in the early stages of colonial settlement, believing it to be a proposal for the future.

An odd mixture of medieval ideas and advanced concepts of toleration, the Fundamental Constitutions prescribed a hierarchical society with a landed nobility consisting of "landgraves" and "caciques" (also spelled "cassiques") at the top; next would come commoners who might be lords of manors, followed by freeholders and yeomen. A freeholder and yeoman had to own fifty acres of land to cast a vote.

The landgraves were permitted to hold four baronies of 12,000 acres each, or 48,000 acres. A cacique might hold 24,000 acres. The lord of a manor could not hold less than 3,000 acres nor more than 12,000. By the accumulation of 3,000 acres or more, a freeholder could, by petitioning the Proprietors, rise in the social scale to the position of lord of a manor. Shaftesbury made at least that concession to social fluidity. But the most unrealistic provision of the land-tenure system was a provision that the great estates would have a lower order of peasantry attached to them in perpetuity, a class of serfs called "leetmen." How Shaftesbury or anyone else thought he could induce a person voluntarily to become a serf in a new land is a dreamer's mystery. Lowest of all were the slaves. Such in brief was the tenurial system provided by the Fundamental Constitutions. The Proprietors expected recipients of land grants to pay them a penny an acre quitrent in perpetuity. That, they believed, would insure them and their heirs a rich revenue forever. They did not foresee the unwillingness or inability of settlers in the new land to raise money for quitrents.

Shaftesbury—like John Winthrop in Massachusetts Bay—was fearful of "erecting a numerous democracy" and sought to establish an aristocratic government so balanced that the aristocracy would not tyrannize over the people. To that end, he provided for a parliament in which both nobles and commoners would sit. An upper house, the Grand Council, composed of members of an elaborate administrative court system, would have all administrative responsibility. The parliament could not initiate legislation. It could only approve or reject laws proposed by the Grand Council. Although one freeman might be elected from each precinct, provided he owned at least 500 acres of land, the freeman could be outvoted by nobles who sat in parliament by statutory right. These were some of the provisions of the Fundamental Constitutions for governing Carolina.

The Fundamental Constitutions did contribute something to South Carolina's legal development: they provided for trial by jury, freedom from double jeopardy, religious toleration, and various other provisions, advanced for that time. Efforts to establish an aristocracy failed, though several landgraves were created and received appointments as governors under the Proprietors. Despite the collapse of the scheme for a nobility, the acquisition by colonial families of large tracts of land worked by black slave-labor in effect established an aristocracy of sorts that persisted for nearly two centuries.

The Carolina Proprietors were less successful and less permanent than the proprietary governments of Maryland and Pennsylvania. Though they held nominal control of North and South Carolina for a little more than fifty years, they had difficulty collecting quitrents, spent more than they gained, and lost effective control before the area was taken under the wing of the royal government.

The original Proprietors spent large sums trying to establish the colony and got almost nothing in return except title to vast acreages that they failed to develop. After the death of the original grantees, proprietorships passed to negligent heirs or were sold to speculators who, usually, had little competence or interest in the permanent development of the land.

Although the ultimate wealth envisioned by the original Proprietors proved illusory, they began their activities with enthusiasm and energy. Indeed, their advertising campaigns anticipated real estate promotion characteristic of land speculation in America for centuries to come.

Planters in the rich sugar island of Barbados, who found plantations there increasingly scarce and expensive, were eager to find more extensive and cheaper land. They had already learned to exploit their semi-tropical island with black slave labor, but families were finding it difficult to provide for their younger sons. Newcomers in Barbados discovered that they were not welcome and were unable to break into the sugar monopoly. Some of these moved on to Jamaica, but others had hopes of finding greater opportunities on the mainland of North America.

Some of these Barbadians, in touch with the Lords Proprietors of Carolina, organized a voyage of discovery in the summer of 1663 under the leadership of Captain William Hilton. His objective was to find a suitable place for colonization by Barbadians and others. In the autumn of 1662, Hilton, then a resident of Massachusetts Bay, had explored the Cape Fear River and the adjacent coast at the behest of New Englanders in search of unoccupied territory. Encouraged by his enthusiastic report, settlers from Massachusetts arrived at Cape Fear in the winter of 1663, but soon left. Hilton himself, apparently disgruntled over an unfavorable land deal in Massachusetts, sailed for Barbados. Barbadian promoters persuaded him to return to the Carolina coast to gain a more detailed description of the country.

Hilton sailed on August 10, 1663, in his own ship *Adventure.* He visited the Port Royal region, where he found several shipwrecked Englishmen and took them aboard. Hilton Head Island, southeast of Port Royal Sound, commemorates this voyage of 1663. After exploring the area, he returned to the Cape Fear and again sailed up that river. His new report pleased both the Barbadians and the Lords Proprietors. An account of this voyage, published in London the next year, was clearly intended to advertise the infinite opportunities of Carolina.

Hilton was at some pains to counteract the New Englanders' unfavorable comments about the Cape Fear region. His pamphlet, *A Relation of a Discovery,* asserted: "We . . . found as good tracts of land, dry, well-wooded, pleasant, and delightful as we have seen anywhere in the world . . . the woods stored with abundance of deer and turkeys everywhere . . . also partridges great store, cranes abundance, conies [rabbits] . . . great store of ducks, teal, widgeon, and in the woods great flocks of parrakeeto's." Hilton was also pleased with the magnificent timber: "Oaks . . . also a very tall large tree of great bigness which some do call cypress (the right name we know not) growing in swamps. Likewise walnut, birch, beech, maple, ash, bay, willow, alder, and holly; and . . . innumerable of pines, tall and good for boards or masts. . . . We saw several mulberry trees, multitudes of grapevines, and some grapes which we did eat of." [2] In short, Hilton made the region south of the upper Cape Fear River sound like a veritable Eden.

Hilton's *Relation* added a note:

> Whereas there was a writing left in a post at the point of Cape Fair [Fear] River by those New-England-men that left cattle with the Indians there, the contents whereof tended not only to the disparagement of the land about the said river but also to the great discouragement of all those that should hereafter come into those parts to settle: In answer to that scandalous writing, we whose names are under-written do affirm that we have seen, facing on both sides of the river and branches of Cape Fair aforesaid, as good land and as well timbered as any we have seen in any other part of the world, sufficient to accomodate thousands of our English nation, lying commodiously by the said river.[3]

This statement was signed by Hilton and two of his companions, Anthony Long and Peter Fabian. As a reward, the promoters agreed to grant these three men "and their heirs forever one thousand acres of land apiece upon the said river, harbor, or creeks, on such places as they shall desire, not taken up before." [4] To insure a favorable report by all the sailors in this expedition, they too received lesser grants of land: 500 acres each to two shipmasters, and 100 acres to the others.

The *Relation* concluded with terms on which immigrants could obtain land: those who went in the first fleet were guaranteed 100 acres with an additional 100 acres for each manservant taken along; in the second voyage, immigrants were to receive 70 acres each, and in following voyages, 50 acres each.

2. William Hilton, *A Relation of a Discovery Lately Made on the Coast of Florida* (London: Printed by J. C. for Simon Miller, 1664), pp. 13–14.

3. Hilton, *Discovery,* p. 22.

4. Hilton, *Discovery,* p. 29.

After Hilton's *Relation,* other tracts continued to emphasize the opportunities in Carolina. *A Brief Description of the Province of Carolina,* attributed to Robert Horne and published in London in 1666, described the abortive settlement on the Cape Fear that the Barbadians, led by Sir John Yeamans, had made in 1665 and was specially intended to advertise that enterprise. It also held out promises of happiness and prosperity to any immigrants who might seek homes on the Proprietors' lands in Carolina. At this time the Proprietors were contemplating the division of their territory into three huge "counties" with separate governments. Already Albemarle County was being settled, mostly with Virginians and a few pioneers from New England. Governor Berkeley of Virginia, himself a Carolina Proprietor, in 1664 had appointed a Scottish merchant, William Drummond, as governor of Albemarle. His name is preserved in Lake Drummond in the midst of the Great Dismal Swamp. The Proprietors designated the Cape Fear country as Clarendon County, and they proposed to create Craven County farther south in what became South Carolina. Horne's *Description* was intended to emphasize opportunities in all of Carolina. The tract was characteristic of the Proprietors' propaganda during this period of active promotion.

Despite heady promises, settlement of Carolina was delayed, in part by unforeseen circumstances in London and in part by dissension among prospective Barbadian immigrants. In 1665 the Great Plague disrupted London and sent businessmen fleeing to the country to escape infection. The next year an even greater disruption was caused by the Great Fire of London. At last, however, in August 1669, the Proprietors organized an expedition of three small vessels commanded by Captain Joseph West, loaded the ships with a contingent of immigrants with their servants, and ordered West to sail for Port Royal, where he was instructed to make a settlement.

The fleet, consisting of two frigates, the *Carolina* and the *Port Royal,* and a sloop, the *Albemarle,* suffered a series of misfortunes. A storm sank the *Albemarle* after it reached Barbados. Sir John Yeamans, head of the Barbadian promoters for colonization in Carolina, who had replaced West as fleet commander and governor of the new colony, hired another sloop, the *Three Brothers,* to carry passengers rescued from the wrecked *Albemarle.* The expedition again got under way, but another storm grounded the *Port Royal* in the Bahamas, drove the *Carolina* into a haven in the Bermudas, and swept the *Three Brothers* past Cape Hatteras all the way to Virginia. Finally, in March 1670, the *Carolina* and a sloop rented in Bermuda reached Port Royal Sound with fewer than 100 bedraggled and sea-weary passengers. These were to be the vanguard of South Carolina's colonial population.

In Bermuda Sir John Yeamans decided to return to Barbados and appointed a veteran of Caribbean settlement, eighty-year-old William Sayle, to take his place as governor. West, a much better choice, was passed over, but he went along anyway and subsequently became one of the best of the early governors.

Sayle did not fancy settling at Port Royal because it was too close to the Spaniards and to hostile tribes of Indians. While Sayle waited at anchor in nearby St. Helena (Santa Elena) Sound, the cacique of Kiawah, a tribe further up the coast, visited the governor and urged him to settle on the Kiawah River (soon to be named the Ashley).

The cacique had made contact in 1666 with Robert Sandford of Barbados, who was exploring the region, had displayed his friendship for the English, and had declared his enmity to the Spaniards. Sandford had left with the friendly Indians a young ship's surgeon, Dr. Henry Woodward, who volunteered to remain and learn the language. Woodward was to prove of immense help to the South Carolina colonists. In talks with Sayle, the cacique of Kiawah told about the ferocity of the Westo tribe of "man-eating" Indians who had recently devastated the Cusabos, to which the Kiawahs belonged. The cacique was eager for allies against the warlike Westos. Sayle, reasoning that friendly Indians hostile to both Spaniards and predatory natives might make good neighbors, sailed to Kiawah and went ashore on the west side of the Ashley River a few miles upstream from the Battery in modern Charleston. The settlers called the spot Albemarle Point; the Proprietors, however, named the village Charles Town in honor of the King. (The name of the town was sometimes spelled *Charles Town,* sometimes *Charlestown;* after 1783 its name was formally declared *Charleston.* For consistency in this book, the town will henceforth be referred to simply as Charleston, except in quoted material.)

In late May 1670, after many mishaps, the *Three Brothers* found its way into the Ashley River with a few more settlers to bring the total to 148 persons. They immediately began to fortify Albemarle Point, a site now occupied by a park, a zoo, and other tourist attractions. Ten years after their first landing, the settlers moved to Oyster Point, the peninsula between the Ashley and Cooper Rivers. There modern Charleston began.

The decade at Albemarle Point was a period of danger and uncertainty for the inhabitants. In August, a few months after their arrival, an expedition of Spaniards and Indians marched on the settlement but withdrew when friendly Indians rallied to the support of the English. But the colonists for a long time to come would remain in peril from the Spaniards and their Indian allies.

Mere survival was also a problem, for, like nearly every early colony in America, the settlers were slow to realize that subsistence farming was essential. Few of the first arrivals at Albemarle were experienced in planting food crops, and nobody had yet thought of instruction in "survival techniques" such as modern military establishments employ. Game and fish were plentiful, to be sure, but the English depended upon Indians for their major supply of such food. They also bartered for Indian corn, beans, and squash. The promoters of the enterprise, of course, furnished some food and munitions, but the imported supplies were rarely adequate.

Another major problem was the production of commodities for export, products that would insure profit. The earliest saleable commodities were deerskins, furs, timber—and Indian slaves. Although the Proprietors had enjoined the settlers against enslaving Indians, unscrupulous traders never hesitated to buy captives brought in by friendly Indians after forays against their enemies. These slaves were in demand in the West Indies, though they were of little use in Carolina, because they could too easily escape into the woods. The Carolinians themselves from the beginning depended upon black African slaves.

The first contingent of settlers consisted of emigrants from England with a few individuals picked up in Barbados and Bermuda. Soon, however, Barbadians began to move into Carolina. Sir John Yeamans, who had left the first expedition in Bermuda and returned to Barbados after appointing Sayle as governor, led a group of some fifty Barbadian settlers to Carolina in the summer of 1671. As a landgrave and a long-time promoter of Carolina, he organized the Barbadians into an effective political clique who centered in the Goose Creek area. M. Eugene Sirmans, the most recent historian of colonial politics in South Carolina, describes the "Goose Creek Men" as unscrupulous opponents of proprietary rule, intent upon disfranchising Dissenters and abolishing the Proprietors' promise of religious toleration. They openly engaged in the Indian slave trade and in trade with pirates and were concerned only with feathering their own nests. Sirmans is harsher than older Carolina historians, who praised the Barbadians for their vigor in developing the early settlements. There is no question, however, that the Barbadians' greed and their hostility to Dissenters resulted in destructive factionalism for decades to come.

In March 1671 Governor Sayle died. On his deathbed, he appointed Joseph West temporary governor until the Proprietors could make a permanent appointment. But a year later, Yeamans, asserting his rank as landgrave, won approval for his own appointment as governor and replaced West. His regime did not last long, because he too died, in 1674, after antagonizing both Proprietors and settlers by his greed and corruption. The Proprietors created West a landgrave to insure his status and made him governor. West had his troubles and made his mistakes, but he proved one of the ablest of the early governors of Carolina.

Although numerous Barbadians had come to the colony, the Proprietors were not altogether enchanted with these immigrants because of their overt opposition to Dissenters whom the Proprietors were trying to lure to their possessions. It is true that the Proprietors intended that the Anglican Church would become the established church of Carolina, but they did not want to discourage the free worship of other faiths. Their main hope of finding abundant settlers lay with Dissenters, who were being persecuted in England with increasing intensity. The Proprietors also directed some of their publicity to distressed French Protestants, Huguenots who had fled to Holland and England. These refugees increased to a flood after Louis XIV's revocation of the Edict of Nantes in 1685.

A scattering of French Huguenots had reached Carolina between 1670 and 1680. In the latter year, the first large group, some forty-five in all, arrived at Oyster Point on April 30 and received grants of land. Two of their fellow countrymen had organized the group and lent them money for their initial equipment. From this time onward, French immigration increased. By the end of the seventeenth century, an estimated 500 Huguenots were living in and around Charleston.

The Huguenots were particularly favored by the Proprietors, who believed that they might be skilled in the production of silk, wine, and olive oil—commodities that England was anxious to produce in its own imperial possessions. Although the Huguenots never were able to supply any of these products in commercial quantities, they contributed in other ways, far beyond their numerical strength, to the development of the colony. They were hard-working, highly intelligent, and frequently skilled in various essential or desirable trades. At last, persecuted Frenchmen, who long before had tried under Jean Ribaut to gain a foothold in South Carolina, had won a permanent place in the social fabric of Carolina.

3

Diversity of People
—and Broils in Plenty

*O*F all the English colonies settled in the seventeenth century, only Pennsylvania exceeded Carolina in the diversity of its population—and in the controversies and quarrels that ensued. People of varied types and religions came early to Carolina, and although the great influx of non-English settlers arrived later in the eighteenth century, the advertising campaigns of the first Proprietors attracted many kinds of adventurers and land-hungry pioneers, some in search of new opportunities for prosperity, others hoping for both prosperity and freedom from religious persecution.

Pennsylvania and Carolina held out the promise of religious toleration to immigrants of all faiths, a promise having an immense appeal to persecuted minorities in Great Britain and countries across the English Channel. The Lords Proprietors of Carolina were not demonstrating a broad spirit of toleration that had come to them like a benevolent revelation; they were merely businessmen in search of profits from the sale of land and from quitrents. They knew that the quickest way to get settlers to Carolina was to offer inducements greater than they could find at home or elsewhere.

The Proprietors had no intention of encouraging heretical doctrines or even of divorcing church and state in their dominions. In God's good time, they would encourage the formal establishment of the Anglican Church. In the meantime, the granting of permission to other faiths to worship as they pleased would encourage immigration. Eventually, when Carolina was a settled colony, the taxpayers might be required to support a state church.

Such was the thinking of the Proprietors, for toleration was not yet widely accepted. William Penn and his fellow Quakers looked more kindly upon religious freedom than other folk, but most religious groups wanted freedom only for themselves. When Lord Baltimore was planning his own proprietary colony of Maryland as a refuge for persecuted Catholics, he thought it expedient and necessary to promise freedom of worship to other sects. It is significant of the times, however, that when dissenting Protestants gained a majority of the population in the mid-seventeenth century, they abolished the earlier Act of Toleration. Whatever the Lords Proprietors themselves would have preferred, they knew that they could not settle their vast land holdings rapidly without appealing to groups eager to escape pressures for religious conformity. Consequently, they widely advertised freedom of worship in Carolina for all who believed in God and wished to set up a church of their own. Even heathen were not to be molested in their unbelief. This propaganda had the desired effect.

During the reign of Louis XIV, persecution of French Protestants, the Huguenots, became acute, especially after the revocation of the Edict of Nantes. In the last fifteen years of the seventeenth century, thousands of the most talented people of France fled to Switzerland, Holland, and England. In England, these Huguenots had become something of an embarrassment because of their competition with English workers, and the government was glad to have the Carolina Proprietors direct publicity to them. Furthermore, English mercantilists perceived a great advantage in having skilled French emigrants settling in the new land; ever since England had sought to colonize portions of North America, statesmen and merchants had dreamed of the production of exotic commodities the purchase of which caused a continual drain of money. In other words, if English colonies could produce silk, wine, olive oil, dates, figs, raisins, currants, and dye stuffs, the home country's balance of payments would improve. The French Huguenots were known to be experienced silk and wine makers. They would therefore make ideal colonists for Carolina, which most Englishmen still believed to be a semitropical paradise.

Out of a Carolina population of approximately 4,000 in 1695, the Huguenots numbered about 500, concentrated on the Santee River in Craven County; some had settled around Goose Creek, and a few remained in Charleston. At this time South Carolina was divided into three huge counties: Craven in the east, Berkeley in the center, and Colleton in the west. Granville County, still farther to the west, was virtually unsettled. The Huguenots, outnumbering the English in thinly settled Craven County, sent six representatives to the legislative assembly. Berkeley and Colleton counties each sent seven. Thus the French, with a large voice in legislation, aroused the hostility of the English, who sought to have representation from Craven County discontinued, on the ground that the population there was too sparse to warrant it. In 1697, however, the assembly granted full privileges of citizenship to the French and to other foreigners on petition to the governor within three months.

Because Englishmen had an ingrained prejudice against Frenchmen, a certain amount of ill-will, even against fellow Protestants of French birth, persisted for a number of years. For their part, the French were disgruntled over efforts at discrimination against them. For example, the English tried to keep them from building or owning ships by invoking a clause in the Navigation Acts disqualifying ''foreigners'' for such ownership, even though the Huguenots had already been given the rights of citizenship.[1]

The Huguenots were Calvinists, with some of the qualities of the Puritans, including a fondness for Biblical first names such as Noah, Isaac, Peter, Daniel, Jacob, Joseph, and Elias. They founded six churches in the colony, one of which, the Huguenot

---

1. M. Eugene Sirmans, *Colonial South Carolina: A Political History, 1663–1763* (Chapel Hill, N.C.: University of North Carolina Press, 1966), p. 66.

Church of Charleston, has endured to the present day. Dissenting sects naturally expected the Huguenots to affiliate with them, but they were disappointed: most Huguenots joined the Anglican Church, after the Act of 1706 made it the established church supported by taxation. Practical Frenchmen, they saw no reason to pay taxes for one church and then contribute to support their own clergymen. The simplest solution was to join the establishment—and perhaps take it over with their ministers. In the course of time, some of the most distinguished clergymen in the Episcopal Church were of Huguenot origins. The union of Huguenots with Anglicans dismayed the nonconformists and contributed to their dislike of Frenchmen.

The Huguenots proved a versatile and industrious increment of the Carolina population. Contrary to romantic tales, most of the Huguenots were not nobleborn but were skilled craftsmen of one sort or another: carpenters, coopers, blacksmiths, weavers, sail-makers, silk workers, vignerons, leather workers, gold- and silversmiths, shipwrights, gardeners, farmers. A few professional men, doctors and clergymen, were among the emigrants, and some were already experienced in trade and ready to set up as merchants. In time, many Huguenots grew rich, rose in the social scale, married into the best families, and became leaders in the Low Country aristocracy. The phrase "rich as a Huguenot" was proverbial. Such names as Laurens, Manigault, St. Julien, Huger (pronounced Ugee), Dupre, Gaillard, Ravenel, Mouzon, Porcher, and Petigru—to list only a few—illustrate the enduring merit of distinguished Huguenot families.

The rise of the Manigaults typifies the industry and shrewdness of these French families. The first of this name in the colony were two brothers, Pierre and Gabriel, who reached Charleston in 1695 with a small amount of capital and one black slave. Gabriel, a carpenter, fell off a scaffold and died. His brother Pierre acquired a tract of land on the Santee, tried farming, but soon gave it up to run a tavern. One of his shrewdest moves was to persuade Judith Giton, a widow, to marry him. Judith had helped her first husband to clear land, saw lumber, and work in the fields. Her heroic endurance and amazing diligence, often with scanty food in the early days, is indicative of the stamina, courage, and determination of the French refugees, qualities that made them successful pioneers.

Judith and Pierre Manigault soon left tavern-keeping to operate a distillery, erect a woodworking shop for barrel making, and finally to build a warehouse and store on the Charleston docks. When Pierre died, in 1729, he was a prosperous owner of land, slaves, warehouses, and mercantile establishments. His son Gabriel increased his patrimony and became one of the richest men in all the American colonies. Succeeding Manigaults continued to prosper and to occupy positions of honor and influence in South Carolina.

A similar story might be told of other Huguenot families. The Laurens dynasty was founded in Charleston by an industrious saddler whose son, Henry Laurens, born in 1724, acquired great wealth as a merchant-planter and ultimately was a hero of the American Revolution.

Although Huguenots settled in other colonies, notably New York and Pennsylvania, their heaviest concentration was in South Carolina. The thrift and diligence which brought wealth to many of them made the envious accuse them of being preoccupied with the pursuit of this world's goods; but they also showed a deep concern with self-improvement and acquired learning and a high degree of cultivation. They made important contributions to the cultural, social, and political development of the colony.

Many French Huguenots had fled to Switzerland, and it was to them that a Swiss promoter, Jean Pierre Purry of Neufchatel, in 1724 held out the promise of a new life in Carolina. Swiss Huguenots were believed to be ideal colonists. Purry had made a contract with the British government—which by this time had taken over from the Lords Proprietors—to recruit 1,200 Swiss emigrants. By the autumn of 1726, Purry's publicity had attracted more than 600 would-be emigrants, but when the British failed to provide promised transportation, Purry had to flee from his disappointed and riotous countrymen. Only twenty-four of this group managed to reach Charleston in December 1726.

Purry did not give up, but continued to publicize Carolina. In 1732 he made another deal with the royal government for a grant of 12,000 acres on the east side of the Savannah River, some twenty-five miles from its mouth, provided that he transport at his own expense 600 emigrants in the next six years. This he contrived to do and settled them on his grant, one of several newly created "townships" on the frontier which the colonial government hoped would serve as protective outposts against the Indians. The promoter named his settlement Purrysburgh. Purry's colonists were expected to develop silk and wine production; but the venture did not prosper. The marshy site was mosquito-ridden, and many of the settlers died of malaria and other ailments. Survivors drifted away to better territory. The village lingered out its existence until the early nineteenth century and even produced a little silk but not enough to be commercially profitable. Although the silk delusion remained an obsession for generations, not even the ingenious French were able to produce enough to supply the English market. Silk production required skilled labor, an eternal lack in the colonies.

Nevertheless, faith in French Huguenots as potential producers of silk and wine persisted for many years after the Purrysburgh fiasco. Almost on the eve of the Revolution, Huguenot colonists were given land in what is now McCormick County in the rugged Up Country, provided with tools, and told to produce silk and wine. The group, led by two Calvinistic ministers, Jean Louis Gibert and Moses Boutiton, named their settlement New Bordeaux. It was southwest of Abbeville, also settled by French, as the name indicates. New Bordeaux, a year after its settlement in 1764, had some 300 French inhabitants. For a time they actually produced some silk but gave it up for more profitable crops. Until the beginning of the present century, Abbeville could still show a few ancient grapevines planted by French colonists, decades earlier.

Early in the present century, a great-aunt of mine, living at Ninety Six, boasted of learning to make silk from the French. She had a grove of mulberry trees on which her silkworms fed. Robert Mills, in his remarkable book *Statistics of South Carolina* (1826), noted that "in 1759 South Carolina produced 10,000 lbs. of raw silk." Describing Abbeville County, he commented that "the culture of silk was carried on here to some extent formerly, but what is now made is for domestic use.'' [2]

Calvinists were not the only Frenchmen to find refuge in South Carolina. In 1755 the English governor of Nova Scotia deported thousands of unfortunate Acadians and scattered them up and down the Atlantic coast. More than 1,000 were landed in Charleston, where they were unwelcome guests: the inhabitants worried lest they burn down the town or stir up a slave rebellion. Nevertheless, the legislative assembly voted funds to assist these French Catholic refugees and sent as many as possible into the country. A few settled on the Santee, but many died and most of the survivors eventually drifted away, some to Haiti and others to Louisiana. The Acadians were suspect because they were Roman Catholics and hostile aliens.

Scottish settlers of three sorts, with vastly different temperaments and dispositions, played an important part in South Carolina history from the days of Proprietary rule onward.

There were Lowland Scots from Scotland proper; Ulster Scots from Ireland, frequently and ambiguously designated Scotch-Irish, or, in early records, simply "Irish"; and, lastly, there were Highland Scots, who came in droves, chiefly to North Carolina, though some drifted into South Carolina. Although a popular impression exists that English authorities deported many Scots to the colonies to avoid executing them after the Jacobite rebellions of 1715 and 1745, most of these Scots came voluntarily to improve their economic lot, for times were hard in the late seventeenth and eighteenth centuries in both Scotland and Ulster. Some Scots brought a little capital and were able to acquire large tracts of land; most, however, could do little more than raise enough money for their ocean fare and needed bounties offered by colonial governments for the bare necessities in getting started in a new land; others had to indenture themselves for a term of years to pay for their transportation. However they got here, they made important contributions to the settlement of the back country, though they were often clannish, contentious, and difficult to assimilate into other groups. Scottish interest in the

2. Robert Mills, *Statistics of South Carolina* (Charleston, S.C.: Hurlbut & Loyd, 1826), p. 155, p. 353.

southern region continued for years. Scottish traders very early found their way to trading posts among the Creeks and Cherokees. Later, Ulster Scots, filtering down from Pennsylvania, helped to settle Piedmont Carolina.

Several Utopian schemes for establishing southern enclaves were evolved by Scots. One of the most colorful was the brainchild of Sir Robert Montgomery of Skelmorly who dreamed of an empire in what is now Georgia on land then claimed by the Lords Proprietors of Carolina. In 1717 Montgomery published *A Discourse Concerning the design'd Establishment Of a New Colony To The South of Carolina, In The Most delightful Country of the Universe.*

Like others before him, Sir Robert described this country, which he named Azilia, as "our future Eden," and further declared that "Paradise, with all her virgin beauties, may be modestly suppos'd at most but equal to its native excellencies." [3] The Lords Proprietors were more than glad to encourage for this territory Scottish settlers who would serve as protection against the Spaniards in Florida and the French in Louisiana. Accordingly, they granted permission to Sir Robert and his colleagues to settle Azilia.

In a literary genre characterized by optimism, Sir Robert Montgomery's *Discourse* is surely one of the most hopeful ever printed. Azilia, as he describes it, "lies in the same latitude with Palestine herself, that promis'd Canaan . . . 'Tis beautiful with odiferous plants, green all the year. . . . The orange and the lemon thrive in the same common orchard with the apple, and the pear tree, plums, peaches, apricots, and nectarines bear from stones in three years' growing." [4] To Scots and Englishmen, who knew oranges from Seville and lemons from Portugal merely as symbols of luxury, this country, in the same latitude as Palestine, must have appeared indeed as a new Canaan.

Montgomery's plans for Azilia came to naught, but he was soon followed by another Scot, the erratic Sir Alexander Cum-

3. Quoted by Louis B. Wright in *The Colonial Search for a Southern Eden* (University, Ala.: University of Alabama Press, 1953), p. 53.

4. Wright, *Colonial Search,* p. 54.

ing of Coulter, who conceived a notion of settling 300,000 Jews on Cherokee tribal lands in South Carolina. Sir Alexander set out in 1729 on a self-appointed mission to Carolina and the Cherokees. His travels read like a chapter from *Don Quixote.* Leaving Charleston on March 13, 1730, the Scottish baronet traveled during the following month nearly a thousand miles through the Cherokee tribes. Armed to the teeth and boasting of the power and brilliance of his king, George II, the baronet convinced his Indian hearers that he was a great chief representing a king whose power reached even to the hills of South Carolina. At a tribal council he persuaded the chiefs to kneel and swear allegiance to King George—or so he thought—and he had himself acclaimed the king's viceroy. So persuasive was Sir Alexander's eloquence that he induced six Cherokees—a minor chief and five warriors—to set out with him for London and the king's court. Near Charleston they were joined by another Indian. When they all reached England, the chief was a king and the other Indians were described as generals or chiefs.

On June 18, 1730, King George received the Scot and his Indian protegés. During the next three months the Cherokee "king" and his fellow "chiefs" were the sensation of London. They were entertained, feted, and taught English vices. On September 28 the play *Orinoco* was performed in their honor at Lincoln's Inn Fields, and so great was the public excitement over the Indians that the theater's box office receipts trebled that night. When they returned to their tribesmen, the Indians' report of the glories of the English nation probably helped to keep the Cherokees loyal to England in the succeeding wars with France.

Fantastic as were Sir Alexander Cuming's schemes for Cherokee-Jewish utopias in the foothills of Carolina, the publicity they received helped to focus further interest on the Southern colonies.

The Proprietors and later the English colonial authorities, eager for diligent settlers of any persuasion, followed William Penn's example of advertising Carolina in the Rhineland and encouraging the immigration of Germans. Six townships, established before 1732 by the Royal government, offered to grant fifty acres to every immigrant; and the authorities also promised to supply transportation to the township sites and provide a small amount of essential equipment.

In addition to the Swiss immigrants who settled in Purrysburgh township, there came, in the summer of 1735, 220 German Swiss to Orangeburg township and began the settlement there. In the same year, Germans began occupying land in Saxe-Gotha township (modern Lexington County). A section known to this day as the "Dutch Fork," between the Saluda and the Congaree rivers, was early peopled by Germans— "Dutch" in this instance meaning *Deutsch,* German. Like the Scots, the Germans were clannish and did not readily assimilate with other groups. A few became members of strange religious cults, the oddest being the Weberites, who affected nakedness and believed that Jacob Weber was the Lord God and a neighbor named John Peter was the reincarnation of Christ. Later Weber received a revelation that Peter was not Christ, but the devil, and forthwith murdered him. For this Weber was hanged in 1761. Traffic in the occult was long attributed to some of these Germans. A lingering remnant of occultism in this region was evident in my youth when the "Dutch Weather Prophet," a resident of the Dutch Fork, solemnly made predictions each autumn for the winter's weather after a judicious viewing of goose-bones.

In 1736 a group of Welsh Baptists from Newcastle, Pennsylvania (now in Delaware), obtained a grant to some 175,000 acres on both sides of the Great Pee Dee River in the region between the present towns of Bennettsville and Hartsville. Two years later they founded a Baptist Church near the river crossing, not far from Society Hill, and endeavored to keep out interlopers of other faiths, lest discord arise. The small town of Society Hill was the center of what became known as the "Welsh Neck."

About the time of the migration from Pennsylvania of the Welsh Baptists, a few Ulster and Lowland Scots made their way overland from Pennsylvania to the fringe of settlements on the upper edge of the Low Country. Scottish and English settlers near the present town of Camden cleared small farms along the

Wateree or grazed cattle in the lush bottom lands. David Duncan Wallace, in his *South Carolina, a Short History,* comments on the abundance of thieves and rogues in this locality—''some so notorious as to be advertised for in the *Virginia Gazette''*—that "plagued the magistrateless settlement as they did other South Carolina frontiers of the period.'' [5] Although a few cabins dotted the southern edge of the Sand Hills of South Carolina by the 1730s, the filling up of the back country had to wait until a later period.

Already, however, the growth of a plantation economy based on the cultivation of rice in the Low Country had created an increasing demand for laborers, and South Carolina quickly became the largest mainland importer of African slaves. Slavery had proved successful on the sugar plantations of Barbados, and the early Barbadian settlers had brought some slaves with them.

The Royal African Company, in which several of the first Proprietors of Carolina had an interest, eagerly pushed the sale of slaves. Even before the development of rice planting, black slaves were used in cutting timber and making naval stores in the coastal pine forests. The discovery that river swamps could be reclaimed for rice fields made an increasing supply of labor imperative. African slaves were believed to be less susceptible to swamp-induced diseases than white laborers—even if sufficient white indentured servants had been available. Hence black slavery was inexorably fastened upon South Carolina— with all of its subsequent tragedy.

From an early date these unwilling immigrants created problems. As they grew in numbers, the danger of slave revolts increased. By 1708, Negro slaves in the Low Country almost equalled the number of whites, and by 1724 they outnumbered whites by three to one. Although legal codes to curb potential rebellion were enacted from time to time, and punishments were often severe, between 1711 and 1740 more than a half-dozen incidents occurred that frightened slave owners. The most terrify-

5. David D. Wallace, *South Carolina: A Short History, 1520–1948* (Chapel Hill, N.C.: University of North Carolina Press, 1951), p. 155.

ing was an uprising in 1739, known from the name of the leader as the Cato conspiracy, in which some thirty whites and more than forty Negroes died.

*   *   *   *   *

With a diverse population of different social conditions, different regions, and different economic potentials, it is small wonder that early South Carolinians were quarrelsome and in a constant state of political discontent. Indeed, political unrest has been a characteristic of the people from that day to this.

South Carolina's proprietary rule was less successful than similar regimes in Pennsylvania and Maryland, or even the somewhat chaotic proprietary regimes in East and West Jersey. It was never popular because the Proprietors were more concerned about their own profits than with altruistic aims for the inhabitants of their domain, particularly since their profits proved consistently elusive. The original eight Lords Proprietors, possibly excepting Shaftesbury, with his coadjutor, John Locke, had small interest in Carolina except as a source of revenue. They knew little about the region and learned little if anything at first hand. Only the Barbadian, Sir John Colleton, had any colonial experience, and Colleton was a greedy, cynical self-server. As the first Proprietors died, their shares were bought by speculators, most of whom had even less concern for the welfare of the region than had the original owners. For example, one Seth Sothel, who bought the Earl of Clarendon's portion, used his prerogative as Proprietor to declare himself governor of South Carolina in 1690 when the Assembly voted to banish Governor James Colleton, brother of Proprietor Sir John Colleton. Sothel had previously established a record as one of North Carolina's most notorious and ineffective governors. Among the few good things that can be said about him is that he tried to achieve justice for the Huguenots and other foreign-born Carolinians; he sought to improve conditions in the Indian trade and tried to suppress the sale of liquor to the tribesmen; and he made an effort to improve various civil regulations that needed reform.

Although officials appointed by the Proprietors were

frequently incompetent or corrupt or both, not all of them were bad. Governor Joseph West, who served from 1674 until 1682, saw the infant colony through trying times and did much to save it from failure. In 1695, a Quaker, John Archdale, who had bought a Proprietorship in the name of his son, came out as governor because his colleagues believed that only a man with the authority of a Proprietor could quiet the squabbles between themselves and the people. Archdale reformed the laws, revised land tenures and quitrents in favor of the people, set an example of religious toleration, and departed after a year in the belief that he had settled the broils that wracked the country. He named as his successor a respected and honest man, Landgrave Joseph Blake, who did his best to follow Archdale's precepts and example. These were among the better appointees. The success of the colony during the Proprietary period, however, resulted from the enterprise of the colony's private citizens.

Some Proprietary officials were competent but corrupt. For example, Nicholas Trott, appointed attorney general in 1698 and later made chief justice, was a man of unusual learning, who compiled the provincial statutes (not printed until 1736). Yet Trott was violently hated for his bigoted support of the Anglican establishment and for other partisan acts and was accused of various corrupt practices in office.

When, for a time, the Lords Proprietors tried to monopolize the Indian trade, the settlers and free-lance traders resisted strenuously. When the Proprietary governors tried to rig representation in the legislative assembly, dissenting groups resisted successfully. By political trickery, however, partisans of the Proprietors contrived in 1704 to establish the Anglican Church as the state church supported by taxation. Nonconformists, disfranchised, raised such a storm of protest that the Church Act had to be modified in 1706. The franchise was restored to non-Anglicans but the established church endured until after the Revolution.

The legislative assembly, created with an elected Commons House and an appointed Council that served as an upper house, was constantly irritated by the Proprietary veto of laws enacted for the welfare of the colony. The Proprietors also showed little concern for the military protection of Carolina. An accumulation of grievances against Proprietary rule came to a climax in 1719. The legislative Assembly in November of that year rebelled against the Proprietors. It was an orderly revolution; the Assembly merely voted to disregard the Proprietors' vetoes of laws it had passed and requested the Proprietary governor, Robert Johnson, to "hold the reins of government for the King till his Majesty's pleasure be known." His Majesty was slow to make his pleasure known, and it was not until May 1721 that the sovereign sent Sir Francis Nicholson to serve as provisional governor. South Carolina was clear of the Lords Proprietors, who did, however, retain a tenuous hold on North Carolina until 1729.

Although the period of Proprietary rule was one of confusion and factionalism, the colony survived and managed to prosper. It also developed a spirit of independence and discovered the potentials of self-government through its own elected Commons House of the Assembly. The early years of royal government were sometimes hardly better than the period of Proprietary rule, but the colony developed resources within itself for survival and growth.

4

Hope of Prosperity: Indian Trade
and Products of the Land

*F*ROM the time of the first settlement at Jamestown, Virginia, until the establishment of Georgia, last of the thirteen original colonies, the mother country had dreamed of finding a source in the New World of all those products that she had been forced to buy from other countries. For example, the principal suppliers of cochineal and indigo, used to dye army uniforms, were France and Spain, England's inveterate enemies. By the early eighteenth century, England's annual bill for silk was something on the order of £500,000—money down the drain in the eyes of mercantilist economists of that day. All those silken garments affected by both men and women of the upper class cost hard money that financial experts thought England could ill afford to spend with other nations. King James I himself had written a preface to a book by a Frenchman describing silk culture and had commanded Virginia colonists to read the book, follow its instructions, and made silk.

Because South Carolina was situated in a latitude believed favorable to tropical products, colonial authorities in London were hopeful that it would become a source of silk, olive oil, sugar, wine, oranges, lemons, dates, figs, and other exotic products. For decades after the arrival of the earliest colonists in South Carolina, hope ran high that this new region would become a profitable source of products that had failed in the more northerly settlements. Much experimentation took place, but results were not precisely what the economic planners expected. As tobacco in Virginia displaced all other commodities in commercial value, so in South Carolina deerskins, rice, and indigo established the economic stability of the colony.

The good things of the earth, fertile as was the soil, proved of secondary importance in the South Carolinians' earliest efforts to achieve prosperity. For generations, trade with the Indians influenced the development of South Carolina and had a profound impact upon the imperial politics of England, Spain, and France. Indian trade, centered in Charleston, determined peace and war between tribes and nations of the aborigines, as well as between the English and their foreign competitors.

As the hucksters of modern advertising have created desires for products sometimes useless or injurious, so traders quickly taught Indians to yearn for the white man's goods and vices. The introduction of rum, to which Indians became immediately addicted, caused the destruction of some groups. The sale of guns and ammunition to increase the production of deerskins was also a calamity. The Carolinians pointed out, however, that "their Indians" had to protect themselves from traditional enemy tribes armed by other Europeans. The Spaniards, it should be noted, had tried to keep guns out of the hands of tribesmen in their jurisdictions.

The promoters of Carolina in England were already keenly aware of the immense profits from the fur trade. Some of them had been instrumental in organizing the Hudson's Bay Company. All were aware of the wealth to be obtained from the exchange of English goods for skins and furs. Virginians had a long-established trade with interior tribes, and Sir William Berkeley, formerly governor of Virginia and a Lord Proprietor of Carolina, for years had been deeply involved in the Indian trade.

Carolinians soon found also that Indian slaves were a profitable commodity in the West Indies. Some Indian slaves, to be sure, were kept at home for heavy work, but they could too easily escape into the woods to prove satisfactory as a consistent labor force. In the West Indies, however, where escape was less easy, they could replace Africans on the sugar plantations. A considerable market for Carolina Indian slaves also existed in New England.

Although the Lords Proprietors had forbidden trade in Indian slaves, probably for fear of depleting hunters and customers for English goods rather than for humanitarian reasons, the Carolinians generally ignored the prohibition from London. For many years, hard-bitten traders continued to bring into Charleston slaves from the interior, sometimes laden with bundles of deerskins. Both the transport and their freight thus turned a neat profit.

Slavery had from time immemorial been traditional with the Indians themselves. Captives were sometimes tortured and, in certain tribes, were occasionally eaten ritually, although most captives were kept as drudges. Many a prisoner lived out a miserable existence as a slave. When Indians discovered that white traders would gladly exchange guns or rum for stout young captives, their eagerness to raid weaker tribes received a new incentive. The slave trade helped to wipe out groups unable to defend themselves against stronger tribes. In the intermittent conflicts between colonists and Indians, the conquering whites sold without a qualm their captives to the West Indies or to New England.

Indian traders from Carolina actively served the ends of British imperial expansion. By the early eighteenth century, they had made contacts with tribes in the lower Mississippi valley, western Florida, and Alabama. Pushing up river valleys and across the southern ranges of the Appalachians, they reached tribes that the French were trying to hold as their own.

In general, the Indians preferred English blankets and other English goods, but the traders themselves were not always as successful as the French *coureurs des bois* or the Spanish missionaries in making friends with the natives. Indeed, many British traders were bad examples on the frontier, and their short-sighted behavior frequently resulted in hostile incidents. Nevertheless, they were a potent factor in pushing English influence on distant frontiers, especially in the southeast.

The names of most of these pioneers of trade and empire are lost to history or preserved only in sparse colonial records, but the career of one of the earliest and most famous, Dr. Henry Woodward, is fairly well documented. Woodward, who began his professional life as a ship's surgeon and accompanied Robert Sandford's exploration of the Port Royal region, elected to stay with the Indians to learn their language. Later captured by Spaniards and taken to St. Augustine, he was rescued by a raiding English pirate. Subsequently wrecked in another vessel on the island of Nevis, Woodward was again rescued, this time by the first shipload of immigrants bound for Carolina, and he went with them to the Ashley River settlement.

Because Woodward knew some of the Indian languages and already had friends among the coastal tribes, his services were crucial. For many years he proved an able forest diplomat, so valuable that the Lords Proprietors paid him on occasion the equivalent of the governor's salary. Well they might, for he looked after the Proprietors' interests when they were trying to monopolize the trade with tribes west of Port Royal. As the special agent of the Earl of Shaftesbury, Woodward wrote the Earl on December 31, 1674, about an expedition he had made to the Westo Indians at what was then their principal town, on the Savannah River in the vicinity of modern Augusta: "They are well provided with arms, ammunition, trading cloth and other trade from the northward for which at set times of the year they truck [trade] dressed deerskins, furs, and young Indian slaves." [1] The "northward" source of their goods was Virginia, and Woodward soon had this traffic flowing to Charleston.

In 1685 he led a small expedition to the Chattahoochee River to establish trade with the Creek Indians. So pleased were these tribesmen with their new source of goods that, when the Spaniards tried to block it, the Indians moved in a body to what is now mid-Georgia to be nearer Woodward's men. Woodward

---

1. Henry Woodward, *A Faithful Relation of My Westo Voyage,* 1674, *Narratives of Early Carolina, 1650–1708,* edited by Alexander S. Salley, Jr. (New York: Charles Scribner's Sons, 1911), p. 133.

was followed by other enterprising agents from Charleston who succeeded in diverting to the Carolina port much of the traffic that had been a Spanish monopoly.

In a traffic that soon became a cutthroat enterprise—sometimes literally that—Dr. Henry Woodward was not universally liked in Carolina. A Scottish nobleman, Henry Erskine, Baron Cardross, eager to establish his own hegemony over tribes beyond the Savannah River, arrested Woodward and forbade him to cross the territory of an abortive Scottish colony in the Port Royal country. Woodward, who had made a good thing out of trade with the Westo Indians, both for himself and the Lords Proprietors, earned the hatred of private traders in Charleston who stirred up a war with the Westos. With the help of an alien tribe of Savannahs of Shawnee stock, they wiped out the Westos and sold the remnant to the West Indies.

Minor Indian conflicts were desirable, for war meant slaves, and slaves meant profits. Greed later precipitated disastrous Indian attacks, but as yet the colonists felt secure in their ability to keep tribes fighting each other and bartering their prisoners for beads, blankets, and rum. None of this was very high-minded, of course, but though our colonial ancestors were mightily concerned about religion, they were rarely troubled by ethics.

Although Indian slaves in the early days were a profitable sideline of the interior trade, deerskins were the staple commodity. Carolina teemed with deer, so numerous that an Englishman in 1682 observed that "there is such infinite herds that the whole country seems but one continued park." [2] The slaughter of deer, continued for more than a century, might be compared to the slaughter of buffalo on the Great Plains in the nineteenth century.

Deerskins were in great demand in Europe and even elsewhere in the American colonies because they made excellent leather for clothing and other uses. Some idea of the extent of the skin trade may be gained from the fact that between December 1706 and December 1707, Carolina shipped to London

---

2. Thomas Ashe, *Carolina, or a Description of the Present State of that Country* (London, 1682), *Narratives of Early Carolina*, p. 150.

121,355 hides. Until the full development of rice production in the eighteenth century, deer hides were the most profitable commodity exported from Carolina.

Charleston was the metropolis for Indian traders from the whole of the southeast. Unlike the fur traders of Canada and the northern tier of English colonies, the Indian traders of Carolina could not transport their wares by canoe. Although the southeast is drained by many rivers, none provided continuous navigation from the trading posts of the interior. Hence traders had to transport their goods by pack horse or human burden bearers. Indians could carry as much as 100 pounds of skins or trade goods, or a heavy keg of rum from the seacoast to the mountains.

In the spring, Charleston's streets rang with the horse bells of pack trains bringing to merchants' warehouses on the wharves the past season's collection of skins and furs. Open taverns invited the now affluent trader to squander his wealth. Like later trappers in the West at such rendezvous as Jackson Hole, the Carolina traders often blew their whole earnings in one glorious spree in Charleston. Once more sober and poor, they set off on their ponies for another season among the Creeks, Chickasaws, Choctaws, Cherokees, or Catawbas.

These long-forgotten frontiersmen, the equivalent of the mountain men who trapped beaver in the West, were a colorful lot. They took Indian squaws as concubines and wives and fathered hosts of half-breeds. At first, most were of English origin, but soon Scots were numerous in the hinterland. Many earned the respect and friendship of the Indians, but others cheated them with false weights and measures, or got them drunk on rum and took their deerskins for a pittance. Although the Indians had flexible ideas of chastity, they complained of the traders' insatiable concupiscence that led to the corruption of their wives and daughters without proper compensation. In short, dishonest and short-sighted traders laid up a store of grievances that would one day break out in devastating attacks on the frontiers.

The government made an effort to regulate and control the backwoods traders by licensing them each year and by appointing agents to attempt overall supervision. But no law was effective in distant reaches of the forest.

Some of the early Indian agents, however, were men of energy and vision. Two in particular deserve to be remembered: Thomas Nairne, a Scot, and Price Hughes, a Welshman. Both tried to enforce fair dealings with the Indians, and both dreamed of expanding English imperial dominion from Carolina to the Mississippi and the Gulf of Mexico.

Nairne, himself a planter of St. Helena, was appointed Indian agent by the legislative assembly in 1707; for the next eight years, he struggled to maintain an enlightened policy of friendship with the Indians of the southeast and to weaken Spanish and French influence in the region. He planned an attack on the French outpost at Mobile, journeyed to the Choctaws and made peace with them, and urged the Society for the Propagation of the Gospel to send missionaries to the Yemassees and other tribes; he pointed out that to destroy Spanish missions which had brought "something of Christianity" and again to reduce the Indians to "downright barbarity and heathenism" was neither Christian nor politic. As Verner W. Crane suggests, in *The Southern Frontier,* Nairne wisely believed it would be beneficial to have among the Indians "persons not interested in trade to protect them from injustice and to send the government intelligence of Indian affairs." [3]

But Nairne's brilliant schemes were thwarted by Governor Sir Nathaniel Johnson, whose slave trade Nairne attempted to stop. Johnson charged Nairne with treason and threw him into jail. Released and restored to his agency by Governor Charles Craven in 1712, Nairne continued his efforts for peace and fair dealings with the Indians. His labors came to naught with the outbreak of the Yemassee War in 1715. On a peace mission to this tribe, he was slaughtered on April 15, 1715, tortured by having lightwood splinters stuck into his flesh to burn slowly and inflict maximum pain. Thus perished the best friend the Indians had in this period.

3. Verner W. Crane, *The Southern Frontier, 1670–1732* (Durham, N.C.: Duke University Press, 1928), p. 146.

Some years earlier, on a visit to England in 1710, Nairne had met Price Hughes, a well-to-do Welshman, who soon concocted a scheme to bring over many of his fellow Welshmen as colonists. His plan to settle Welsh poor in Carolina did not materialize, but Hughes himself became a volunteer forest diplomat of extraordinary skill and energy. He was soon writing to members of Queen Anne's court, outlining schemes for expanding English authority from Charleston to the Mississippi and beyond. Between 1713 and 1715, he went from Carolina on missions to the Cherokees, Creeks, Chickasaws, and Choctaws in an effort to alienate them from French influence. During this period, British agents from Charleston, ranging as far away as the Illinois with trade goods and gifts, succeeded in subverting many tribesmen who had previously been loyal to the French. South Carolina agents even succeeded in employing some French *coureurs des bois*. A South Carolina dream of western expansion seemed about to come true. But Hughes was made a prisoner by French and Indians in April 1715 as he floated down the Mississippi. Taken before acting French governor Sieur de Bienville at Mobile, Hughes stoutly asserted English claims to the central Mississippi valley by reason of "occupation" by established traders. Courteously treated by Bienville and released, Hughes went on to Pensacola to negotiate with Spanish officials. Then, setting out for parleys with Alabama Indians, he was waylaid and murdered by a tribe that had suffered from unscrupulous Carolina slave catchers. So perished another forest statesman.

South Carolina, the southern frontier before the establishment of Georgia in 1732, was drawn into all of the colonial wars between Great Britain, France, and Spain—and was involved in Indian conflicts of its own. During Queen Anne's War (1701–1713), Charleston stood in constant fear of Spanish invasion from St. Augustine. Believing that offense was the best defense, Governor James Moore in September 1702 attacked the fort at St. Augustine from the sea, but was frightened off by the arrival of two heavily armed Spanish ships. He burned his own vessels but abandoned his supplies to the enemy. After setting fire to the town and burning its churches, Moore made his way overland to Charleston. "The debt incurred by the expedition led in 1703 to South Carolina's first issue of paper money, beginning a derangement of the currency that lasted for eighty years,'' [4] David Duncan Wallace comments. Moore redeemed his defeat in the winter of 1704 by an expedition which devastated the interior of Florida all the way to the Gulf.

Although Charleston was threatened by the French and Spanish more than once during Queen Anne's War, the Carolinians beat off attacks. After the Peace of Utrecht concluding that conflict, South Carolina suffered its greatest danger, retribution for slave-catching and other corruptions in the Indian trade. In the spring of 1715, the Yemassees precipitated an uprising that involved some fifteen tribes and Indian nations. The ensuing Yemassee War cost South Carolina at least 400 lives, an increased colonial debt and inflation, and the loss of prestige among Indians with whom the colony had traded.

The Yemassees were a warlike tribe who had removed from Georgia and settled in South Carolina between the Combahee and the Savannah rivers. Resentment against cheating traders and white encroachments upon their tribal lands finally came to a head, and the Yemassees managed to arouse other resentful Indians, especially the powerful Creeks in what is now Georgia. Only the Cherokees stayed out of the Indian alliance, but on terms that humiliated the whites, for they knew their advantage and contemptuously forced the Carolinians to make concessions. From this time onward, it became a fixed element in South Carolina Indian policy to keep the Creeks and the Cherokees fighting each other, or, as a contemporary quoted by Wallace phrased it, "to keep both friendly with us and assist them in cutting one another's throats without offending either.'' [5]

The war dragged on, guerrilla fashion, until late in 1717 when the colony finally made a peace treaty with the Creeks. The war was a disillusioning experience for South Carolina, for she got only scant support from the other colonies or from England. Virginia was even accused of selling guns and ammunition to the Indians and of taking advantage of the war to pre-

4. Wallace, *South Carolina*, p. 69.
5. Wallace, *South Carolina*, p. 91.

empt South Carolina's trade on the frontiers. Colonial solidarity was still long years in the future.

In spite of heavy losses, increased debts, and continued neglect by the Proprietors and the royal government, South Carolina pulled itself together and continued its expansion. Fortified trading posts near modern Augusta and near Columbia at the Congarees, a few miles below the mouth of the Saluda River, paved the way for the development of the back country. South Carolina citizens showed immense resiliency, as they have in every great emergency. Within a few years they had regained their lost trade with the Indians. The hostile Yemassees fled to Florida; the disaffected Creeks moved back to their former tribal lands on the Chattahoochee; the Catawbas promised to keep the peace; and the Cherokees agreed to remain brothers of the English "as long as the rivers run"—a pact that the Carolinians sealed with appropriate gifts and pledges of more. The Yemassee War had taught the colonists two important truths: they must attempt fairer dealings with the Indians, and they must rely on themselves in any crisis.

During the last flicker of the Yemassee War, South Carolina had to battle a pest of pirates that cruised off her coast and seized valuable cargoes. Piracy had long been a curse in the American colonies. Frequent wars resulted in the issuance of letters of marque to privateers who often continued their habits of preying on commerce when the wars were over. On May 22, 1717, a notorious pirate, Edward Teach, called Blackbeard, anchored off Charleston harbor and threatened to burn the shipping and batter the town about the citizens' ears unless they sent him a chest of medicine. Other pirates were equally bold and arrogant, for they found easy shelter in the numerous inlets of North Carolina and felt secure.

In the summer of 1718 Colonel William Rhett was commissioned a vice-admiral, given two vessels, and sent cruising against the pirates. On September 27 Rhett captured Stede Bonnet, a well-educated Barbadian turned pirate; Bonnet and twenty-nine of his crew were tried and hanged at low tide off what is now the Battery in Charleston. In November of the same year Governor Robert Johnson himself led an expedition which encountered a pirate named Richard Worley and killed him and twenty-six of his crew. Of twenty-four survivors, nineteen were convicted and hanged. The execution of forty-nine pirates at Charleston within a month was discouraging to other freebooters. Although pirates occasionally captured vessels off the Carolina coast after this time, their depredations were greatly diminished.

The emphasis placed on the Indian trade in the early years does not imply that other sources of revenue were neglected by the Carolinians. Forest products—timber, and naval stores—had been the most obvious commercial assets from the beginning. Immense forests of pine provided pitch, rosin, tar, and turpentine, essential in the construction and maintenance of wooden ships. Tall cypress trees and pines also supplied sturdy masts. Cypress and white cedar lumber were highly prized.

The Indians from prehistoric times had made dug-out canoes from both long-leaf pines and cypress trees. White settlers learned to make pirogues by hewing out tree trunks in a similar fashion. The Charleston Museum has an Indian pine-tree dugout made long before Columbus reached America. It also has a plantation river craft made by hollowing out a huge cypress tree, sawing it apart down the middle, and fitting a keel and floor between the halves. A boat of this type, capable of carrying a considerable cargo and a number of laborers, provided essential transportation between plantations. Although ship-building did not become an important South Carolina industry, local craftsmen built needed river and coastal vessels.

The earliest and most important money crop to be discovered by Carolinians was not one of the exotic tropical products that the Proprietors had dreamed of; it was rice. Rice had been suggested by the Proprietors as a possibility, and some had probably been planted before 1685. By 1700 it had already become a fairly profitable crop, for in that year South Carolina shipped 300 tons to England and 30 tons to the West Indian islands.

The rapid development of rice growing from this time onward transformed the agricultural economy of South Carolina, determined the social structure of the Low Country, and left a romantic heritage of legend and literature. The cultivation of rice for nearly two centuries brought enormous wealth to a few great planters. Then its profits faded in the face of competition from Louisiana and Texas, where it could be raised at less expense and with fewer hazards from hurricanes and freshets, recurring calamities in Carolina that wiped out whole crops from time to time and brought the growers to the verge of ruin. Today decaying banks and the remains of old dams mark the outlines of once prosperous rice plantations, but the land has reverted to swamp, and marsh grass sways in the breeze where rice once grew. Not a grain of rice is now produced commercially in South Carolina. A few of the most productive plantations now lie beneath the waters of Lake Marion and Lake Moultrie, while others have gained resurrection as hunting lodges and game preserves for wealthy capitalists from the North.

Well-established legend attributes the introduction of the famous "Carolina gold rice" to Captain John Thurber, who put into Charleston harbor for repairs to his ship in 1685 and gave to Dr. Henry Woodward less than a bushel of rice seed from Madagascar. This excellent rice was called "gold" from the color of the husk, for the long grains were white. Another variety, called "white rice" (again from the color of the husk), was later introduced from India. As late as the post-Revolutionary period, when Jefferson was U.S. minister in France and John Adams was minister to England, these two statesmen were writing back and forth about the introduction of another species of rice liked by the Portuguese with whom they were negotiating trade agreements. On July 1, 1787, Jefferson wrote from Paris to Adams in London that he was entrusting to him a small packet of Italian Piedmont rice seed which he had obtained in Italy, to be forwarded to William Drayton, chairman of the South Carolina Society for Promoting and Improving Agriculture. For nearly two centuries, Carolina rice was an important commodity in international trade.

The Carolina swamp country proved ideal for rice growing because the mucky soil was fertile, and fresh water was available in ample quantities for flooding the fields. Inland swamps near the coast were the first sites of rice plantations. Using canals and dams, the planters managed to impound fresh water for irrigating the fields. The swamps were not heavily wooded, and fields could be cleared with relative ease; but how the laborers avoided the cottonmouth moccasins has always puzzled one who has no love of snakes. At any rate, few records exist of snakebite of planters or their laborers, both of whom slogged through the muck as fields were laid out and drained.

Salt water is deadly to rice, and from time to time marshes nearest the coast were drowned with sea water blown in by hurricanes. When that happened, in the growing season or near harvest time, a crop could be wiped out overnight and the planter would be faced with ruin, not only from the loss of his year's work but from destruction of dams and irrigation canals.

Because of this recurring hazard, planters moved upstream when the danger of Indian attack lessened. They built dikes along the rivers, impounded fresh water in holding ponds to be used as they needed it, and canalized fields in the river marshes. Their greatest initial problem was the necessity of clearing land more heavily forested than the coastal marshes. Such labor required larger numbers of slaves, who increased rapidly after the mid-eighteenth century.

The rice planter was never altogether free from the calamities of nature, even on his new river plantations, because most of these rivers, the Pee Dee, the Santee, the Edisto, the Combahee, and others were parts of long drainage systems, and heavy rainfall in the mountains might bring freshets to the lowlands which sometimes swept over the dikes and ruined crops.

But by and large, the cultivation of rice, though laborious, was highly profitable, and planters grew rich, built handsome homes on the bluffs overlooking their fields, and frequently had town houses in Charleston. They also resorted to places in the Sand Hills or elsewhere to avoid summer heat, mosquitoes, and "swamp fever." Rice planting was not for small farmers. It was big business and required large amounts of capital—capital invested in black slaves imported from Africa or the West Indies.

Many of these slaves were brought straight from Africa and sold in Charleston to the planters. They knew no English and had no knowledge of the work they had to do. To teach and direct them, experienced slaves were put in charge. The leader

was known as the "driver" and had authority under the over-
seer, whose duties were too multifarious for him to direct all the
work personally.

Students of slavery frequently forget that slave society had its
own hierarchies and social gradations. House servants, of
course, were at the top, but there were various grades of craftsmen: blacksmiths, carpenters, boatmen, and canal tenders, as
well as hunters, fishermen, and field hands.

The African newcomers gradually learned English, or at least
a patois. The more isolated groups retained many African
words, and they modified English words to suit their ears and
vocal cords. To this day, the coastal Negroes retain a dialect
known as Gullah, a term of disputed origin. A few linguists
think it derives from Angola, homeland of some of the slaves.
The Africans brought with them a body of interesting folklore,
animal tales, superstitions, folk medicines, song rhythms,
dances, and one vegetable that soon became a Carolina favorite:
okra.

Tragic as was slavery, some reformers' imaginary descriptions of slave life on the rice plantations contain more myth than
fact. For example, the notion that bloody-minded overseers
roamed the fields with lash in hand, beating at will the helpless
chattels, is not borne out by either statistics or factual accounts.
Nor is the notion true that planters discouraged family unity,
sold off surplus children for profit, and promoted slave breeding
like that of livestock. Men of sound business judgment do not
abuse or destroy valued property, and slaves represented heavy
capital investments. It was in the planters' interest, even if they
had no humanitarian instincts, to keep their costly labor pool as
calm and contented as possible. And the bald facts are that
many plantations maintained the same families of Negroes for
generations, even long after emancipation. That sadistic cruelty
occurred occasionally, as it does in all societies, no one can
deny; but the profit motive, if no other, helped to ameliorate the
lot of the laborers in the rice fields.

In *Seed from Madagascar* (1937), Duncan C. Heyward describes in some detail, realistically and unromantically, the life
of the rice-field laborer, both before and after emancipation.

From the papers of the Allston family, J. H. Easterby, in *The South Carolina Rice Plantation* (1945), gives for the nineteenth century a vast amount of documentation of the economics and labor practices on rice plantations. Enlightening, if controversial, statistics about slavery are given in Robert W. Fogel and Stanley L. Engerman, *Time on the Cross: The Economics of American Negro Slavery* (1974). No civilized human being today will attempt to romanticize slavery, but we ought to understand how this labor system operated and maintained consistent family structures of stable workers. Whether they were contented is another question, but they were not driven to desperation so that they fled wholesale from persecutors.

Archibald Rutledge, poet and chronicler of life in the Low Country, has written nostalgically about the rice plantations of the Santee delta and adjacent territory. His own family home, Hampton, was the focal center of a two-thousand-acre tract on the south side of the Santee, not far from McClellanville, off modern U.S. Highway 17. In *Home by the River* (1941), Rutledge gives the flavor of plantation life: the hard work, the hazards, the profits when crops were good, the final debacle of rice culture, and the abandoned plantations, now only ghosts in the marsh grass—places with such names as White Oak, Lone Pine, Wampee, Broad Ditch, Daisyland, Eagle's Nest, Rice Queen, and Tranquility.

Generations of Rutledges lived at Hampton, including Edward Rutledge, one of the signers of the Declaration of Independence. Archibald Rutledge, who restored the plantation house, spent the later years of his life there and experienced a few of the amenities of his ancestors' existence, especially such field sports as hunting deer, wild turkeys, and ducks, once more plentiful in coastal Carolina. He also studied the descendants of the slaves, many of them still resident in the region, and wrote sympathetically about them. He was particularly impressed with their keenness of observation and their gift for apt expression. One of his black friends had a favorite prayer: "O Lord, prop me up in all my leaning places."

But the Lord did not prop up the rice economy in all its leaning places, and even in the first century of Carolina's existence, men were avidly searching for other sources of agricultural wealth. But for generations after Captain John Thurber left his bag of seed in Charleston, rice continued to enrich great planters in the Low Country.

Tourists today can get a vague impression of what a prosperous rice plantation was like when they visit Middleton Place, developed about 1741 by Henry Middleton, later president of the First Continental Congress. Faint outlines of some of the dikes along the Ashley River can still be made out. Middleton Place became one of the most prosperous plantations in the Charleston region. There lived Arthur Middleton, a signer of the Declaration of Independence, and there he is buried in a huge stone mausoleum. Most tourists, however, will be more interested in the ancient camellias, introduced just after the Revolution by a French botanist, André Michaud, suspected of mixing botany with espionage for France.

Another old rice plantation, now familiar to tourists visiting Charleston, is Magnolia Gardens, once the seat of the Draytons. Early in the nineteenth century, a clerical member of the family, the Reverend Grimké Drayton, started planting azaleas and created a garden now probably more profitable than ever were the Draytons' rice fields. Brookgreen Gardens, near Murrells Inlet, also once a rice plantation, is now a garden of statuary, the gift to the public of Archer Huntington and his wife, Anna Hyatt Huntington, herself a sculptress of note.

The most productive rice plantations in the eighteenth century were in the Georgetown region, especially on the Pee Dee and Waccamaw rivers. An excellent rice museum in Georgetown gives visitors detailed information of the way rice was grown, husked, and prepared for market. The best seed rice, for reasons not quite clear, was grown on the Cape Fear River in North Carolina.

The most profitable crop after rice was indigo, a weedy plant from which growers produced the blue dye much in demand in the period before the invention of aniline dyes. From indigo came the blue for British uniforms and the blue for dress coats greatly favored by eighteenth-century gentlemen.

In 1739 the price of rice was depressed by the outbreak of

war with Spain and the subsequent war with France, and planters were eager for substitute crops. Indigo had been tried much earlier, but greater profits from rice had discouraged its cultivation. With an over-production of rice and curtailed shipments to England on account of the war, new experiments began with indigo, ginger, lucerne (alfalfa), cotton, "Guinea corn"—a species of millet—and other plants.

Curiously, the leader in these experiments was a seventeen-year-old girl, Eliza Lucas, daughter of Lieutenant Colonel George Lucas of Antigua, who in 1738 moved his ailing wife and his energetic daughter to a plantation he owned on Wappoo Creek, up the Ashley River six miles by water from Charleston. When Lucas had to return to Antigua because of military duties, he left his daughter to manage Wappoo Plantation and other properties.

In 1740 Eliza began her agricultural experiments and soon concentrated upon indigo. After three or four years of trial, she managed to make a crop and processed it into blocks of the blue dyestuff that London merchants proclaimed excellent. Her story is told in a biography by her great-granddaughter, Harriott Horry Ravenel, *Eliza Pinckney* (1896) and more recently in a publication of her letters preserved in the South Carolina Historical Society, *The Letter Book of Eliza Lucas Pinckney* (1972), edited by Elise Pinckney with a useful introduction by Walter Muir Whitehill.

The endeavors of this intelligent teen-age girl helped to establish a new and profitable crop in South Carolina. Indigo could be grown on upland fields out of danger of floods. The plant, about the size of a thin cotton stalk, had to be cut when mature, macerated, and soaked in vats with a certain amount of lime. The process was laborious, messy, and stinking. Yet the price was high; in 1748 Great Britain granted a bounty of six pence a pound to producers. This generosity of the home government, David Duncan Wallace comments, came about because "Great Britain detested paying money to the French," [6] her ancient enemy, previously the principal source of the dye.

6. Wallace, *South Carolina*, p. 190.

An English correspondent, enthusiastic over Eliza Lucas's indigo, was quoted in the *South Carolina Gazette* for April 1, 1745, as declaring that Eliza's indigo was just as good as the French, from whom, he understood, England was buying £200,000 worth of the stuff each year. No wonder the government was pleased at the prospect of stopping this drain. So rapid was the development of the industry that by 1748 South Carolina shipped to England 134,118 pounds of indigo cakes, and it remained a profitable crop until the Revolution.

Eliza Lucas, pioneer of the indigo industry, in 1744 married a widower, Charles Pinckney, and became the mother of two sons who ultimately were national leaders after 1776: Charles Cotesworth Pinckney, a member of the Constitutional Convention of 1787, and Thomas Pinckney, who served as minister to both Spain and Great Britain.

Moses Lindo, a Sephardic Jew, who arrived in Charleston in 1756, also played an important part in promoting indigo. Jewish merchants in London were large importers of dyestuffs. Lindo represented one of these London firms. Within a year after his arrival, he was advertising in the *South Carolina Gazette* a promise to pay the highest prices for indigo, and incidentally offering a reward of £500 for information about anyone impugning his credit. Although Jews had been welcome in South Carolina from the earliest days of settlement, and no prejudice had been shown against them, Lindo's aggressive campaign to purchase indigo had aroused the jealousy of other merchants dealing in the dye.

One other product, cotton, was to alter both the economy and the society of South Carolina. Although some cotton had been grown since early days, it did not become a significant commodity until after the Revolution.

By the mid-eighteenth century, forest products, rice, and indigo had brought prosperity to the great landowners of the Low Country, but small farmers could have little share in enterprises that required vast acreages and many slaves. They had to move to the back country and make a living as best they could.

The lot of the great planters, however, was not one of halcyon ease. They themselves had to work hard to make their plantations pay. Slave labor, which they believed essential, was usually inefficient. And, as in imperial Rome, the fear of servile rebellion hung over them. By 1724 the white population of South Carolina numbered approximately 14,000, and black slaves numbered some 32,000. Although the colonial government made efforts from time to time to curb the import of slaves and to encourage the immigration of white settlers, slaves continued to outnumber whites by a large proportion. If the planters were troubled by anything beyond the fear of revolts, they probably salved their consciences with the threadbare cliché that they were providing African savages with opportunities of Christian salvation. That, at least, was the pious excuse of Puritan slave traders in New England who pocketed their profits and thanked God that they were the instruments of saving so many heathen souls for Christ.

5

Pioneers in the Back Country

$\mathcal{T}$OURISTS motoring to Florida or to such South Carolina resorts as Myrtle Beach, Charleston, or Hilton Head roar along superhighways at sixty or more miles an hour, crossing creeks, rivers, and swamps that once were impassable barriers to communication and trade between the sparse settlers of the Up Country and the civilized Low Country. To this day, most tourists think of South Carolina in terms of the azaleas and camellias of the Charleston region in the spring and the beautiful old houses of that city, or of the white sands of the Carolina beaches in summer, or the semitropical golf courses of Hilton Head and other playgrounds in winter. A few may know about the horse-loving society of Aiken and Camden or the shooting preserves on abandoned rice plantations along the Waccamaw, Pee Dee, Edisto, and other rivers. But not many travelers who race across the state over double-lane highways take time to read historical markers or to ponder the folders that hospitality centers on the main arteries hand out to visitors. Speed, even in an age of energy shortage, prevents much contemplation of local history.

Although superhighways from the Canadian border to the tip of Florida reduce the bordering landscape to a common denominator of sameness, even the fleeting traveler may discern striking differences as he moves from region to region of South Carolina. If so, he may pause to wonder what impact the changing terrain has had upon the inhabitants, past and present. For example, U.S. Interstate 26, from the mountains at Asheville, North Carolina, to the ocean at Charleston traverses almost every geological variation in the state and skirts significant historic sites. U.S. Interstate 85 from the Virginia border via Durham, Salisbury, Charlotte, and Gastonia, North Carolina, and then across the top of South Carolina via Gaffney, Spartanburg, Greenville, and Anderson, and on into Georgia, crosses routes by which many immigrants filtered into South Carolina from the northern colonies. It also cuts across the old hunting grounds of the Catawba and Cherokee Indians who long blocked the development of the back country. U.S. Interstate 95 from Raleigh, North Carolina, bisects the middle region—the upper limits of the Low Country plantations—until it crosses Lake Marion, once the Santee River and part of its swamp; when completed, U.S. 95 will drop sharply southwest to Savannah. U.S. 17 follows the coast from the north to Florida. U.S. 1, from Cheraw to Augusta via Camden and Columbia, meanders through sand hills and red claybanks, bordering the fall line of streams that once spread out into swamps below it. Many other highways crisscross a land that in colonial times was made inaccessible by rivers and creeks too deep or too swift to ford and miles-wide swamps of jungle and quagmire. The network of hard-surface roads that has now brought villages and towns within minutes of each other makes it hard for modern travelers to realize that a difficult terrain isolated these same localities from each other until well into the nineteenth century.

Numerous waterways running from the highlands to the sea caused immigrants to parallel the streams instead of crossing them except where a few fords and an occasional crude ferry made transit possible. The earliest penetration of the back country was made by river boats up the navigable streams. But shoals and rapids at the fall line ended navigation until the era of canal building that began in the late eighteenth century. Even some of the deep-water rivers and creeks near the coast spread out into swamps so choked with vegetation that only an experienced pilot could find a channel.

When water navigation failed, immigrants to the back country depended on pack horses or trudged on foot along ancient trails that the Indians had marked. Most famous of the routes to the interior was the Cherokee Path that Indian traders and warriors had beaten long before the white man came. It led from the northwest corner of the state, in modern Pickens and Oconee counties, to the Saluda River valley by Greenwood and Ninety Six to the Congaree valley west of Columbia. Thence, it roughly paralleled U.S. Interstate 26 to Charleston. Another trading path led from Charleston to the Indian settlement of the Congarees just south of Columbia and from there due north to the Catawbas in York County. A third great Indian trail crossed the Savannah River at Augusta and angled southeast to Charleston. This was the route usually followed in the eighteenth century to the Creek, Chickasaw, and Choctaw nations in Georgia and Alabama.

Other Indian trails less well known also opened ways for traders and settlers to gain access to the Up Country. By following river valleys and avoiding impassable swamps, the Indians discovered routes that in time would serve as roads for the pack horses and carts of settlers. But, at best, the Indian paths were long, narrow, and rough. The settlement of Ninety Six derived its name from the traders' estimate of distance from the Cherokee town of Keowee; other landmarks got similar names from weary traders who stopped to rest at Six Mile, Twelve Mile Creek, or some other "mileaged" spot. No easy way led to the fertile uplands promised farmers by the propaganda of immigration agents.

Fear of both Indian raids and slave insurrections influenced tidewater planters to make an effort to stimulate the immigration of white settlers for the back country. Placed strategically, these newcomers might serve as a buffer against marauding Indians and could be drafted into the militia in case of a black rebellion. By the mid-eighteenth century, the more prosperous rice growers had overreached themselves as their greed for the extension of plantations induced them to import increasing numbers of African slaves. The excess of blacks over whites gave many a planter sleepless nights. By 1760 Lieutenant Governor William Bull reported that the slave population numbered

57,253 and that white males over sixteen years of age were not "more than 6,000," a condition that David Duncan Wallace quoted him as saying "must raise in our minds many melancholy reflections." [1]

Bull might indeed feel melancholy because his fellow planters had done little to reduce the menace. For years, the legislative assembly had wrestled with the problem of the growing slave trade. From time to time, a tax on imported slaves had been levied, and in some instances increased, but planters and merchants contrived to evade any effective curtailment of imports. In 1751 the assembly voted a curious tax on imported slaves in accordance with their height. On a black slave four feet, two inches tall, the importer had to pay a duty of £10, but the duty on shorter slaves was less. It is not recorded that this import tax did more than ease the conscience of some legislators.

Part of the duty collected on slaves was designated for use as bounties to be paid white Protestant immigrants who needed help in getting started. To receive a bounty, however, they were required to settle for at least three years not more than forty miles from the coast in a strip extending from the Savannah to the Santee rivers. Convenient as this area might be for the planters in case of need, not much land suitable for small farms was available; the best had already been granted to rice planters. Consequently restrictions on how far inland new immigrants might settle had to be removed, and they pushed on into the more distant, more fertile, and more dangerous back country.

Since 1730 the colony had tried to promote settlement beyond tidewater by means of a township scheme proposed at that time by Governor Robert Johnson. His plan to create townships on the frontiers, to settle them with poor Protestants from Europe, and to provide the immigrants with necessary tools paid for out of provincial customs duties had been approved by the Board of Trade in London.

The townships consisted of areas six miles square in which the great planters of the tidewater would not be allowed to claim grants. In other words, these lands would be reserved for poor

---

1. Wallace, *South Carolina*, pp. 218–219.

immigrants. Although the land hunger of old tidewater residents resulted in frequent violations of the plan, the townships on this early frontier fostered development of the middle country between the fall line and tidewater plantations.

Only nine townships were surveyed and established: Purrysburgh, on the east bank of the Savannah River; Orangeburg, north of the Edisto River; Amelia in modern Calhoun County; Saxe-Gotha in the lower part of Lexington County; New Windsor, across the Savannah from Augusta, where the town of Hamburg later developed; Williamsburg with modern Kingstree at its center; Kingston in Horry County, north of Conway; Queensborough, west of Kingston on both sides of the Great Pee Dee River; and Fredericksburg, east of the Wateree River, surrounding the present town of Camden. Purrysburgh proved a disappointment, but gradually the other middle-region townships acquired inhabitants of various nationalities and opened the way for further expansion inland.

Rich alluvial land, interspersed with swamps along the Wateree, and fertile red-clay-and-sand plateaus among the hills induced Charleston planters to compete with incoming immigrants for grants in this area and other favored spots in the middle region. Hence both rice and indigo plantations, worked with slaves, developed alongside small farms operated by the owners and their families. A settler could expect a grant of fifty acres for himself and each member of his household, including servants or slaves that he might bring along. Ony an occasional immigrant, however, owned a slave, and few had indentured white servants.

The settlers were a mixed lot: Germans, English, Welsh, Ulster Scots, Lowland Scots, and an occasional Highlander. Some migrated from Charleston and other tidewater localities where they had served out their time as indentured servants and now sought freedom and opportunity in a new area. Increasing numbers drifted down from Pennsylvania, Maryland, and Virginia. A steady stream came from overseas in immigrant ships in which the treatment of passengers was often as bad as or worse than that suffered by Africans in slave ships.

Records show the arrival of many ''poor Irish Protestants,'' meaning Ulster Scots, or Scotch-Irish, as they also were called. As early as the autumn of 1732, Ulster Scots were being directed to Williamsburg and settling around what became Kingstree. Beginning in the 1730s, many German-Swiss and Rhineland Germans came to Orangeburg and Amelia. By 1750 Saxe-Gotha was filling up with Swiss and Germans of the Reformed faith. A few Lutheran Germans were among the early immigrants. Although the Germans were inclined to create close-knit enclaves, both English and Scots settled in the same townships. In time many of the Germans anglicized their names, and a man named Miller might have begun as Müller. Consequently, it is not always easy to determine from names the national origins of families.

In one locality, the fork between the Broad and the Saluda rivers—the so-called ''Dutch Fork''—the Germans clung clannishly together and retained the German language until the mid-nineteenth century. English settlers tended to avoid localities thickly settled by Germans, but nearly all communities had mixed populations.

In the ''Far West,'' New Windsor, opposite Augusta, with Fort Moore at its center, was thinly settled. Beginning in 1736, a trickle of German-Swiss moved into the area. The principal leader of this group was Johannes Tobler, a well-educated Swiss. His son John began publishing the *South Carolina Almanac* in 1752, though he had announced it two years earlier. This was one of the first literary productions of the back country. New Windsor needed something to add lustre to its name, for it had achieved a reputation for ungodliness. Land in the region was not productive, and New Windsor's principal source of income was derived from the Indian trade. George Galphin, who established a base at Silver Bluff, a few miles below Fort Moore, carried on a thriving business with the Creeks from about 1750 to the Revolution.

One of the most populous and prosperous communities of the middle region was the Welsh Tract, not properly one of the townships but having some of their characteristics. Situated on the east side of the Great Pee Dee, north of the township of Queensborough, it had water communication with both Georgetown and Charleston. The land was fertile and suitable for indigo, which after 1750 became a profitable money crop. By 1757 the Welsh Tract had some 3,000 white settlers and 300 black slaves. Many of the Welsh Baptists who had come from Pennsylvania had persuaded others of their faith to emigrate from Wales. Some were small farmers but others acquired substantial holdings, bought a few slaves, and became planters specializing in indigo and corn.

The swamplands of the back country provided abundant forage for cattle, summer and winter, and many settlers were what in later days would be called ranchers. They drove their fattened beeves to the Charleston market. A few enterprising Germans made cheese and butter on a commercial scale. Tanneries supplied leather for local use and for sale on the Charleston market when transport was available. Hogs abounded, and cured bacon and hams were saleable commodities, when they could be got to a market. Unfortunately, much of the back country was cut off from practical communication with the prosperous Low Country.

Isolation from legal authority also caused hardships to honest settlers. The people of the Welsh Tract, for example, were constantly complaining about a plague of horse and cattle thieves—rogues from Virginia and North Carolina.

The provincial government, prompted by the Board of Trade in London, tried to stimulate the production of hemp, flax, and wheat. Not much hemp was raised, and only enough flax for local use, but wheat did well on the high ground beyond the swamps. Several mills were erected on streams that had sufficient fall, and settlers in Orangeburg, Amelia, and the Welsh Neck boasted that they made as good white flour as that from Virginia.

But by the mid-eighteenth century, settlements still did not extend far beyond the fall line and the sand hills. The Cherokees claimed as their hunting grounds the territory to the mouth of the Saluda River. The Congarees, a small group, held out below Columbia on the Congaree River. The Catawbas in the north contended with the Cherokees for hunting rights in the territory between the Broad and Catawba rivers, and by tacit agreement both nations hunted there. A few traders had settled among

Cherokees and Catawbas, but few white settlers ventured into Indian territory. The rolling, forested lands of the Piedmont were yet to be exploited.

The key to further expansion into the interior lay in negotiations with the still-powerful Indian nations, especially the Cherokees and the Creeks. The Catawbas were already weakened, diminished in numbers, and dependent upon traders for supplies. Indian diplomacy was infinitely complicated by internal feuds among the tribesmen themselves, the abuses of white traders residing among them, the frequent wars between the English and French, French efforts to win over Indians allied to the English, and even the rivalry among the colonies for the Indian trade. For example, after the founding of Georgia in 1732, that colony interfered with South Carolina traders doing business with the Creeks and Chickasaws, and on occasion seized South Carolina boats on the Savannah River. Virginians following trails from Roanoke into Tennessee attempted to win over the trade of the Overhill Cherokees—tribesmen living across the mountains from the Cherokees of the Lower Towns in what is now northwest South Carolina. All the Indians, of course, were shrewd enough to play one faction against another: the French against the English, or Carolinians against Virginians.

South Carolina expansion was also contingent upon imperial policies. While some Charleston merchants would gladly see the Cherokees and Creeks at war with each other—so long as they could trade with both. Because of the frequent wars with France, strategy required efforts to keep peace with all the Indians on the frontiers lest they accept French overtures to attack vulnerable English settlements.

Various royal governors had made efforts to keep peace with the Indians, but Governor James Glen, a forty-two-year-old Scottish lawyer who arrived in Charleston in 1743, virtually made a career of Indian negotiations. He served as governor for nearly thirteen years, the longest term of any colonial governor, and labored unceasingly, if often in vain, to cement friendly relations with the red men on the frontiers.

Energetic and flamboyant, Glen stepped on many toes in Charleston and made enemies who accused him of submitting to humiliating Indian insolence. Yet, despite frequent failures and setbacks, his negotiations helped to extend the borders of South Carolina into Cherokee territory and made possible settlements in the Piedmont. Wallace calls him the "most progressive and active of any of our royal governors," an administrator who "traveled through the province oftener and farther than any provincial governor before or after him to see 'what improvements have been made' and what ought to be done, and to win the friendship of the Indians and encourage the back settlers." [2]

Glen's first foray into the back country began in 1746 with a cavalcade of 200 militiamen and fifty gentlemen-volunteers to meet the headmen of the Catawbas at the Congarees, the Cherokees at Ninety Six, and the Creeks and Chickasaws at Fort Moore. One main objective was to persuade the Indians to attack the French, in which he failed, but he made a lasting impression. The next year he bought from the Cherokees of the Lower Towns "all their lands south and east of Long Canes Creek . . . and a line running in general northward and northeastward from its head." [3] This embraced much of later Abbeville County and land beyond. Though the Overhill Cherokees declined to ratify the sale, it was a beginning of efforts ultimately successful to acquire Cherokee lands in upper South Carolina.

Glen's negotiations with the Cherokees were long, tedious, and frustrating. During 1751 and 1752, progress was stopped by a war between them and the Creeks. The Cherokees had many grievances against the white traders, whom they occasionally murdered. They complained about their men being debauched with rum and their women being violated. The traders had even cut short their yardsticks with which they measured deerskins. Glen at least made amends for this by sending the chiefs new steel yardsticks.

At last, in 1753, he agreed to build a fort at Keowee to protect the Indians from northern enemies, such as raiding Senecas. In October of that year Glen set out for Keowee and erected

---

2. Wallace, *South Carolina,* p. 163.
3. Wallace, *South Carolina,* p. 164.

Fort Prince George on a site now covered by Lake Keowee. Because neither side was completely satisfied, Glen called a great powwow at Saluda Old Town, below Ninety Six, in June 1755.

The ruling chief of the Overhills, Connecorte, known to the English as "Old Hop," and the principal chief of the Lower Towns, Attakullakulla, known as "Little Carpenter," came with some 500 warriors. Not to be outdone, Glen arrived with nearly as many militiamen and gentlemen, splendidly garbed—and with horse-loads of presents without which no Indian conference could hope to succeed. The upshot of the conclave was that Glen promised to build another fort at the junction of the Little Tennessee and the Tellico rivers to protect the Overhills from their enemies. Completed in 1757, it was named Fort Loudoun. In return, Old Hop agreed to cede to King George II all the Cherokee lands in South Carolina except the northwest corner comprising present-day Greenville, Anderson, Pickens, and Oconee counties. The ceded land was actually unoccupied by the Indians, but whether they intended to open it for white settlement is a moot question.

Whatever the intention of the Cherokees might have been, the problem was resolved in the next seven years by subsequent purchases, war, and treaties. North Carolina built Fort Dobbs near modern Salisbury on the route that immigrants from Virginia and Pennsylvania followed into North and South Carolina. From the mid-eighteenth century onward, pioneers straggled down the Yadkin valley into South Carolina. But life was hazardous on the frontier, and periodic hostility by dissident groups of Cherokees resulted in the killing of both traders and settlers. The whites retaliated sometimes with savagery equal to that of Indians. The peace that Glen had hoped to achieve evaded him. On the way to supervise the erection of Fort Loudoun in the summer of 1756, he learned that he had been superseded by William Henry Lyttleton, a baron and former ambassador to Portugal, who felt confident of his ability to handle any problem, certainly one dealing with a few rude savages.

A series of frontier killings precipitated a state of war in September 1759, when the Indians attacked Fort Prince George.

Lyttleton led an expedition to the fort in December and made a short-lived peace, retaining twenty-two hostages until the Cherokees surrendered the murderers of a number of whites. Open war broke out in January of the next year. Cherokees sent raiding parties against Ninety Six and settlements to the south, killing as they went. The soldiers at Fort Prince George, in retaliation for the murder of one of their men, slaughtered the twenty-two hostages. For the next two years the frontier blazed with gunfire. Meantime, in April 1759, Lyttleton returned to England and left the colony in better hands, those of Lieutenant Governor William Bull.

Among the devastated settlements was one in the Long Canes, occupied by Ulster Scots. As they were evacuating to take refuge in Augusta, a party of nearly 100 Cherokee warriors fell on them and butchered men, women, and children, variously reported from twenty-three to fifty-five persons, including the mother of Patrick Calhoun and grandmother of John C. Calhoun.

The provincial government, threatened with widening warfare on the frontiers, appealed for aid to General Sir Jeffrey Amherst, over-all commander of British troops in North America. To the rescue he sent Colonel Archibald Montgomery with a battalion of Highlanders and four companies of Royal Scots, numbering about 1,200 men. Enlisting as many of the militia as he could, Montgomery marched from Monck's Corner in the spring of 1760 and reached the Lower Towns of the Cherokee on June 1. Burning villages, cutting down the growing corn, and killing or capturing as many Indians as he could, he relieved Fort Prince George and continued into North Carolina where he engaged in a battle near modern Franklin. Montgomery had learned little about Indian warfare since Braddock's defeat and lost twenty men killed and seventy-six wounded.

Boasting that he had "chastised" the Indians, Montgomery took all except 400 of his Scots back north to join Amherst, but his destruction of Cherokee homes and crops had succeeded only in infuriating the tribesmen. Soon after his departure, the Overhills isolated and starved out Fort Loudoun. Although the Indians promised to let the 200-man garrison depart in safety, they ambushed them, killed thirty, and made the rest prisoners.

The renewal of war in 1761 induced Lieutenant Governor Bull to ask Amherst again for aid. This time he sent another Scot, pugnacious and obstinate Lieutenant Colonel James Grant, with 1,200 regulars to add to the 400 already in South Carolina. Enlisting additional militia, the troops marched over the mountains and fought a bloody battle near where Montgomery had been attacked. Grant succeeded in burning the Cherokee towns, completely destroying their crops, and driving the Indians into the mountains to starve. The Cherokees had to sue for peace and make a humiliating treaty that left the Piedmont open to immigrants.

The Cherokee War was hardly over before Scottish pioneers and others were pouring down from Virginia and Pennsylvania and moving up from Charleston to stake out homes for themselves. Within the next fifteen years, the Up Country would be dotted with settlements as small farmers cleared land, planted corn and wheat, turned cattle loose to forage in the cane brakes and fields of wild pea-vines, and let their hogs fatten on acorns in the forests. It was a promising land for farmers who expected little except subsistence. It was too far from distant markets to attract planters who hoped to get rich from the labor of slaves. Few in the Up Country for many years to come would own a slave or benefit from labor other than their own and that of their families. A scattering of Low Country planters, perhaps with clairvoyance about the future, contrived to get grants in the Up Country, but greater opportunities, opening up about the same time in Georgia, for rice and forest products resulting from slave labor, sent most tidewater planters scrambling for new land grants there.

To encourage small farmers to settle in the western part of the colony, the provincial government set aside three large townships west of a line from Ninety Six to Due West: Boonesborough on Long Canes Creek; Hillsborough on Little River; and Belfast or Londonborough on Hard Labor Creek. Eager to bring in settlers, the provincial assembly in 1761 provided passage money of £4 sterling for "respectable poor Protestants" from Great Britain and Ireland. Children aged from twelve to two would receive £2 passage money. In addition, bounties would be given for the purchase of tools. This generosity resulted in a flood of Ulster Scots as well as some Lowland Scots, Welsh, and English emigrating to the Up Country. A few French settled at New Bordeaux and Abbeville. A sprinkling of Germans also came from overseas, and still others came down from Pennsylvania and Maryland. Before the outbreak of the War of Independence, the Up Country had a well-established citizenry of industrious farmers, grateful for the opportunity to own land on which they had been promised exemption from taxes for ten years.

The rapidity with which upper South Carolina was settled after the middle of the eighteenth century was phenomenal. Even before the Cherokee menace was diminished, settlers were streaming down the mountain valleys to the vicinity of Salisbury, North Carolina, whence they fanned out into North and South Carolina. The defeat of General Braddock in 1755 in his attempt to capture Fort Duquesne (later Pittsburgh) discouraged pioneers on the Pennsylvania and Virginia frontiers and sent many searching for safer homes in the Carolinas. After the elimination of the French in 1763 at the conclusion of the Seven Years' War, many more settlers from the northern colonies came through the Shenandoah Valley, the "Great Wagon Road," and through Blue Ridge gaps into the Carolinas. Most managed to get legal grants to their lands, but a fair number were simply squatters. Among these immigrants, who met others coming up from the coast, were some rascals and rogues who were to cause infinite trouble in the back country, safe from the arm of the law.

Many of the settlers came with only a pitiful supply of this world's goods: a horse and a cow if they were lucky, the clothes on their backs, the simplest of cooking utensils (one or two pots, two or three pewter spoons, and a knife or two), one or more quilts apiece, and often little else. Not every immigrant owned a long rifle but most contrived to procure some sort of firearm—if not always one of the prized Lancaster-made rifles later known as the Kentucky rifle. One indispensable article every man carried was an axe.

With his axe, the frontiersman cut down saplings and made his first crude brush lean-to, to be replaced as soon as possible by a log cabin. With his axe, too, he hewed out a frame for a bed, laced across with vines on which he piled pine bows until he could procure a tick-and-straw mattress. Puncheon benches served in place of chairs. On wooden pegs he could hang such clothes as he could spare from his body. The floor at first was dirt, tamped down and sometimes covered with rushes or pine needles. Cooking was done over an open fire, at first outdoors, but after the building of a cabin with its stick-and-mud chimney, in the fireplace. Such was the simple equipment of many a backwoodsman whose courageous wife shared both his privations and his hardest labor.

Not all immigrants, of course, were so destitute, and some came with better tools, more household goods, and ample livestock. A surprising number had whipsaws with which they made clapboards and floor boards for their houses. Very soon simple dwellings of two rooms—with an ell for a kitchen, fireplaces at each end, a loft, and a porch across the front— replaced log cabins on the more prosperous farms. Some were even more commodious. A good example of a larger structure is the Kate Barry house a few miles south of Spartanburg, built before the Revolution when Indian attacks were still a hazard. Paint was virtually unknown in the Up Country and houses for years to come weathered to a soft gray.

By the decade before the Revolution, a few rough wagon roads connected with water transport on the Wateree or with a more central wagon road that led through the site of Columbia to Charleston. The journey was long and hard, but with difficulty the backwoods farmer could take to market wheat—or flour after mills were built—peas, corn, cured meats, butter in wooden tubs, cheese, and skins and furs obtained in winter hunting or trapping. Such products he exchanged for sugar, tea or coffee, powder and shot, cutlery, and utensils that he could not make for himself. He might also procure cloth and a few articles of clothing. Spinning and weaving, both of wool and flax, however, provided most households with needed apparel. Leisure, obviously, was not a problem for our ancestors in the Up

Country as they struggled against the forces of nature for subsistence and a modicum of prosperity.

The backwoods people had little time to devote to cultural improvement—and few opportunities, if they had had the time. Some were religious and brought along a Bible and maybe a spelling book and a reader for the instruction of their children. Schools at first were nonexistent, and few itinerant teachers were available. Literate parents did their best to teach their children the rudiments of reading, writing, and arithmetic. It is a matter of wonder that the level of literacy remained relatively high.

Churches in the back country were few and far between for some years after the first settlement, but too much has been made of the irreligiousness of frontier folk. Many of them were Scots of rigid Presbyterian background, but the intensity of piety varied with each individual. The German-Swiss were prevailingly of the Reformed faith, though late-coming German immigrants from communities in Pennsylvania were sometimes Lutherans, sometimes Mennonites or one of the related cults. The French Huguenots were of course Calvinists, but they soon espoused the Anglican communion. The Welsh were for the most part Baptists. Those in the Welsh Neck built a church as early as 1744. Anglicans, who dominated the Low Country, were scarce in the hinterland; but in 1768 they were numerous enough in Cheraw to build a church. Not until after the Revolution did the Methodists become a significant religious group in South Carolina.

The ferocity of religious hatred in this period is evident in the journals and sermons of Charles Woodmason, an Anglican parson, who was a self-appointed missionary to the back country from 1766 to 1768. A strange, twisted personality, he could find no good in anybody outside the Anglican communion—and of these he found so few as he traveled through upper South Carolina that his fanatical anger boiled. Upon Baptists and "vile" Presbyterians he heaped abuse and obscene invectives in purported descriptions of their ignorance and iniquity. In September 1768, after a foray on the west side of the Wateree, preaching and baptizing "heathen," he complained of the provincial government's lack of zeal "to promote the interest of the Church of England." And he ruminated: "Hence it is that above £30,000 sterling have lately been expended to bring over 5 or 6,000 ignorant, mean, worthless, beggarly Irish Presbyterians [Ulster Scots], the scum of the earth and refuse of mankind, and this solely to balance the emigration of people from Virginia, who are all of the Established Church." [4] Such commentary fills his letters and journals. But Woodmason cannot be taken at face value, as some historians have been inclined to do, though his comments on the poverty and backwardness of some areas, often exaggerated, sometimes have a ring of truth.

Woodmason did have the shrewdness to realize that neglect of the back country was laying up trouble for both present and future, and he drafted a protest to the provincial government that made a stir in Charleston. The background of this protest, reflecting the discontent of thousands of settlers beyond tidewater, had a profound significance for the history of colony and state. It represented the deepening resentment of the Up Country over the domination of Charleston, a resentment never resolved until a political revolution in the late nineteenth century altered the balance of power.

The tidewater planters were eager for a multitude of small white farmers to occupy the middle country and the Piedmont to insure help in case of slave insurrections, made more and more inevitable by the continued import of thousands of black Africans to tend rice and indigo fields. The planters openly referred to the growing black population as "the internal enemy," and several abortive insurrections gave color to their fears. That they could feel confident of backwoodsmen marching to their rescue when they had done little to win the back country's sympathy merely indicates the self-assured complacence of the planter class. It did not occur to them that all of Carolina would not weep over their plight if they were threatened. Coming events would unnerve some planters but would stir others to contemp-

---

4. Charles Woodmason, "Journal," 1766–1768; *The Carolina Backcountry on the Eve of the Revolution,* edited by Richard J. Hooker (Chapel Hill, N.C.: University of North Carolina Press, 1953), pp. 60–61.

tuous reference to the inhabitants of the hinterland as "idle vag-
abonds, the mere dregs of mankind," [5] a view that Lieutenant
Governor William Bull had the wisdom to refute.

Violent trouble began because the back country could not
protect itself against organized bands of thieves and robbers
who drove off their cattle, stole their horses, rode over and
ruined their crops, sometimes violated their wives, and burned
down their houses. Appeals to Charleston did little good. The
criminals openly defied the few constables sent to arrest them.
At length the frontiersmen, like citizens of San Francisco in
Gold Rush days, took the law into their own hands and organized vigilantes—only they called the law enforcement group
"Regulators." But so strong and well organized were the criminals that they sometimes outfought and horsewhipped the Regulators and even had the gall to take some of them to Charleston
as law-breakers and "insurrectionists."

Not only was the exposed back country unprotected from
organized crime, but it had no local magistrates, no courts, and
no legal machinery nearer than Charleston. The recording of a
deed or the proving of a will required the long, arduous journey
to the capital, the payment of fees to Charleston officials, and
often the employment of Charleston lawyers. All criminal cases
and civil suits, wherever they originated, had to be heard in
Charleston. Equally annoying was the fact that undeveloped
land in the hills was taxed at the same rate as the most productive rice plantations. Furthermore, backwoodsmen pointed out,
this was "taxation without representation," because they had no
members in the Commons House to look after their interests. To
remedy these inequities, they demanded courts and representation in the legislative assembly.

Governor Glen in 1753 had urged the establishment of courts
beyond Charleston for the greater convenience of the citizens,
but a bill to establish them died in the Commons House. The
Charleston lobby knew a good thing and was determined not to
permit the dispersal of the legal business of the colony. In 1767
Charles Woodmason drafted a petition from 4,000 backcoun-

5. Wallace, *South Carolina*, p. 226.

trymen, demanding a redress of grievances. They were talking of marching on Charleston to present the petition in a body; hotheads even talked of taking over some of the plantations.

In the meantime, the Regulator movement was complicating the protest, for the Regulators had refused to recognize or obey orders from the legal authorities in Charleston. They had even fought a pitched battle on the Great Pee Dee River with a Charleston posse sent to carry out a legal order against them and had killed one member of the posse. The whole back country was in an uproar. A Regulator movement in North Carolina, which resulted in a pitched battle at Alamance in 1771, was partially stimulated by the activities of the South Carolinians. The Up Country was ripe for rebellion, and the lamentations of the Low Country over the tyranny of Great Britain in passing the Stamp Act had fallen on deaf ears beyond the fall line. A nearer tyranny bothered the small farmers.

At length, after several efforts, a circuit court act became law and was approved by the king on November 25, 1769. The act provided for seven court districts and for courts to meet three times each year in Charleston and twice annually in Beaufort, Orangeburg, Ninety Six, Camden, Cheraw, and Georgetown. The first courts were held in these districts in November 1772. Before the outbreak of the War of Independence the back country had elected three representatives to the legislative assembly, including John C. Calhoun's father. It was not much, but it was a beginning.

The ill will aroused by Charleston's long disdain of the people on the frontiers helps to account for the unwillingness of backcountrymen to throw up their hats and cheer for the "Patriots" when the War of Independence broke out. As Wallace comments, the memory of the bitter struggle over the court act "made many a man a few years later scorn to follow, against the sovereign who had given him his land, the cross-country politicians from whom he felt he had suffered far greater wrongs than any imposed by Parliament or King." [6]

6. Wallace, *South Carolina*, p. 229.

6

Charleston:
The Culture of a City-State

*C*HARLESTON, like Venice in its heyday, was a city-state, ruled by an intelligent and cultivated oligarchy of great families who managed to monopolize control, generation after generation. Perhaps it is only coincidental that the Prioleau family, one of Charleston's oldest, traced its ancestry to the princely Venetian house of Priuli. The origins of most of the Charleston aristocracy, however, were less pretentious. Most of the great families who rose to prominence by the mid-eighteenth century owed their eminence to money earned as planters or merchants, or a combination of the two. Whatever their beginnings, the rich and powerful very early gained control of the colonial government; and for more than a century they concentrated all political power of the colony in Charleston.

Again like Venice, Charleston, the only town worthy of designation as a city until long after the War of Independence, extended its political and economic power far beyond its own precincts. A few outlying communities served as satellites as Charleston drew trade from distant Indian nations, from the whole back country, and from all the plantation area.

As Venice had extended its influence over Verona, for example, so Charleston made a financial and social tributary of Georgetown. As Verona erected in its market place a marble column bearing the lion of St. Mark, so Georgetown imitated the social institutions of Charleston with visible evidence: in 1758 it chartered the Winyah Indigo Society, at first dedicated, like some of Charleston's organizations, to philanthropy, but soon to become a social club that is still extant.

Camden, by the middle of the eighteenth century, became another little satellite. Charlestonians, seeking relief in summer from mosquitoes, malaria, and yellow fever in the High Hills of Santee on the east bank of the Wateree, looked with favor upon that region, acquired such land as they could, and by the time of the Revolution had made of Camden a little enclave of Low Country aristocrats.

But in the hinterland beyond Camden, the tidewater grandees could find few inhabitants worthy to be acknowledged as social equals. No Venetian member of the Council of Ten could have been more scornful of a peasant of the Veneto than a Meeting Street merchant was of a barbarian from beyond the fall line.

The concentration of political power in the hands of a few Charleston families began early in the town's history, even before the colony had shaken off Proprietary rule. After South Carolina became a royal province, and rice culture, combined with the Indian trade and the profitable import of black Africans, had established the economic independence of a few large landholders and merchants, these newly rich colonists began a long contention with royal governors and often with the Council. The Council, appointed by the king, served as the upper house of the Assembly. Members, whose terms were not limited, were usually elderly, prominent, conservative merchants and planters. Gradually, over the years, the Commons House whittled away the power of the Council; the Commons were especially concerned over any efforts the Council might make to interfere with money bills. The Commons House maintained that it had the same prerogatives as the House of Commons in England, and it usually made its decisions stick.

To believe that the Commons House was a great bulwark of democracy, ever ready to combat the minions of the king, is sheer romanticism. Through most of the colonial period, the Commons House was composed of members of an upper class

more intent upon furthering their own interests than in supporting legislation in behalf of the people as a whole. Furthermore,
no Venetian council could have been more arbitrary and tyran-
nical than the Commons House. "Imprisonment at the pleasure
of the Commons, so long as their session lasted, was inflicted
with great frequency for anything from disrespect toward them
in tavern gossip to attempts to defend legal rights by appeals to
the courts," Wallace comments. "For such arbitrary imprisonment there was no remedy." [1]

The constant conflict between the appointed Council and the
elected Commons, or between Governor and Commons, gave
Charlestonians experience that proved useful in the later controversies and conflict with Great Britain. The tradition of arbitrary authority exercised by a few men of property, however,
carried over into a later day and made reform tedious and slow.
Charlestonians came to believe that they had a God-given right
to rule and were loath to be separated from their power.

At an early stage, the franchise was restricted to free white
Christians possessing fifty acres of land or paying taxes in the
amount of twenty shillings. Since elections were held in the Anglican churches, supervised by the church wardens, the defini-
tion of Christianity was sometimes interpreted as membership in
the state church. To be a representative in the Commons House,
one had to possess 500 acres of land and 10 slaves or own other
property worth £1,000. Before the Revolution, backwoodsmen
had little or no representation in the legislative assembly, and it
is small wonder that they did not get excited about the purported
trespass on their rights by a British Parliament far across the
seas.

South Carolina and Virginia in the colonial period developed
aristocracies that bore some resemblance to the gentry of England, but the upper classes in the two colonies differed
markedly. The great Virginia families who came over earlier in
the seventeenth century were more conscious of an ancient tradition of gentility and were more deliberate in their efforts to
reproduce patterns of life similar to those of the county families

1. Wallace, *South Carolina*, p. 108.

in the home country. Many Virginia immigrants brought along Renaissance books on the rationale of behavior; their libraries revealed immense interest in the heritage of the past going back to Greece and Rome; and their correspondence discloses profound concern for the lessons that the classics and the writers of the Renaissance had to teach.

The great families of South Carolina were founded by men who came later in the seventeenth and early in the eighteenth centuries. They were not a bookish lot, and the inventories of the estates of many of these founding fathers are notably lacking in titles of books that display a concern for the past. These were men on the make, and they looked to Augustan London for models of behavior—if, indeed, they thought much about the matter. Some of the wealthiest—the Manigaults, for example— were not even English in origin, though they sent their sons to England for schooling. This is not to say that the South Carolina gentry were less conscious of status than their Virginia brethren, or less concerned to assert their privileges and to display the outward manifestations of an upper class. But they reflected the social patterns of the London of Queen Anne and the Georges, rather than the older traditions of English county families. Many Virginians of the eighteenth century, it is true, were also influenced by the behavior of Georgian London—sometimes to the disgust of their parents who had sent them overseas for education—but the county family heritage in Virginia was much stronger than in South Carolina.

Another factor making for differences in the aristocracies of Virginia and South Carolina was the early development of an urban society in Charleston, something that Virginia lacked until after the Revolution. Virginia's capital at Williamsburg had social occasions of considerable glitter during meetings of the Council of State and the House of Burgesses, but it was not a commercial center of any importance. Although it had a theater where occasional plays were acted and a printing office and newspaper, Williamsburg remained a small town glorified only by the presence of the royal governor in his palace and the Capitol at the end of the Duke of Gloucester Street.

Charleston, on the other hand, almost at once became a busy

mart of trade. Ships from the West Indies, from New York, the Rhode Island ports, Philadelphia, London, Bristol, Liverpool, and Glasgow put into the harbor to load rice, corn, tar, turpentine, pitch, and indigo. They brought manufactured products, from window panes to wedding gowns. They also brought an endless procession of slaves from the coast of West Africa. Wholesale merchants of Charleston were in direct communication with commercial houses in the northern colonies and in Great Britain. The wholesale merchants supplied retail tradesmen of Charleston with goods which they sold to the local inhabitants; the merchants also furnished back-country traders with goods in exchange for deerskins and other products. It should be remembered that the term *merchant* meant a wholesaler, who stood on a different social plane from the retailer, or humble shopkeeper.

During the first two generations of the colony, trade provided the quickest way to wealth. Not until the development of rice culture on a considerable scale could a planter hope to acquire the riches needed for the full trappings of aristocratic life. Many families who rose to prominence began in trade. Brewton, Drayton, Middleton, Laurens, Manigault, Gadsden, Grimké, Guerard, Pringle, Brailsford, and Roper are only a few of the family names of merchants and traders who early gained both wealth and prestige in the market place. Once possessed of money, merchants bought land, some for the additional profits to be made from growing rice, others to insure their social status. By the end of the colonial period, the great wealth of the planters was beginning to give them an edge over the merchants, and a few were already looking down their sunburned noses and asserting the superiority of their social position. An overweening pride, first of the Seven Deadly Sins, which was to afflict aristocratic families in the years to come, would ultimately have a ruinous impact upon South Carolina and the country as a whole.

Few better insights into the developing commerce of Charleston can be gained than by reading *The Papers of Henry Laurens* in the edition begun by the late Philip M. Hamer. Four volumes, for the most part letters, carry the reader from September

11, 1746, to August 31, 1765. Laurens, son of a prosperous saddler of Charleston, intended to enter a commercial house in London, but the plan fell through; he then came home to become the partner of George Austin in general trade. The firm prospered; Laurens grew rich, bought land, and became a planter. From 1771 to 1774, he lived in Europe, chiefly in England, supervising the education of his sons at London and Geneva. After the outbreak of trouble with Great Britain, Laurens was elected president of the Continental Congress.

Although he later declared that he hated slavery and wished he could free his own bondsmen, Laurens for many years was one of the principal slave importers. His letters, beginning in January 1749, are filled with instructions to dealers in Liverpool and Bristol for the shipment of slaves. In a letter to John Knight of Liverpool, dated January 20, 1749, he advised that if he wished "to try a cargo of slaves at Carolina, I can venture to assure you there is a prospect of pretty good sales as rice promises fair to be a good commodity." He adds that a cargo destined for Charleston might also include wines from Madeira and rum and sugar from Barbados and the Leeward Islands, "always in demand but most from September to February." Charlestonians early developed a palate for good wines and a need for rum, useful both for punch and for trade.[2]

The demand for slaves was influenced directly by the price of rice and indigo. As the market for both products expanded, the price rose, and planters were eager to extend their fields. To a Bristol slave dealer, Laurens wrote on August 1, 1755, that buyers were so avid for a recent cargo of slaves that "there was such pulling and hauling who should get the good slaves that some of them [the would-be purchasers] came to collaring and very nearly to blows." They bid up the price of the "fine men" to £300 each. "There was people enough in town that day to have taken off a thousand good slaves."[3]

Slave dealing, however, was tricky. A cargo might arrive

2. *The Papers of Henry Laurens,* edited by Philip M. Hamer et al. (Columbia, S.C.: University of South Carolina Press, 1968) 1:205.

3. *Papers of Henry Laurens,* 1:308.

with smallpox, and then the vessel had to lie in quarantine a month or two. If the slaves looked sickly or scrawny, buyers might turn them down. Calabar tribesmen from the delta of the Niger River were disliked because they were given to suicide, Laurens asserted; stout fellows from Gambia, the Windward Coast, and Angola found the readiest sale.

Both sellers and buyers were much concerned about the health and welfare of their charges, because each slave represented a heavy investment, often on credit. Risky—and distasteful—as the trade might be, the potential profits were high, and most of the great Charleston merchants sold slaves when they could procure them. The largest dealers were Miles Brewton, Henry Laurens, and Samuel Brailsford. Few in the eighteenth century were concerned about the moral wrong of treating human beings as commodities, but many South Carolinians worried endlessly about the growing imbalance between the white and black population and the increasing possibility of slave insurrections.

Laurens and his contemporaries-in-trade imported vast quantities of luxuries, as well as the usual necessities required by the colony. Many Charlestonians had spent time in England and Europe and had acquired a taste for the good things of life. Their houses held fine furniture, mirrors, porcelains, silver, damask, linens, wallpaper, draperies, pictures, and occasionally books.

An illustration of the abiding interest of Charleston in all things connected with London is found in a letter of Laurens to Richard Shubrick, his agent in London, dated October 12, 1756, ordering two landscapes, of Kensington and of Hyde Park, wanted by his brother-in-law Elias Ball. Ball owned a plantation named Kensington, on the Cooper River. Ball's brother, John Coming Ball, had named his plantation Hyde Park.

A rare reference to an order for books occurs in a letter to a London stationer, Samuel Hirt, dated November 10, 1747, in which Laurens complained that, in a set of the *Spectator,* the first two volumes were the *Tatler* instead of the *Spectator,* a defect that had caused him to lose money on the sale. He thanked the stationer, however, for sending "5 volumes of Rapin's *History . . .* which are come safe to hand." [4]

Although good wines, especially those from Madeira, were in constant demand, the amount of rum imported was enormous. Occasionally the market was literally flooded, and Laurens from time to time had to write his agents that he could see no immediate sale for any more of that commodity. At one point Laurens approached Gabriel Manigault about attempting to corner the market in rum to stabilize the price, but Manigault shrewdly thought it would not work out to their advantage. Rum was not merely an article of trade with the Indians: rivers of it were consumed in cooling drinks beloved of Charlestonians then as later. Current recipes for planters' punch may derive from Singapore, but eighteenth-century South Carolina had its equivalent.

Dr. David Ramsay, a Charleston physician who wrote a *History of South Carolina* first published in 1809, made some telling comments about the long Carolina tradition of alcoholic absorption. "Drunkenness," he remarked, "may be called an endemic vice of Carolina. The climate disposes to it, and the combined influence of religion and education too often fail to restrain it. . . . Several persons are contented with the beverage of nature, and maintain good health and spirits without any artificial liquor whatever; but a much greater number drink water only when they can get nothing else." [5]

Physicians, Ramsay regretted to say, had recommended spirits to rectify water. "The general position being once admitted that the addition of rum, gin, brandy, or whiskey is an improvement of water, it is no easy matter to stop at the precise point of temperance," he added. From the beginning, South Carolinians have held to the doctrine that branch water is much improved by spirits of whatever kind available. Idleness of the gentry, Ramsay thought, accounted for much drunkenness in high place:

4. *Papers of Henry Laurens,* 1:79.

5. David Ramsay, *History of South Carolina,* 2nd ed. (Newberry, S.C.: W. J. Duffie, 1858), 2:217.

To these [working men who drank too much] may be added the
gentlemen who spend their afternoons and evenings over their wine.
By the help of semi-annual fits of the gout, they sometimes make
out to live for several years, though they seldom go to bed sober.
. . . Perplexity, from debt and other embarrassments or troubles, is
in Carolina a common cause of inebriation. . . . When all the pre-
ceding classes are taken into view, the number of strictly temperate
people is far short of what is generally supposed.[6]

This picture of our ancestors, sitting around of an evening in a
sodden stupor, is not one that romanticists usually portray, but
in London and in its small reflection, Charleston, contemporary
accounts often bear out Dr. Ramsay's description.

Drunk or sober, however, Charlestonians of the eighteenth
century were an enterprising and acquisitive people. They ac-
cumulated great wealth and the power that wealth assured them.
They created a small replica of London with most of the amenities that a visitor from England would have expected to find at
home.

Some of the more prosperous Charlestonians, like Henry
Laurens, for example, paid long visits to England or the Continent for pleasure, to educate their children, or to seek an improvement in health. Intermarriage between Carolinians and the
upper class of Great Britain was not uncommon. Social contacts
helped to cement ties with the mother country that were hard to
break in 1776.

Like Venetians of the sixteenth century, who felt obliged to
possess a handsome palazzo on the Grand Canal regardless of
any villas they might own elsewhere, so the wealthier South
Carolina planters believed it essential to build a fine house on
the peninsula between the Ashley and Cooper rivers regardless
of how comfortable a home they might already have on the
Edisto, Combahee, Cooper, or one of the other innumerable
rivers of the land. This conviction was more compelling in
South Carolina than in Venice, because summers on the rivers
were dangerous to health. Malaria was endemic, and no one had

6. Ramsay, *History of South Carolina*, 2:219.

yet contrived a way to eliminate mosquitoes, had they even known that the pests were carriers of disease.

A few of the planters' houses in Charleston have survived to the present day to illuminate the culture of the period and to excite the admiration of tourists. Fortunately, Charleston was not betrayed by affluence in the nineteenth century, and its denizens had to make do with their old houses instead of replacing them with Victorian monstrosities of gingerbread now venerated by conservationists. In late years, Charleston has set a worthy example to the rest of the country in zealously preserving its architectural heritage.

The houses on the peninsula were highly practical, often beautiful. Sometimes built of wood and sometimes of Charleston-baked brick, many were three stories high, one room wide with high ceilings, and set with the end to the street, facing south to catch the evening breeze. A piazza on each floor made an outdoor sitting room. Some houses had fine paneling and carved mantels of local cypress. Henry Laurens writes constantly of importing marble slabs for mantels, table tops, and other household uses. The houses were built for both comfort and the entertainment of guests. Servant quarters were usually in a side yard or on the ground floor, which frequently had brick flooring built up to be above normal flood levels. The kitchen and cellars were usually on this floor. The drawing room and dining room were reached by high steps leading from the street or the garden.

Gardens were prized by Charlestonians. Although space around their town houses was limited, they made the most of what they had. Carolina jessamine with fragrant yellow flowers in spring climbed fences and pillars and mingled sometimes with white star jessamine. Ferns grew rampant in the shade, and oleanders bloomed in sunny spots. Frequently orange trees in tubs stood in the open except in the coldest winter weather.

Henry Laurens and his wife illustrate the growing interest in gardening in the later eighteenth century, again an interest imitative of the taste of Londoners. In a letter of May 20, 1763, to Isaac King of London, ordering a variety of articles for the decoration of his house, Laurens included a request that King seek out some flower seeds and bulbs, apologized for troubling him for things so out of his line, and explained: "Mrs. Laurens, who has a good garden and takes great delight in it, comes now with a winning request that I write to England for a few garden seed and roots." [7] Mrs. Laurens's order included "colly flower" and carnation seed, and bulbs of mountain lilies, daffodils both white and yellow, ranunculuses, peonies, and anemones. Under bulbs, she listed nasturtiums, which was clearly her error.

The critical Dr. Ramsay in his *History of South Carolina* reproached South Carolinians for neglecting gardens in their greed for profitable crops; but he almost contradicts himself in his enthusiastic descriptions of Charleston gardens. Of especial note, he declared, was the Laurens garden:

> About the year 1755 Henry Laurens purchased a lot of four acres in Ansonborough, which is now called Laurens Square, and enriched it with everything useful and ornamental that Carolina produced or his extensive mercantile connections enabled him to procure from remote parts of the world. Among a variety of other curious productions he introduced olives, capers, limes, ginger, guinea grass, the alpine strawberry bearing nine months in the year, red raspberries, blue grapes; and also, directly from the south of France, apples, pears, and plums of fine kinds and vines which bore abundantly of the choice white eating grape called *Chasselates blancs*. The whole was superintended with maternal care by Mrs. Elinor Laurens with the assistance of John Watson, a complete English gardener. [8]

Ramsay also praised Watson for developing his own botanical garden "on the ground now occupied by Nathaniel Heyward, and afterwards on a large lot of land stretching from King Street to and over Meeting Street." [9] Ramsay mentioned the exotics planted by Charles Drayton on his Ashley River plantation (today's Magnolia Gardens) and the introduction of camellias by André Michaux at Middleton Place. It should be remembered that one exquisite white flower, the gardenia, was named after a

7. *Papers of Henry Laurens,* 3:458.
8. Ramsay, *History of South Carolina,* 2:128.
9. Ramsay, *History of South Carolina,* 2:128.

Charleston physician and scientist, Dr. Alexander Garden; he is not to be confused with a contemporary of the same name, a sour ecclesiastic serving as "commissary" (official representative) of the Bishop of London, who had jurisdiction over the Established Church in the colonies.

After the passage of the Church Act of 1706 making the Anglican communion the Established Church of South Carolina, Charleston became the religious center of the colony, but in name only. Although the commissary of the Bishop of London labored earnestly to bring about conformity, his work was a losing game. South Carolina Dissenters might grit their teeth and pay their taxes to support the Church in Charleston, but they refused to bow the knee to Baal; the colonial Rome had no power except occasionally to harass the voters at election time, to attempt to stop Dissenting ministers from performing marriage ceremonies, and to assume a haughty social superiority. The tolerance that the Lords Proprietors had commanded in the beginning lasted throughout the colonial period. If Dissenters had to pay taxes to support the state church, they were not prohibited from building their own. Jews suffered no handicaps and by 1750 had organized a congregation. Some of the most talented South Carolinians are descended from Sephardic Portuguese and Spanish Jews who early found refuge in Charleston. They added an important intellectual leaven to colonial society.

In the early days of settlement, although Anglicans and Dissenters quarreled mightily, nobody got around to building a church for fourteen years—a neglect not equalled in any other colony. Finally, in 1682, St. Philip's was organized and a structure erected on the site now occupied by St. Michael's. When St. Philip's outgrew its first building, it moved to its present location at 146 Church Street. In 1685, Dissenting Presbyterians built their White Meeting House where the Circular Church now stands. The name of the Presbyterian edifice gave its name to Meeting Street. The French Huguenots, most of whom in time were absorbed into the Anglican establishment, began a church of their own in 1687. The present Huguenot Church in Church Street is the fourth structure on this spot. Once a year, a service using the French liturgy is still held there. The cornerstone of the most famous of Charleston churches and the oldest church building still intact, St. Michael's, was laid in 1752, and the first services were held there in 1761.

Even though Charleston had churches, religious conditions in the colony were less than satisfactory to Anglican authorities in London. To improve the morals and piety of the colony, the Society for the Propagation of the Gospel sent out scores of missionary preachers to save Carolinian souls. These missionaries were not intended for the far back country, where Presbyterians and Baptists were taking care of themselves; they were needed to fill the pulpits of churches in the tidewater region. "Of the thirteen parishes in 1723, six including several rich and populous, were served by missionaries of the Society for the Propagation of the Gospel," Wallace points out. "Four were vacant. It is an interesting speculation what would have been the fate of the Anglican Church but for the interest of this great missionary society, which made South Carolina one of its favored fields; for the bland tolerance displayed by such a large proportion of the ruling class was the outcome, by all contemporary testimony, of a considerable indifference to religion." [10] Even the Society for the Propagation of the Gospel wearied at last of paying preachers to serve in rich parishes and in 1759 abandoned the practice.

The parsons themselves were not always exemplary shepherds of such flocks as they could corral. Several were dismissed for drunkenness or for openly keeping concubines. Dissenting ministers were also sometimes guilty of similar offenses. The eighteenth century in South Carolina was not a period of great moral fervor. Even the appearance of George Whitefield, the eloquent evangelist who stirred the multitudes during the religious revival known as the Great Awakening, aroused Charleston to nothing more than a controversy in the *South Carolina Gazette*. On later visits, the evangelist did attract crowds to Dissenting churches. The city, however, was not deeply moved; it showed little addiction to "enthusiasm," a word in that day connoting religious fanaticism.

For many years, schools were scarce or virtually nonexistent

10. Wallace, *South Carolina*, p. 208.

in Charleston and the surrounding country. Unlike Massachusetts Bay and Virginia, South Carolina made no effort to found a college to insure a supply of ministers and leaders. In Charleston, the wealthy could hire tutors; the poor could pass on to their children such learning as they possessed. In 1712, the legislative assembly passed a free school act which promised each parish £ 12 to help defray the cost of a schoolhouse and £ 10 toward the pay of a schoolmaster who was required to be an Anglican, approved by the vestry. As elsewhere in colonial America, "free school" did not mean what the words connote today. A free school was required to teach a few of the indigent poor without charge, but was expected to collect fees from all able to pay.

The missionaries of the Society for the Propagation of the Gospel sometimes combined teaching and preaching. For example, the Reverend Francis Le Jau and his wife, in the early years of the eighteenth century, took a few pupils into their home at Goose Creek, but soon abandoned the effort. A schoolmaster, Benjamin Dennis, sent out from England at Le Jau's request, arrived in 1711 and the next year was reported to have twenty-seven white pupils, two Indians, and one Negro. Although schools did not flourish, Wallace comments on the "high degree of educated intelligence in the province." [11]

Throughout the colonial period, occasional small bequests were made for schools and education, but not many schools were actually founded as a result. Education remained a matter of private enterprise, with many schoolmasters and schoolmistresses advertising their services in the *South Carolina Gazette*. Women teachers usually offered reading and needlework, sometimes French and dancing. Men emphasized arithmetic, surveying, navigation, reading, and the keeping of accounts. In 1723, the Reverend Thomas Morrit was conducting the Charleston Free School, but its history is vague. The lack of highly organized schools did not prevent Charlestonians and other tidewater folk from getting the essentials of an education, for there is ample evidence of their intelligence and literacy.

On June 26, 1755, Henry Laurens wrote to John Knight of

11. Wallace, *South Carolina*, p. 81.

Liverpool thanking him in behalf of his business partner, George Austin, for "the kind information you have given him of his boy [Austin's son]. Believes he must make a voyage to England next year to place him somewhere more to his advantage than to pore over Latin and Greek authors of little utility to a young man intended for business." [12] Clearly Austin was displeased at the classical curriculum of the English school where he had sent his son. Carolinians, like Virginians, sometimes asked their merchant correspondents in England to place their sons in schools and report on them from time to time.

If Charleston in the eighteenth century could boast few schools of note, the city was not without concern for education, even education of the poor. The South Carolina Society in the 1760s and 1770s hired schoolmasters to teach twenty or thirty children of the poor. Other philanthropic Charleston societies also took upon themselves the duty of supplying some modicum of education to the indigent.

One reason for Charleston's failure to create good schools of its own, Frederick P. Bowes suggests, in *The Culture of Early Charleston,* was the consistent belief of the upper class that the only good education was to be had in England. The practice of some families of residing for a time in England, that their children might benefit from the schools, had obvious cultural benefits; but only the wealthy could afford it. Charles Pinckney, for example, took his family to England in 1754 so that his children might be properly educated; his son Thomas spent nearly twenty years attending Westminster School, Oxford, and the Middle Temple. Henry Laurens also went abroad for the education of his three sons, but disliked what he found in England and took his two older boys to Geneva to be instructed by Swiss teachers.

Oxford and Cambridge had fallen to a low state in the mid-eighteenth century, and only a few Carolinians went there. An English university education at the time chiefly fitted a man to be a clergyman, a teacher, or a roué. Carolina fathers preferred that their sons enter one of the Inns of Court, usually the Middle Temple, for legal training which they found useful back home in business or politics.

12. *Papers of Henry Laurens,* 1:271–272.

SOUTH CAROLINA

A photographer's essay by Bruce Roberts

Photos in Sequence

Beach at Huntington Island State Park near Beaufort.
Cotton harvester near Summerville.
Worker in the Springs textile mill at Chester.
Sailboats on the Ashley River, Charleston.
Avenue of the Oaks, Boone Hall Plantation, Mt. Pleasant.
Cadets on parade, the Citadel, Charleston.
Guns at Fort Sumter,, Charleston Harbor, Charleston.
School children in class, the Lancaster Public Schools.
Owner of water-powered grist mill, Westminster.
Farmers Market, downtown Charleston.
Early morning on the Battery, Charleston.
Angel Oak, St. Johns Island, south of Charleston.
Cobblestone street near St. Philip's Church, Charleston.
Basket seller, street market, Charleston.
Cattle egret and Black Angus on a plantation near Georgetown.

Despite Henry Laurens's caveat about classical education, many of the Charleston ruling class in the later eighteenth century were well versed in Greek and Latin literature and could toss off a Latin tag in their political oratory. Christopher Gadsden resigned in a huff from the Charleston Library Society in 1765, when it voted to stop buying classical works.

From the mid-eighteenth century onward, Charleston showed a greater interest in books than had been evident earlier. The most important cultural event of the period was the formation in 1748 of the Charleston Library Society, an organization that was to grow in distinction and influence with the years. It has survived to the present day and has preserved invaluable historical documents. The aim of the Society was to create a fund for the purchase of books and current periodicals and pamphlets. But it soon developed more grandiose ideas, and proposals were made to purchase scientific apparatus, to hire a professor of mathematics and natural philosophy, and to foster the establishment of an academy—in short, to become a sort of Charleston version of London's Gresham College. Fortunately, plans to diffuse the activities of the Society fell through, and it stuck to its original program of being a library. Its meetings, however, provided a forum for the liveliest intellectual conversation in the city. It also bought some scientific apparatus, for one must remember that this was the beginning of heightened interest in science, especially in chemistry and physics, and chemical experiments and demonstrations of static electricity always excited attention.

Leadership in scientific speculation and investigation was taken by Charleston's physicians. Busy as they were in an area constantly afflicted with epidemics, they took time to write scientific papers, discuss scientific problems, and make contributions of note in their time. Many of the physicians were graduates of the universities of Leyden or Edinburgh. Perhaps the most original scientific mind was possessed by Dr. John Lining, a Scot, who arrived in Charleston about 1730 and for many years combined the practice of medicine with painstaking research. He made a detailed study of metabolism, using himself for his observations. He made an elaborate investigation of weather, and some of his meteorological data, including rainfall

measurements for Charleston during fifteen years, were published in the *Transactions of the Royal Society* of London. Lining, like Franklin, was interested in electricity, and he corresponded with Franklin about the kite experiment. Thanks to
Lining and Franklin, some Charlestonians put lightning rods on
their houses, though a few objected that this was an impious interference with "God's artillery."

Controversy over inoculation for smallpox raged in Charleston, as it did in Boston and elsewhere, with doctors arguing on
both sides of the issue. During the epidemic of 1738, Dr. James
Killpatrick employed inoculation with considerable success, but
was so violently opposed by both fellow physicians and laymen
that the legislative assembly finally prohibited its use. As in the
case of lightning rods, some citizens argued that inoculation
constituted an interference with the divine plan for the disposi-
tion of mankind.

Botany and agriculture naturally attracted intense interest, for
advances in these fields had practical applications. The inves-
tigations of Dr. Alexander Garden, another Charleston physician, were notable. Garden corresponded with such well-known
naturalists as Linnaeus in Sweden and John Bartram in Philadelphia, as well as with scientists in Great Britain. The Royal
Society published his contributions and in 1773 elected him a
Fellow. After his retirement to England, he remembered the
South Carolina Low Country with nostalgia, especially the birds,
the fireflies, and the "fine peaches . . . when full ripe exceeding
in richness and flavor any other fruit, or whatever fancy can
suggest." [13] Many another South Carolinian in later times was
to remember the delicacy of tree-ripened peaches.

The interest of Charlestonians in natural curiosities and the
phenomena of nature led to the founding in 1773 of the Charleston Museum, the first in America. A room in the Charleston
Library Society was set aside for collections that citizens were
asked to contribute. Frederick P. Bowes comments that the
Charleston Museum "was a community project and thus reflected the interest in science among Carolinians generally. For

13. Frederick P. Bowes, *The Culture of Early Charleston* (Chapel Hill, N.C.: University of North Carolina Press, 1942), p. 91.

not only did the colony have its men of science . . . but also it could boast a cultivated gentry who valued the achievements of science and were eager to promote its cause.'' [14]

After 1731, a printing press and a newspaper provided an opportunity for Carolinians to express themselves in print. From this time onward, controversies frequently resulted in a rash of pamphlets, sometimes written in heroic verse, for the meters of Alexander Pope were easy to imitate even though both thought and measure might limp.

The legislative assembly having offered a bounty for the establishment of a printing office and newspaper, three printers had turned up in 1731, but two of the earliest soon died, and in 1733 Lewis Timothy, a French Huguenot sent from Philadelphia by Benjamin Franklin, began publishing the *South-Carolina Gazette*. After Timothy's death in 1738, his widow Elizabeth continued to edit and publish the paper, and she was followed by her son Peter. Thus the *South-Carolina Gazette,* under the control of the Timothy family from 1733 until the end of the Colonial period, reflects the social, political, and intellectual interests of Charleston and the colony.

That Charlestonians did not improve their opportunity to become men of letters is not surprising. Colonial citizens were usually too busy about other matters to consider literature as a serious vocation or avocation. Furthermore, Charlestonians looked to London for their reading matter and were not moved, themselves, to make original contributions beyond occasional verse and satirical essays in the *Gazette*. The newspaper did give an opportunity for the discussion, sometimes violent, of current political and social problems.

The pleasure-loving and sophisticated class that developed in colonial Charleston delighted in theatricals. Beginning in 1735, with a performance of Otway's *The Orphan,* the town enjoyed drama for generations. The very next year, 1736, Charleston's first theater was erected in Queen Street and opened with a comedy by George Farquhar, *The Recruiting Officer.* Shakespeare also had an enduring popularity on the Charleston stage.

Wealthier Charlestonians in the late colonial period had their

14. Bowes, *Early Charleston,* p. 91.

portraits painted in London by the reigning artists of the day—
Romney, Gainsborough, Reynolds, and others. But much earlier, local artists limned the faces of the prominent and sometimes painted crests and devices on their coaches. In 1735, a
certain Bishop Roberts advertised in the *Gazette* that he was
prepared to do portraits, landscapes, and house painting. His
wife Mary offered to do "face-painting." Charleston's best-
known colonial artist was Jeremiah Theus, a German-Swiss who
operated a drawing school in Friend Street, did portraits of
scores of well-to-do citizens, and gained enough money and
prestige to buy a pew in St. Michael's.

Music attracted the most prestigious interest. The *Gazette* is
filled with notices of both vocal and instrumental concerts, of
singing lessons offered, and of music lessons on almost every
instrument from the harpsichord to the French horn. On November 22, 1737, St. Cecilia's Day, Theodore Pachelbell advertised a cantata suitable for the occasion.

Charleston can rightfully claim the distinction of supporting
the first paid orchestra in the English colonies. In 1762, the St.
Cecilia Society was organized and, for a number of years, supported an orchestra, promoted classical music, and attained
fame as far away as Boston, where it advertised for musicians.
In time, however, the St. Cecilia Society forgot its high endeavors for music (or got tired of the financial burden of paying
for an orchestra) and declined into a social club known primarily for its pride and exclusiveness. Generations later, a story
circulated that South Carolina's great Confederate hero, General
Wade Hampton, was forbidden to bring Minnie Maddern Fiske
as his guest to the annual St. Cecilia Ball because she was an
actress, albeit the most famous of her day.

As the Charleston upper class grew wealthier, its sophistication increased, as did its appetite for amusement and entertainment. During the social seasons, especially on holiday occasions—Christmas and the days before Lent—Charleston was a
city of gaiety, with receptions, card parties, balls, and much
elaborate entertainment in the town houses of the great. Social
clubs by the dozen sprang up, to last for a few months or for
generations; a club was available to cater to any taste. In the

summer, planters often took refuge in their Charleston houses from mosquito-ridden rice plantations. "The summers offered such diversions as horse-races, cock-fights, and outdoor musical programs at the Orange Gardens," one social historian observes. "Later in the period a number of Charlestonians went to Newport [Rhode Island] for the summers, so many in fact that the town was called the 'Carolina hospital'." [15] Also many business and professional men as well as planters who could get away frequently sought healthier climates in the Sand Hills and the Up Country. Nevertheless, the summer season, especially in the period before 1750, was a time of much social activity. The great houses of the city were built to insure comfort, with broad piazzas on each floor, so placed that they could catch the ocean breezes.

Sophisticated Charleston was noted for good conversation. Hospitality was unbounded, and a gentleman, from any part of the world, was always welcome. Perhaps the give-and-take of conversation on every subject under the sun, from the political complexities of Portugal (with which Charlestonians had commercial contacts) to the latest essay in the *Spectator,* did more to stretch the minds of Carolinians than the perusal of books in isolation on their plantations. By the end of the colonial period, few areas equalled Charleston in polish and cultivation.

But not all the entertainment was either polite or cerebral. From an early time, horse racing and cockfighting were popular sports. Two courses near the city made it easy for all classes to view the races, where considerable sums were lost and won. Cockfighting had less prestige with the elite, but it was widely attended.

Studies of Charleston in the colonial period are likely to give the impression that the city was inhabited only by the rich and their servants. Actually, the city had a large and growing population of artisans, craftsmen, shopkeepers, and other folk engaged in one business or another. It is often stated that competition from slave artisans, hired out by their masters, tended to retard the development of a community of white craftsmen.

15. Bowes, *Early Charleston,* p. 9.

Although advertisements in the *Charleston Gazette* indicate a considerable number of slave carpenters, coopers, shipwrights, and other skilled workers, the number of whites in a multiplicity of trades continued to increase. Thus Charleston was not merely a city monopolized by a high social caste; it was also the focal point in the colony of a thriving industrial class that one day would bring prosperity to the region when the planters had become only a memory.

From its founding, Charleston demonstrated remarkable vigor and resilience in the face of every sort of danger and disaster. Until the settlement of Georgia, it was on the frontier, in constant danger from Spanish and French attack by both sea and land. For many years, hostile Indians remained a menace. Before the city was well established, between 1697 and 1699, it was ravaged by both smallpox and yellow fever. Plague even killed the cattle. Fire burned down a third of the town, and an earthquake terrorized the populace. As if that were not enough, a hurricane in the autumn of 1699, first of many to follow in later years, flooded the houses on the peninsula, wrecked vessels in the harbor, and drowned many people. Through the years, Charleston has suffered many more destructive fires, disastrous hurricanes, and devastating plagues of smallpox and yellow fever. But its citizens never wavered in their vigor and determination to rebuild and advance. From the ship chandlers on the wharves and the small tradesmen on Market Street to the great merchants in their counting houses on East Bay Street, Charleston's men and women were determined, intelligent, ambitious people. They made a great city, and if they wanted to become a small replica of London, they succeeded in making a city-state more like Venice of old. Charleston's virtues—and its vices—would influence South Carolina for all succeeding generations.

7

Reluctant Rebels; Violent Partisans

$\mathcal{O}$OUTH CAROLINA was potentially the most loyal of the British colonies when the controversies began that erupted eventually into the War of Independence. In the beginning, few South Carolinians dreamed of breaking away from the mother country. Grievances and complaints they had in plenty, as others had; but at the end of the French and Indian War, no one could foresee that American guns would be firing on British troops at Lexington and Concord within a scant dozen years. The merchants of Charleston were prospering from trade with London, Bristol, Liverpool, and Glasgow. The rice planters were getting richer from abundant crops shipped overseas to British markets and to foreign ports south of Cape Finistere. Indigo, thanks to a bounty paid by the British government for every pound produced in the colonies, was bringing in additional revenue to planters and even to small farmers in the middle region of Carolina.

The back country was filling up rapidly with immigrants moving down from Pennsylvania, Maryland, and Virginia, and from a lesser tide moving inland from the port of Charleston. These back-countrymen in many cases received small bounties for farm equipment along with land grants from the government; others simply squatted on unclaimed land in the backwoods. They had no grudge against any overseas authority. In short, South Carolinians in 1763 at the time of the Peace of Paris were as content as human beings are likely to be in this imperfect world.

How Great Britain contrived to alienate an influential minority and make rebels of prosperous merchants and planters in so short a time is a revelation of tactless bumbling by King George III's ministers and of the intransigence of a few hotheads in South Carolina. As has so often happened in the commonwealth's history, the voices of moderates went unheard and extremists carried the day. The leader of the extremists was a well-to-do merchant named Christopher Gadsden, soon to be acclaimed the greatest patriot of them all.

In the Revolutionary epoch, as in later periods of South Carolina's history, events were shaped to a large degree by the persuasive characteristics of a few leaders. All states, of course, are influenced by the quality of their leaders, but South Carolina always has been peculiarly susceptible to political oratory. The Revolutionay years were to illustrate the effect of the magnetic impact of a few Whig voices from Charleston, soon to be known as Patriots. The first of these was Gadsden.

The source of Gadsden's deep-seated hatred of British authority would make a fascinating problem for a psychiatrist. Gadsden had been educated in England, had served for a time as a purser on a British man-of-war, had returned to Charleston to prosper as a merchant and a planter, and had fought with distinction in the Cherokee War. Perhaps an incident in that campaign may have triggered some latent dislike of the British.

Gadsden was a close friend of, and junior officer under, Thomas Middleton, colonel of the militia. When General Sir Jeffrey Amherst placed Lieutenant Colonel James Grant, a Scot, in command of some 1,600 regular British troops and sent him to rescue Carolina from hostile Cherokees, Middleton was disgruntled, for he thought he outranked Grant and should have been given over-all command. Gadsden ardently supported Middleton.

After the fighting was over, Middleton challenged Grant to a duel, which luckily ended without casualties, but Gadsden continued the controversy in the *South Carolina Gazette* and in two pamphlets. This intemperate attack on Grant was too much for

Henry Laurens, a lifelong friend of Gadsden. In reply, Laurens wrote a pamphlet which circulated in manuscript. From then onward, Laurens became a middle-of-the-road influence, and Gadsden became a firebrand.

The arrogance of British officers, both civil and military, in dealing with colonials probably aroused as much animosity as any other single cause. In the eighteenth century, scores of militia officers, including George Washington, had been driven to anger and sometimes to resignation by the arrogance or fatuousness of officers sent out from England. Even Henry Laurens, for all his defense of Grant and other Britons, was frequently irritated by them.

In addition, dishonest customs officers and judges in the court of admiralty caused Laurens to lose faith in English justice. Like many other merchants, he was driven to desperation by arbitrary enforcement of petty rules under the navigation acts. Fraudulent or stupid officers, as much as the injustice of the laws themselves, helped to alienate even moderate men like Laurens.

The passage in 1765 of the Stamp Act, requiring every legal paper and every newspaper to bear a revenue stamp, was followed by a sequence of annoying and alarming acts imposed by the government of George III that set the country aflame from Maine to Georgia. Especially threatening to individual liberty was the requirement that persons accused of treason must be sent to England for trial. Also troubling was the quartering act, which required the colonies to provide billets for troops sent, some believed, to keep colonials in subjugation. The revenue acts, passed by Parliament to help pay for the recent defense of the colonies against the French and Indians, might have seemed reasonable to English M.P.s, but such revenue-raising measures soon produced a revolutionary battle cry of "taxation without representation."

To George III's ministers, the Stamp Act seemed a particularly fair measure that treated all the colonies alike. But no act could have touched so many sensitive—and articulate—areas, for every lawyer had to buy stamps for his documents; every newspaper had to appear with a revenue stamp attached; every bill of lading and all other commercial papers had to be stamped. In short, nobody could escape paying the hated tax. Samuel Adams in Massachusetts and Christopher Gadsden in South Carolina were soon using their eloquence to persuade the populace to resist British tyranny. In Boston, a mob swept through Lieutenant Governor Thomas Hutchinson's house, broke up his furniture, and threw his library into the streets. In Charleston, Gadsden organized mechanics and other tradesmen as Sons of Liberty and harangued them on the iniquity of King George. They chose as their favorite meeting place Isaac Mazyck's pasture under a giant oak soon called the "Liberty Tree." It stood at the Cooper River end of present Calhoun Street. Later, during their occupation of Charleston, the British cut it down. As in Boston, the mob got out of hand and broke into Henry Laurens's house searching for stamps. That act did not sweeten his attitude toward the fire-eating tactics of his old friend Gadsden.

In Virginia, Patrick Henry was denouncing with his own brand of eloquence British audacity in attempting taxation without representation. Stirred by Sam Adams and encouraged by the attitude of Virginia, the oldest colony, Massachusetts issued a call to all the colonies to send delegates to a Congress in New York in October 1765. South Carolina's representatives were Gadsden, John Rutledge, and Thomas Lynch. Gadsden made a highly favorable impression on the Congress by declaring that "We stand upon the broad common ground of natural rights. . . . There ought to be no New England man, no New Yorker, known on the continent, but all of us Americans." [1] The Congress passed a resolution declaring that no taxes could be levied constitutionally upon the several colonies "except by their respective legislatures," and that the Stamp Act in particular tended to "subvert the rights and liberties of the colonists."

The next year, Parliament repealed the Stamp Act, but maintained its authority by passing the Declaratory Act, which stated unequivocally the right of King and Parliament to make laws

---

1. Samuel E. Morison and Henry S. Commager, *The Growth of the American Republic* (New York: Oxford University Press, 1942), 1:151.

"to bind the colonies in all cases whatsoever." Thoughtful citizens on this side of the Atlantic had reason to be concerned about their rights as Englishmen, which they were loudly asserting. Under the Declaratory Act, they were placed under the same subjection as Ireland had been placed by a similar Declaratory Act in 1719.

During the decade between 1765 and 1775, South Carolina, like the other colonies, was swept by continuing controversies over the efforts of the British government through the Townshend Acts to impose revenue taxes on the stubborn colonials. Boston took the lead in resisting, and the *South Carolina Gazette* eagerly reprinted incendiary news items emanating from the New England city. Resistance to the Townshend Acts at first took the form of economic sanctions as the colonies signed nonimportation agreements. Gadsden was the leader in South Carolina in promoting the effort to prevent Charleston merchants from importing anything except the barest essentials from Great Britain. Significantly, firearms were not included in the boycott. South Carolinians were going to get all the guns and powder they could get.

The boycott was not unanimously favored, though it was about fifty percent effective. Some Charlestonians resented the dictation of the mob that tried to enforce the boycott. Lieutenant Governor William Bull, a native South Carolinian and a moderate and wise officer of the king, acted for Governor Lord Charles Montagu, who was frequently absent from his titular post. Bull did his best to keep South Carolina loyal. He was much respected in the colony, but not even Bull's influence was able to prevent Gadsden and others from stirring up mob action against those who refused to join the boycott. Bull was particularly incensed when a few government officials gave encouragement to the nonimportation movement. At length, in April 1770, the authorities in London repealed all the Townshend Acts except that on tea. The tea tax, a measure designed to bail out the East India Company and to show the colonists that the government retained the right of taxation, so infuriated the Bostonians that, on December 16, 1773, they threw a cargo of tea into the harbor—the famous Boston Tea Party. In Charleston, tea was brought ashore, stored in the cellars of the new Exchange building, and later sold for the benefit of rebel patriots fighting the British.

In the meantime, two acts of the South Carolinians annoyed the royal authorities. In 1766, the Commons House appropriated £1,000 sterling to procure a marble statue of William Pitt, which was duly erected at the intersection of Broad and Meeting streets—a traffic hazard, but a symbol of the colony's appreciation of Pitt's labors in getting the Stamp Act repealed. The other act, in the eyes of royal authorities, was downright impudent: in 1769, the Commons House voted to send £1,500 sterling to England as a contribution to help pay the debts of John Wilkes, under attack for allegedly libeling King George in his newspaper, the *North Briton*. Wilkes, a notorious character who would not have been welcomed at the dinner tables of Charleston gentlemen, nevertheless became a symbol of the fight for freedom of the press and support of the Bill of Rights.

The appropriation by the South Carolina Commons House for Wilkes became a constitutional issue, as royal authorities asserted that money could not be appropriated without approval of the governor and Council. The quarrel over the right of the Commons House to have sole authority to enact money bills dragged on until the eve of the Revolution and finally ended in tacit agreement to the authority of the Commons.

As difficulties with Great Britain increased in all the colonies, South Carolina took measures leading ultimately to the organization of representative government in the colony. The tea tax agitation led to the December 1773 mass meeting of citizens of the colony that agreed to import no tea. But an action of greater importance occurred at another mass meeting on January 20, 1774, when the group voted to make its organization permanent and appointed a large committee to enforce nonimportation and other resolutions passed by the general meeting. In June of the same year the general committee elected a committee of ninety-nine composed of fifteen merchants, fifteen mechanics, and sixty-nine planters at large to serve in effect as the governing body of the colony. Charles Pinckney was elected chairman. South Carolina was launched on a course that would lead to a break with Great Britain, even though few except Christopher Gadsden and some of his fellow radicals were yet ready to take so drastic a step.

To the first Continental Congress of all the colonies, held in Philadelphia in September 1774, South Carolina sent five delegates: Christopher Gadsden, Edward Rutledge, Thomas Lynch, Henry Middleton, and John Rutledge. The last two, put up by the merchants, were regarded as conservative in their points of view.

Joseph Galloway of Pennsylvania proposed a plan of union with a legislature to deal with the internal problems of the colonies. Although this measure did not pass, the Congress did agree on a "Continental Association" to enforce the boycotts of trade with Great Britain and to take such other steps as might be deemed expedient. Both Gadsden and Lynch were eloquent in behalf of colonial rights. Gadsden, it was said, outdid even the Boston Sons of Liberty in his advocacy of resistance to British tyranny.

The Continental Congress agreed to allow the continued export of rice to Great Britain. The South Carolina delegation, with Gadsden refusing to go along with his colleagues, argued that, unless rice were exported, South Carolina would be economically paralyzed. Because the export of indigo was forbidden under the nonexportation resolution, the indigo growers raised such a protest that the South Carolinians had to agree to devote one third of the proceeds from the export of rice to subsidizing other crops, chiefly indigo.

South Carolina in January 1775 organized a Provincial Congress which included forty-six delegates from the back country. Although back-country representatives were still in the minority, at least a beginning was being made to include the whole of the province in the government.

Three months later, South Carolina's first overt act of revolution occurred in Charleston. On the night of April 21, 1775, the Provincial Congress's Secret Committee of five, headed by William Henry Drayton, seized 1,600 pounds of gunpowder, 800 guns, and 200 cutlasses—property of the government. After an "investigation" at the behest of Lieutenant Governor Bull, the

Commons House solemnly reported that it was unable to identify the culprits but that evidently the action was taken because of "the late alarming accounts from Great Britain." Thus ended the farce of an investigation with members of the powder party sitting in the House.

A report of the Battle of Lexington in Massushusetts reached Charleston on May 8, 1775, and stirred the town to action. The Provincial Congress, whose president was Henry Laurens, authorized the enlisting and training of 1,500 troops. A rumor reaching Charleston from a correspondent in London asserted that the British were planning to stir up the slaves to revolt and to encourage Indian attacks on the frontiers. An association was formed, with instructions to sign up citizens to oppose the authority of the king and to blacklist as enemies those citizens who refused to sign. This procedure, which opened the way for tarring and feathering and other mob action, incensed Laurens and his fellow moderates, but they could not stem the tide of violence unleashed by the demagoguery of the firebrands. The Commons House authorized the issuance of £1,000,000 in paper currency and then quietly passed out of existence. The Provincial Congress, through its Council of Safety, now served as the governing body.

A new royal governor, Lord William Campbell, arrived on June 18, 1775, and was coldly received. Nevertheless, a delegation from the Provincial Congress requested him to inform the king that his loyal subjects were not desirous of independence. Desirous or not, South Carolinians would soon be caught in the rush of events that would lead to independence. Fifteen months later, Lord William himself would have to slip out of Charleston and be rowed to a British man-of-war, taking with him the Great Seal of the colony, thus ending royal rule.

Emotions were soon running high in Charleston, as the radicals whipped up sentiment against all who disagreed with them. In June 1775, two citizens, James Dealy and Laughlin Martin, accused of speaking ill of the Committee of Correspondence and expressing a hope that Roman Catholics, Indians, and Negroes would be armed, were tarred and feathered. Later in the summer, a gunner from the British garrison at Fort Johnson near

Charleston was also tarred and feathered for something he had said. On August 18, a free Negro pilot, accused of saying he would gladly pilot British warships across the bar of Charleston harbor, was summarily hanged. Charlestonians who opposed the activities of the revolutionary association were vulnerable to mob action. William Wragg, for example, who remained loyal to the king and refused to sign the association's compact, was driven out of Charleston and, finally sailing for England, was shipwrecked and drowned. The reign of violence that would characterize much of Carolina's history had begun.

Although the fiery Whigs could call a meeting of the "Liberty Boys" in Charleston and whip them into a lather against King George, the back country remained lethargic and unexcited. To remedy this situation, the Charleston revolutionaries decided to send William Henry Drayton and William Tennent, a Congregational preacher, to the hinterland to explain to the backwoodsmen that their liberties were threatened by King George and that they must join their Low-Country brethren to save themselves from slavery to Great Britain.

Drayton, a young aristocrat who earlier had been contemptuous of the unwashed multitude, had now become a violent democrat opposed to all British authority. Tennent was a Dissenting preacher with a considerable popular following. They moved up through the middle region by way of Camden and on into the frontier region, preaching the gospel of rebellion against King George. Their message fell on barren ground. The Germans who had received land from the king were unmoved. The Scots of the interior not only were unmoved, they were hostile to the messengers from Charleston. Among the Scottish leaders in the Saluda River region were Patrick and Robert Cunningham, later to become powerful Tories. Another was Thomas Brown, a cultivated, well-to-do Scot living on the Carolina side of the Savannah River near Augusta, who made fun of the Liberty Boys and was tarred and feathered for this impiety. Later, in the guerrilla wars between Whigs and Tories, Brown wreaked repeated revenge upon his Whig enemies. Bitter Whig and Tory animosity was already beginning in the back country.

Drayton persuaded the Council of Safety that anti-Revolution leaders in the back country would have to be arrested, and he sent out squads of men from his headquarters at Ninety Six to search the houses of loyalists. During September, Drayton's Whig followers faced a force of Tories led by Colonel Thomas Fletchall on the Saluda. They came to terms without fighting, but fighting broke out later in the autumn.

The first battle of the Revolution in which blood was shed in South Carolina occurred November 19–21, 1775, at Ninety Six, a strategic outpost in the Up Country nine miles south of the present city of Greenwood. Whigs and Tories were about evenly divided in the region, and tension between them was acute. Tories had captured a wagon train of ammunition being taken to the Cherokees as part of their hunting allowance on orders of the Council of Safety; this supply was deemed essential to keep the Indians at peace with the colonists. The Council of Safety ordered Major Andrew Williamson to recapture the gunpowder in possession of the Tories. Before Williamson could mobilize an adequate force, he learned that more than 1,800 Tories under the command of Patrick Cunningham and Joseph Robinson were marching on Ninety Six.

Only a small brick jail at Ninety Six was available for defense, and it would not serve for the 562 troopers whom Williamson had recruited. Consequently, Williamson built a makeshift fortification across the creek from the jail in a field owned by John Savage. Williamson had one advantage over the Tories: he had three small swivel guns which he mounted so as to sweep a wide area. For three days the two forces exchanged sporadic firing until finally, on the morning of Wednesday, November 22, both factions agreed to a truce and the fighting ended. One Whig lay dead. The Tories admitted to one man dead, but the Whigs claimed several more. Thus ended the first bloodshed by South Carolinians in a war that would increase in bitterness as the years went on.

Whigs continued the attack on Tories in the Up Country for a few weeks in December 1775, in what they called the "Snow Campaign." Desite the truce that Williamson had agreed to, the Council of Safety ordered Colonel Richard Richardson to mobilize the Camden militia, reinforced by militiamen from North

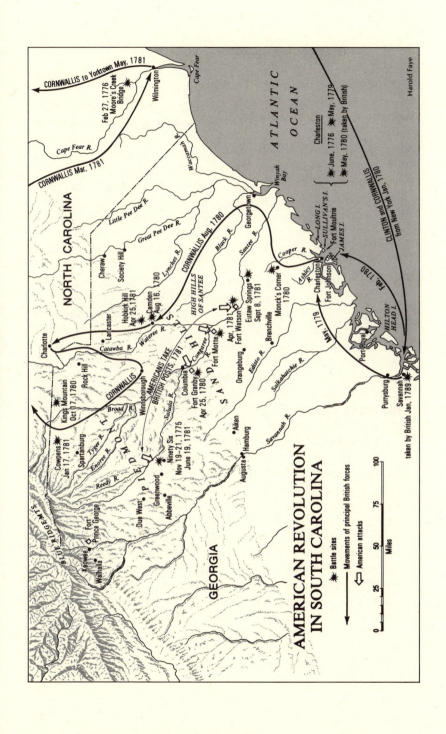

AMERICAN REVOLUTION IN SOUTH CAROLINA

★ Battle sites
→ Movements of principal British forces
⇨ American attacks

Miles
0   25   50   75   100

Harold Faye

ATLANTIC OCEAN

NORTH CAROLINA

GEORGIA

Charleston
{ June, 1776
{ May, 1779
★ May, 1780 (taken by British)

CLINTON and CORNWALLIS
from New York, Jan. 1780

CORNWALLIS to Yorktown May, 1781

Feb 27, 1776
Moore's Creek
Bridge

Wilmington

Cape Fear

Cape Fear R.

CORNWALLIS Mar. 1781

Little Pee Dee R.

Great Pee Dee R.

Cheraw

Society Hill

Lynches R.

Waccamah

Winyah Bay

Georgetown

Black R.

CORNWALLIS Aug. 1780

Santee R.

Cooper R.

Ashley R.

Charleston
Fort Johnson

Fort Moultrie
LONG I.
SULLIVAN'S I.
JAMES I.

Feb. 1780

Lancaster

Hobkirk Hill
Apr 25, 1781

Camden
Aug. 16, 1780

Wateree R.

HIGH HILLS OF SANTEE

Eutaw Springs
Sept 8, 1781

Apr. 1781
Fort Watson

Monck's Corner
1780

May 1779

Catawba R.

Charlotte

CORNWALLIS

AMERICANS TAKE
BRITISH POSTS, 1781

Congaree R.

Fort Motte

Branchville

Edisto R.

Orangeburg

HILTON HEAD I.

Port Royal

Kings Mountain
Oct 7, 1780

Rock Hill

Winnsborough

Columbia

Fort Granby
Apr 25, 1780

Saluda R.

SAND HILLS

Salkehatchie R.

Purrysburg

Savannah
taken by British Jan, 1789

Broad R.

PIEDMONT

Cowpens
Jan 17, 1781

Spartanburg

Tyger R.

Enoree R.

Ninety Six
Nov 19–21, 1775
June 19, 1781

Aiken

Hamburg

Savannah R.

Reedy R.

Greenwood

Due West

Abbeville

Augusta

BLUE RIDGE MT'S

Fort
Prince George

Keowee

Walhalla

Carolina, and to pursue the Tories who had captured the gunpowder destined for the Cherokees. With some 2,500 men, Richardson moved on Ninety Six and then followed the Tories to a camp they had established on the Reedy River at the Great Cane Brake, six miles southwest of Fountain Inn in Greenville County. He killed five or six Tories and captured the rest; these the Council of Safety later paroled. This campaign in the back country led to an uneasy peace that prevailed in most areas until the British captured Charleston in 1780 and encouraged the Tories of the interior to seek vengeance on their Whig neighbors.

A second Provincial Congress of South Carolinians was called into session on November 1, 1775. This time they elected William Henry Drayton president in place of the more moderate Laurens. It has been suggested that this was an adroit move to try to make Drayton less obstreperous and vocal. If so, the plan did not work. He continued to call for resistance to "tyranny" and enlisted other young men in his cause. One was Arthur Middleton, like Drayton an aristocrat turned rabble-rouser. At a meeting of the Congress on March 26, 1776, South Carolina adopted a state constitution and elected John Rutledge president and Henry Laurens vice-president. William Henry Drayton was chosen as chief justice.

Although moderates still hoped for reconciliation with Great Britain, and few yet wanted to break away from the mother country, a declaration by the British Parliament that the colonies were in rebellion and that colonial ships and cargoes could be lawfully seized took the wind out of the sails of all who wanted to prevent separation from Great Britain. In the meantime, South Carolina sent four delegates to the Continental Congress in Philadelphia which was soon debating independence. When, on July 4, 1776, the Declaration of Independence was adopted, the four delegates—Arthur Middleton, Edward Rutledge, Thomas Lynch, Jr., and Thomas Heyward, Jr.—signed on August 2. Henry Laurens declared that separation from Britain caused him to weep and brought him as much sorrow as the death of a son. But many South Carolinians who felt as Laurens did loyally stood by the state and fought its battles.

While the debate on independence went on in Philadelphia, the British were launching an attack on Charleston, the most important port in the South and the strategic key to the whole region. The British had first intended to establish a powerful base in the Cape Fear region of North Carolina where, they had been informed, Highland Scots would rally to the royal cause. Unfortunately for their plans, patriots on February 27, 1776, decisively defeated the Tories at the Battle of Moore's Creek Bridge and thus eliminated the possibility of substantial support for the British.

A powerful force had been destined for the Cape Fear. Sir Henry Clinton, in overall command, was to bring an army by sea from Boston. From Ireland, Admiral Sir Peter Parker was sailing with a fleet of warships and a further contingent of troops under the command of Lord Cornwallis. But when the Cape Fear project went awry, the British forces in June 1776 converged on Charleston.

To defend the city, guns were mounted along East Bay and on the point of the peninsula. Fort Johnson, on James Island, guarding one side of the harbor, was already occupied by Patriots. A second fort, opposite Fort Johnson, was under construction on Sullivan's Island. The strength of the new fort lay in its double walls of bolted palmetto logs sixteen feet apart with sand piled between. This fort was still incomplete when the British fleet appeared.

To take charge of the defense of Charleston, General George Washington, whom the Continental Congress had appointed commander-in-chief, sent down General Charles Lee. He was a former British soldier of fortune with some reputation acquired on battlefields in Europe, but in Charleston he proved both arrogant and incompetent. He did not help morale when he characterized the palmetto-log fort on Sullivan's Island as a slaughter pen. If President Rutledge had not intervened, Lee would have ordered the commander, Colonel William Moultrie, to evacuate it.

At the eastern end of Sullivan's Island, Colonel William Thompson had some 500 men facing 2,000 or 3,000 British troops that Clinton had landed on Long Island (now the Isle of

Palms). Separating the two islands was a narrow inlet that the British believed could be forded at low tide. Providentially for the defenders, unusually high tides required crossing by boat, and Thompson's riflemen, with the help of three small cannon, successfuly fought off landing parties.

In the meantime, on June 28, the fleet had sailed around the point to attack the palmetto fort, which Admiral Sir Peter Parker expected to destroy with a few broadsides from his warships and mortar shells from the bombship *Thunder*. Again nothing went right for the British. Overcharged mortars severely damaged the *Thunder*. Three ships ran aground, and one, the *Acteon*, stuck so hard on a shoal (later used as the site for Fort Sumter) that the crew burned her the next day. Other ships, however, pounded away at the palmetto fort, but to no avail. Their shells lodged harmlessly in the sand and the spongy wood without splintering the walls.

During the bombardment, a shell cut down the South Carolina flag, blue with a silver crescent in the corner. Sergeant William Jasper, at the risk of his life, jumped over the parapet and stuck the flag back on an artillery-sponge staff, a deed immortalized in South Carolina legendry. In this battle, Francis Marion, later to serve so effectively in guerrilla warfare, had his baptism of fire from the British.

Unable to destroy the fort or to land troops at the other end of the island, the British gave up the attack on Charleston harbor and sailed away, not to return until 1779. For the time being South Carolina was safe from further attack by sea. For his defense of the fort, Moultrie was made a brigadier general and a palmetto was added to the South Carolina flag.

The British defeat at Charleston under Moultrie's guns was not the first evidence of the enemy's vulnerability and the shortcomings of its high command. The battle of Breed's Hill and Bunker Hill in Boston had proved a costly victory for the British, and Washington, by March 17, 1776, had forced Sir William Howe to evacuate Boston and retire to Halifax to prepare for an attack on New York. Howe had demonstrated supreme complacence and almost contempt for the employment of any strategy of defense or offense.

Washington, however, was experiencing difficulties that

would plague the patriot forces throughout the war. Congress would authorize only short-term enlistments in the Continental army with which Washington was supposed to fight a war. The militia were subject to the whims of the individual states whence they came. At the expiration of the first enlistments on December 31, 1775, Washington's army at Boston melted away. Someone remarked that his camp looked like moving day as soldiers packed up to leave. While he waited to seek new enlistments for another year, he was left only with such state militia as were willing to remain under arms. Small wonder that Washington was rarely able to mount a vigorous offensive, but he proved a master of skillful retreat, a tactic that allowed incompetent British generals to defeat themselves in more than one campaign. The patriot cause also stood in imminent danger from loyalists, who often outnumbered the rebels. New York, for example, furnished more troops to the British army than to Washington's.

Soon after the attack by the British on Charleston in 1776, the Cherokees swarmed into the northern settlements, scalping men, women, and children and burning the cabins of settlers. The South Carolina militia, reinforced by militia from Georgia, North Carolina, and Virginia, moved against the Cherokees and devastated their territory so completely that many died of starvation. In May 1777, Georgia and South Carolina met with Cherokee chiefs at Dewitt's Corner (later called Due West) and concluded a treaty which gave to South Carolina the northwestern tier of counties: Greenville, Pickens, Oconee, and Anderson.

While Washington was fighting indecisive campaigns from Long Island through New Jersey and Pennsylvania in 1777 and 1778, South Carolina was reasonably quiet. Except for the campaign against the Cherokees and some rather ineffectual aid to Georgia in repelling an attack of the British from Florida, the state had little military activity. Privateers from time to time captured valuable British prizes and brought them into Charleston harbor. Commerce flourished during these years. Though South Carolinians were aware of the suffering of Washington's army at Valley Forge in the desperate winter of 1777–1778, they could do little to help.

In this period, the state revised the Constitution of 1776. The most important change was the separation of church and state by the disestablishment of the Anglican communion. The Reverend William Tennent made a ringing speech in behalf of disestablishment and helped to carry the day in opposition to Charleston conservatives.

One surprising development in this period was the resignation of President Rutledge as head of the state because he still hoped for a reunion of South Carolina with Great Britain. Rawlins Lowndes was elected to succeed him. Later, in 1779, when the chief executive's title was changed to governor and hope of conciliation with England was long past, Rutledge again took office.

If no military actions of consequence took place in South Carolina from 1777 to 1780, it would be a mistake to think that all was tranquility. Agitation between Whigs and Tories often erupted in violence. An effort to make all citizens swear allegiance to the state brought on mob violence. Even Christopher Gadsden now condemned the lawlessness of so-called patriots who would resort to tar and feathers to force loyalists to take the oath. The state was ready to explode in civil war.

Sir Henry Clinton, in his comfortable headquarters in New York in 1778, once more turned his thoughts to the South as a possible theater of war. Although he remembered with some embarrassment the humiliation that he and his colleagues had suffered in Charleston in June 1776, he now thought the time was ripe to pay off old scores in the South, release a horde of loyalists to harass the rebels, and send a victorious British army rolling northward to trap the wily Washington in a pincers movement between British troops operating out of New York and the oncoming army from the South. The army moving up from the Carolina coast would need little in the way of supply, for it could live off the country and would find many friends among crypto-loyalists waiting to cut the throats of rebels who had been threatening them with tar and feathers. The dream of a great rising of loyalists was a constant solace of British commanders.

To begin this new phase of the war, General Augustine Prevost in December 1778 seized Savannah and planned an overland attack on Charleston. He marched north and in May of 1779 crossed the Ashley River and laid siege to Charleston from the land side. The commander whom Washington had sent south to defend Charleston this time was a stolid mediocrity named General Benjamin Lincoln. Lincoln, in the vicinity of Augusta when Prevost reached Charleston, made a hurried march to try to capture the British force, but Prevost slipped back across the Ashley and escaped.

The ease with which Prevost attacked Charleston by land encouraged Sir Henry Clinton to lead a force of some 11,000 men and a strong fleet to the area in March 1780. Lincoln was still in command of the defense and allowed himself to be bottled up on the peninsula. Clinton's forces captured Fort Johnson, and he sent Cornwallis to attack and capture Fort Moultrie from the weak land side. One of his cavalry officers, Colonel Banastre Tarleton, swung around to Monck's Corner and cut to pieces a small force under Colonel Isaac Huger. Just before the last escape route was closed, Governor Rutledge and two aides got away. For the rest of the war, the nominal state government would be wherever Rutledge could find a place of refuge.

On May 12, 1780, Benjamin Lincoln signed capitulation papers, and the British army of occupation moved into the city. Sir Henry Clinton found the Miles Brewton house to his liking and established his headquarters there. Clinton, like Sir William Howe and other British generals, had an eye for luxury and comfort and always managed to find pleasant quarters. Clinton's terms of surrender were generous. He had captured more than 5,000 troops and a large quantity of military equipment. The militia he turned loose on parole; the Continental "regulars" were retained as prisoners of war.

But as Clinton was preparing to return to New York, he issued a proclamation to the conquered territory that made bitter enemies of hundreds who might have remained passively loyal, but would not bear arms for England. Clinton declared that paroled prisoners must take up arms for the king if required or be classified as traitors—and run the risk of being hanged. Lord Cornwallis was left in command in the South and was supposed to implement Clinton's orders. One of Cornwallis's officers, the daring cavalryman Banastre Tarleton, was responsible for an atrocity that also turned many neutrals into patriots. On May 29, 1780, Tarleton's dragoons were in pursuit of a detachment of infantry, under Colonel Abraham Buford, retreating toward Salisbury, North Carolina. Overtaking Buford's men near the Waxhaws, nine miles east of Lancaster, Tarleton slaughtered them after they had surrendered and called for quarter. Henceforth, "Tarleton's Quarter" became a byword because of this massacre. Tarleton had also made the mistake of plundering and burning Thomas Sumter's home in the High Hills of Santee, a deed which made an inveterate enemy of one who soon was known as the fighting "Gamecock." Unwittingly, the British were paving the way for their own defeat.

At the moment, however, South Carolina lay prostrate, a conquered territory, which Clinton and Cornwallis regarded as safe for the rest of the war. Loyalists—Tories—were already riding through the back country plundering, burning, and hanging their Whig enemies. Most of the early leaders of revolt in the state were out of action. Of the four signers of the Declaration of Independence, Edward Rutledge, Thomas Heyward, Jr., and Arthur Middleton were prisoners of the British at St. Augustine; Thomas Lynch, Jr., had previously drowned at sea. Henry Laurens, president of the Continental Congress in 1777 and 1778, was sent as an envoy to the Netherlands in the summer of 1780, but was captured at sea and kept a prisoner in the Tower of London until exchanged for Cornwallis after Yorktown. William Henry Drayton had died of typhus in September 1779. Fiery Christopher Gadsden was confined to a cell in St. Augustine. John Rutledge, the governor, was still at large in the back country. But many erstwhile Charleston patriots were now once more trying to prove themselves loyal subjects of Great Britain.

Washington was not yet ready, however, to concede that South Carolina was completely lost. To attempt a rescue operation, the Congress dispatched General Horatio Gates, the "hero of Saratoga," to attack the British at Camden, where Lord Rawdon, Cornwallis's second in command, had established a base. When Cornwallis heard that Gates was headed for Camden, he hurried to the scene. Gates had with him an able German officer, General Johann Kalb (who had assumed the title of Baron de Kalb), in command of Delaware and Maryland Continentals, the best troops in this army.

By a strange coincidence, both the Americans and British planned a surprise night march and a dawn attack. They met about five miles north of Camden after midnight on August 16, 1780, and Cornwallis quickly defeated Gates's troops. Only Kalb's Continentals stood their ground, and Kalb himself died bravely fighting.

The North Carolina and Virginia militia fled in panic, with Gates himself leading all the rest. The tarnished hero of Saratoga never stopped riding until he reached Charlotte, nearly seventy miles away. Two days later, he was in Hillsborough, 120 miles from Cornwallis. Only about 700 of the 3,000 to 4,000 troops he had at Camden were able to join their commander at Hillsborough. Camden was a disgraceful rout for the Americans. The British retired to the village and fortified an area around a house built by a merchant named Joseph Kershaw. That is now a part of the restored area of "Historic Camden."

The defeat of the patriots at Camden unleashed bands of Tories thirsting for revenge against Whigs who had earlier plundered their homes and farms and in some cases had tarred and feathered them. General Edward McCrady, in his *History of South Carolina in the Revolution,* asserts that 137 battles and minor engagements took place in the state, more than in any other of the thirteen original states. Most of these were guerrilla fights in what amounted to civil war after Gates's defeat at Camden. Most are not even mentioned in general histories and are now forgotten by all except local historians and the Daughters of the American Revolution.

The guerrilla warfare was important, however, for despite the renewed activity of the Tories, a few daring leaders of the patriots managed to pin down substantial bodies of British troops, thus thwarting their strategy of rolling up the South and crushing Washington between armies moving from north and south. Charlestonians who congratulated Cornwallis after his victory at Camden lived to regret it.

After Gates's flight, Washington sent General Nathanael Greene, a cautious, careful Quaker, to command in the South. Greene never won a victory, but he made the enemy pay so dearly for their successes that he wore the British down. He had able guerrilla commanders who also constantly harried the British: Francis Marion, the "Swamp Fox"; Thomas Sumter, the "Gamecock"; Andrew Pickens; and others equally courageous. The South Carolina partisan leaders sometimes had the support of such vigorous North Carolinians as William R. Davie and William Davidson. In a later day, these men would have been called leaders in the resistance movement.

The career of Brigadier General Francis Marion has produced a great body of legend, some undoubtedly true, some the invention of fiction writers. The hook-nosed little Huguenot got his sobriquet, it is said, from a comment by Tarleton, who gave up chasing him and said to his men: "Come, my boys! Let us go back, and we will find the Gamecock [Thomas Sumter]. But as for this damned old fox, the devil himself could not catch him." [2] From this time onward, Marion's admirers called him "the Swamp Fox." The name fit, because he hid out in various camps in the trackless swamps where no traitor was ever smart enough to lead the British to him. With a small body of hard-riding troopers he would sally forth to seize a wagon train of ammunition and supplies, to disrupt British reinforcements, or to capture thinly held outposts. Cornwallis's supply lines from Charleston to the north were in constant jeopardy, and heavy convoys were necessary to insure their safety.

Marion successfully captured a number of strong points along the supply route. In April 1781, building a log tower to give him fire power into Fort Watson on the Santee, he forced the surrender of that fortification. Other outposts soon fell to the patriots as Marion, Sumter, and Pickens kept the Tories off balance and prevented the British from consolidating their position in the Low Country in preparation for Cornwallis's advance to Virginia.

2. Hugh F. Rankin, *Francis Marion: The Swamp Fox* (New York: Thomas Y. Crowell Co., 1973), p. 113.

In the meantime, two victories over the British—at Kings Mountain on October 7, 1780, and at Cowpens on January 17, 1781—disrupted British plans and encouraged neutrals to join the patriot cause. The fortunes of the Tories were beginning to look less rosy.

The battle of Kings Mountain was fought by Americans on both sides; only the British commander, Major Patrick Ferguson, a native of Aberdeenshire in Scotland, was a "foreigner." He had under his command some 1,100 men, Tories he had trained, some from New York and New Jersey, but most from the Carolinas. With Cornwallis moving into North Carolina and establishing a base at Charlotte, Ferguson made a foray into the hill country as far as Gilbert Town (modern Rutherford) to protect Cornwallis's western flank, to recruit more Tories, and to intimidate Whigs.

Backwoods patriots had helped defeat British regulars and Tories at Musgrove's Mill on the Enoree River, twenty-seven miles south of Spartanburg, on August 18, 1780, and Ferguson wanted to put the fear of God and the British into others who might venture to the aid of South Carolina partisans. He made the grave mistake, however, of sending word to the over-mountain men that if they continued to support the enemies of the king, he would march over the mountains, "hang their leaders, and lay their country waste with fire and sword." [3] That did it: the mountain men decided to strike first.

Calling for a rendezvous at Sycamore Shoals on the Watauga River near modern Elizabethton, Tennessee, on September 25, the mountain men prepared to pursue Ferguson to whatever lair he chose. An eloquent Presbyterian parson, the Reverend Samuel Doak, preached a sermon and urged them to take as their battle cry, "The sword of the Lord and of Gideon." Led by Colonel John Sevier, Colonel Charles McDowell, Colonel William Campbell, and Colonel Benjamin Cleveland (the principal officers were all colonels, regardless of the units they commanded), the over-mountain men numbered well over 1,000.

---

3. Lyman C. Draper, *King's Mountain and Its Heroes* (Cincinnati: Peter G. Thomson, 1881), p. 169.

They were typical frontiersmen, dressed in homespun or buckskin, each bringing his own Kentucky rifle and most riding tough horses; a few came on foot. They elected Colonel Campbell as their commanding officer.

Marching over the hills in snow and rain, they swung down by Cowpens (soon to be the scene of another battle) and crossed the Broad River on the trail of Ferguson, who for reasons still a mystery had decided, instead of pushing on to join Cornwallis at Charlotte, to await the enemy on a low plateau of the western ridge of the Kings Mountain range, just south of the border in South Carolina. There the mountain men attacked him on the afternoon of October 7.

Surrounding the ridge, they crept up behind trees and rocks, firing with deadly aim at the redcoats. Ferguson's silver whistle could be heard constantly sounding as he rallied his men to make a bayonet charge each time a squad of the enemy appeared on top of the ridge. The attackers, who had no bayonets of their own, could not withstand cold steel, but would retreat into the woods to reload and pick off more redcoats from behind cover. At length, a rifleman's bullet toppled Ferguson from his horse. Their commander dead, the redcoats surrendered; but the riflemen, remembering Tarleton's Quarter, continued to shoot down the conquered British until Colonel Campbell managed to stop the killings.

Ferguson was rolled unceremoniously into a fresh cowhide left from a beef the British had killed and was buried on the field of battle, along with one of his mistresses who, legend reports, had died with him. The mountain men rested on the field until morning, then took their prisoners and hurried back toward their native heaths. They were afraid Tarleton might pursue them. Near Gilbert Town, they stopped to court-martial Tory prisoners accused of atrocities. Thirty were condemned to be hanged; but after nine had swung, Colonel Campbell stopped the executions. Colonel Cleveland, a huge semiliterate bear of a North Carolinian, was for hanging the lot. He came from a locality where both Whigs and Tories were accustomed to summary executions.

Less than four months after the battle of Kings Mountain, the

British suffered an equally disastrous defeat on January 17, 1781, at Cowpens. General Daniel Morgan, a hardened old fighter who had been a wagoner long ago in Braddock's march on Fort Duquesne, had come out of retirement and joined General Greene's troops. On detached duty with a small army of Continentals and militia, Morgan made a foray southward that frightened Cornwallis into believing that he was headed for Ninety Six, still a British bastion on the frontier. To prevent danger to Ninety Six, Cornwallis ordered Tarleton to pursue and annihilate Morgan.

Tarleton found Morgan at Hannah's Cowpens, a Tory ranch where the over-mountain men had bivouacked on the way to Kings Mountain. Morgan shrewdly chose a slightly elevated battlegound with woods in the rear and on his flanks. Not trusting his green militia to stand and fight in the face of a cavalry charge, the general told them to run, but to fire two rounds first. Morgan had the advantage of several able commanders to assist him. General Andrew Pickens deployed his militia in high grass and behind trees, and instructed his men to aim at the enemy officers—men wearing epaulettes and crossed belts. When Tarleton's men charged toward the crest of the rise and Morgan's center fired and fell back, these obscured riflemen poured a deadly fire into the onrushing redcoats. Colonel William Washington (a distant cousin of General Washington) led a squadron of cavalry in an attack on Tarleton's right flank and rear. After only an hour's fight, Tarleton's feared legion was decimated, with at least 100 dead and 830 captured. Tarleton was forced to withdraw with the remnants of his force, after his famed cavalry refused to charge in the final minutes of the battle. The defeat of this arrogant leader was peculiarly satisfying to the patriots. After the battle, Morgan marched into North Carolina to rejoin Greene.

The disasters of Kings Mountain and Cowpens were blows more deadly than Cornwallis yet perceived, as he attempted to corner General Greene, now deep into North Carolina. At last the two armies met at Guilford Courthouse, now a restored area a short distance north of Greensboro. As Cornwallis made his way toward Hillsborough, Greene evaded him until he thought he had found terrain that would give some advantage. Although forced by Cornwallis to give up the field at Guilford Court-house, Greene exacted a dreadful toll of the victor. When news of it reached London, Charles James Fox exclaimed, ''Another such victory would destroy the British army.'' [4] Cornwallis had to lead his bedraggled army back to the safety of the coast at Wilmington. Greene's lost battle at Guilford Courthouse de-layed Cornwallis's march to Yorktown until the French had es-tablished naval superiority at the mouth of Chesapeake Bay. Thus Greene helped insure the British defeat. After Guilford Courthouse, Greene turned back to South Carolina in the hope of saving the state from further British domination.

Greene moved down into South Carolina by way of Cheraw. On the way, he hoped to enlist enough militia to challenge Lord Rawdon, whom Cornwallis had left in command at Camden. However, at Hobkirk Hill—now a fashionable residential area of Camden—Rawdon surprised Greene's camp on April 25, 1781. Once again the American commander had to retreat. But Rawdon's small force found itself isolated by Francis Marion's previous capture of Fort Watson and the fall of other British outposts; he evacuated Camden and returned to Charleston.

Former British strongpoints in an arc from Augusta to Fort Watson were now in control of the partisans, but Ninety Six, strategically important, was still held by the British. So long as they occupied this outpost, Tories, who outnumbered the pa-triots in this section of the back country, were free to raid, plun-der, burn houses and barns, and frequently hang their Whig enemies. Hangings at Ninety Six had prompted the retaliatory executions after Kings Mountain. Rallying as many partisans as possible, Greene marched from Camden toward Ninety Six, which he reached on May 22, 1781.

A New York Tory, Lieutenant Colonel John H. Cruger, held Ninety Six with 550 Tories from New York, New Jersey, and South Carolina. He had fortified the village with a stockade and an eight-foot ditch. On high ground at the village's eastern

---

4. Hugh T. Lefler and Albert R. Newsome, *North Carolina* (Chapel Hill, N.C.: Uni-versity of North Carolina Press, 1954), p. 237.

edge, he constructed an eight-pointed star redoubt. With cannon mounted on the redoubt, Cruger had made his fort well-nigh impregnable to frontal assault.

With Greene was a Polish engineer, Thaddeus Kosciusko, who immediately ordered trenches dug within seventy yards of the redoubt. British fire soon proved these trenches useless. Greene next tried a wooden tower filled with snipers to fire on the fort's defenders, and he also sent showers of fire-tipped arrows to ignite roofs inside the fort—all to no avail. In the meantime, Kosciusko was driving a tunnel toward the redoubt, which he hoped to blow up with gunpowder. He did not complete his work in time. Greene cut off the fort's water supply, but the garrison sent out black slaves under cover of darkness to bring in enough water to keep the soldiers from perishing.

With reinforcements brought by Colonel Light Horse Harry Lee and General Andrew Pickens, returning from the capture of Augusta, Greene tried to storm the fort on June 19. Because of the loss of life, the Quaker general pulled back his assault force. News had also reached him that Lord Rawdon was advancing from Charleston to relieve Ninety Six. Consequently, Green arranged with Cruger for an exchange of prisoners and withdrew with his army to the High Hills of Santee to recuperate. The American loss was 57 killed, 70 wounded, and 20 missing in action. Cruger lost 27 killed and 58 wounded.

Rawdon reached Ninety Six on June 21, two days after Greene had left, but he conceded that he could no longer hold Ninety Six with all the peripheral outposts—Fort Watson, Fort Motte, Fort Granby, and Augusta—in rebel hands. So Cruger evacuated the fort and followed Rawdon back to Charleston. Once more Greene had lost a battle, but had won the campaign.

Of all the Revolutionary outposts, Ninety Six is the only one still visible. The redoubt, now called Old Star Fort, is being restored, and the outlines of the village are being excavated.

Greene's forces of about 2,000 men, after two months of rest and recreation in the High Hills, were ready again for action. The only sizable British force north of Charleston consisted of nearly 2,000 men commanded by Lieutenant Colonel Alexander Stewart at Eutaw Springs, in an area now near the dam impounding Lake Marion. Most of Stewart's men were Tories, many of them deserters from Greene's own army. Against this force, Greene advanced and achieved a surprise on September 8, 1781. The battle, hotly fought for four hours, was nearly won when American troops fell into confusion, partly because they stopped to plunder the British camp of food and rum. Greene ordered his troops to retreat and marched back seven miles. Both sides claimed the victory, one of the hardest fought battles of the war, but Stewart realized that he had to fall back to Charleston. Greene again was a victor without holding the field of battle. Stewart had lost some two fifths of his whole force, 866 casualties. Greene had 139 killed and 375 wounded. Next day, a detachment of American troops that had been left to observe the retreating redcoats had to watch them smash more than 120 hogsheads of rum and pour the liquor into the creek—a sight to draw tears from wooden Indians.

The last formally organized British forces were now concentrated in Charleston. Cornwallis had achieved his wish of invading Virginia from Wilmington—and on October 17, 1781, had been forced to surrender at Yorktown. The end was in sight; but in South Carolina's back country, bitter civil war still raged as Whigs and Tories continued to raid and burn.

Greene, who had returned to camp in the High Hills of Santee after Eutaw Springs, could muster hardly more than 1,000 able-bodied soldiers. But in November, with reinforcements sent by Washington, he marched down to the Low Country to hold the British in Charleston and to keep them from sending out parties in search of food. Some minor fighting took place. While trying to intercept a British foraging party, Lieutenant John Laurens, the able son of Henry Laurens, was killed at Combahee Ferry on August 27, 1782.

The British finally determined to evacuate Charleston, and a fleet arrived on September 6, 1782, for that purpose. By December 14, the troops, some 3,800 Tories, and more than 5,000 slaves embarked and sailed away. South Carolina at last was independent in fact as well as in name.

Although South Carolina in 1776 had been less than unanimous in its desire for independence, before the war was over, it had made major contributions to its achievement. The battles of Kings Mountain and Cowpens and General Nathanael Green's Fabian retreats so hampered Cornwallis's strategy that Yorktown and its aftermath were inevitable.

Memories of Tory atrocities in the back country resulted in summary vengeance meted out to many when the war was over. In the Saluda River region of Ninety Six District, one of the cruelest Tories had been William ("Bloody Bill") Cunningham. He was charged with committing scores of wanton murders, including women and children. The first elected House of Representatives after the war recommended that the governor offer a reward of 300 guineas for Cunningham, dead or alive, but he apparently escaped to British Florida. Rewards of 100 guineas were offered for lesser Tories. Self-appointed groups frequently warned Tories trying to return to their homes to leave—and soon. In April 1784, a dozen Tories came back to Fishing Creek in Chester County and tried to reclaim their homes. They were given twenty days to move. At the expiration of this period of grace, eight were killed, and the remaining four were sent as emissaries to warn other Tories that they too could expect to swing. When a judge in a Ninety Six court released on a technicality one of "Bloody Bill" Cunningham's henchmen named Love, kinsmen of men whom Love had murdered waited until the judge was out of sight and then hanged Love from the limb of a nearby tree.

Yet, despite sporadic outbreaks of lynch law and a few riots, the country fairly soon settled into ways of peace. Men and women, sick of fighting and bloodshed, wanted to get on with their farming, cattle raising, and other vocations. Even though the back country had suffered most from civil strife, the farmers and traders quickly recovered. They had had little to begin with, and they were resilient. Their plight was less serious than that of many rice planters whose black slaves had been captured and taken away by the British: the planters were left without workers and lacked capital with which to renew their labor force.

The first postwar legislature met at Jacksonborough on the Edisto in January 1782. It voted the state's thanks to Generals Marion, Sumter, and Pickens, along "with the brave militia," and presented Boone's Barony, a plantation south of the Edisto, to General Greene. This property, however, Greene was obliged to sell to pay off debts incurred when he had borrowed money to feed his soldiers. He finally settled on a plantation that Georgia gave him. The populace as a whole soon showed its resentment of any favors to the military, a characteristic of Americans after the need for protection by soldiers and sailors is past.

The legislature elected Christopher Gadsden governor, but he declined on account of ill health, and John Mathews was chosen in his place. Gadsden fought efforts to pass laws confiscating the estates of known Tories; eventually the punitive laws were moderated, and Tories were treated with mercy, if not always with complete leniency. The war, however, bequeathed social and economic problems that would bedevil the state for years to come. Freedom, South Carolina discovered, was not much easier for its citizens than life ''under the British yoke''— to use the term beloved by the propagandists of liberty.

8

King Cotton and the
Road to Ruin

IF a young Yale graduate had not gone to Georgia in the autumn of 1792 with the family of General Nathanael Greene, the social history of the South might have been different. The young man was Eli Whitney, who had been offered a job instructing the children of a South Carolinian. When the tutorship turned out to pay only half the amount promised, Whitney remained in the Greene household on the general's plantation a few miles from Savannah. There he heard much talk about cotton. Planters were interested in new crops to supplement rice production, and cotton was a possibility—if a way could be found to separate the lint from the seed. Picking it off by hand—the only way then known—was slow and prohibitively expensive. Someone suggested to Whitney, who had demonstrated his skill with tools, that he turn his hand to the invention of a device to clean cotton seed. He accepted the challenge.

Two varieties of cotton had been tried in the South: the so-called sea-island cotton, grown principally, as the name indicates, on the coastal islands off Carolina and Georgia. This was a long-staple, silky cotton with smooth black seeds. The lint came away from the seeds of this variety with relative ease. In India, where it had been grown for many centuries, a primitive ginning device had been long in use.

But the cotton suited to the uplands of the South was a hardier, short-staple variety with green seeds to which the lint stuck tenaciously. Separating the seed from the lint by hand was tedious and difficult. Upland cotton could not be produced at a profit until an efficient method of ginning it could be found. That was the task that young Whitney tackled. In 1793 he came up with a practical invention and the next year received a patent.

So eager were planters for cotton gins that many operators were soon infringing Whitney's patent, and he had a lifelong battle defending his rights. The multiplication of gins, with or without Whitney's permission, revolutionized agriculture in the deep South and caused profound changes in the social structure. In 1792, the year before Whitney perfected his invention, the entire South exported only 138,328 pounds of cotton. In 1794, after gins had been in use one year, exports had risen to 1,601,000 pounds. In 1800, the South's production had risen to a phenomenal 35,000,000 pounds of which 17,790,000 pounds were exported.

Already big business, cotton became King and imposed the tyranny of a one-crop system on most of the land, extended the plantation system into the Up Country, vastly increased the demand for black slaves, spread slave-holding to regions hitherto free of the curse, and ultimately divided the nation, as slave states and free states battled over the question of slavery in new states entering the Union. In all of this, South Carolina took the lead as the loudest advocate of slavery and states' rights.

From the end of the Revolution to the beginning of the Civil War, South Carolina made significant cultural and social advances and produced a galaxy of brilliant men. Yet, from the perspective of the twentieth century, these were the most dismal and tragic years of the state's history. Not even the actual war years or the miserable decades of Reconstruction and its aftermath were so tragic. In these later years, South Carolina met disaster with courage and nobility. But during the pre-Civil War period, the state exemplified the ultimate in social and political perversity, the wastage of brilliant minds fighting for futile (and often iniquitous) causes, and the enthronement of that worst of the Seven Deadly Sins, Pride. Even more terrible, South Carolina led the whole of the South to ruin.

Writers of romantic fiction and a few regional historians have sought to endow antebellum society with a rosy glow: white-columned plantation houses, ladies in silks and crinolines, chivalrous men, the desire of every gentleman to demonstrate his physical courage, an eagerness for glory (military if possible), and a disdain for lowly money-grubbing in trade. Labor, in this interpretation, was all performed by happy black slaves, singing and dancing in the dusk in front of their quarters. In the great house, the servants were always smiling with polished politeness. With some exceptions, this picture is false. A few wealthy planters, for the most part in the coastal region, had great white-columned houses, but they were not common. By the end of the Revolution, some of these were encumbered with substantial mortgages. Southern planters were never very good at accounting and fiscal matters. Unfortunately, too much reading of Sir Walter Scott and other romantic fiction stimulated notions of a false chivalry that has been a handicap in the South to the present day.

At the end of the Revolution, South Carolina had a growing population above the fall line—roughly a line drawn diagonally southwest to northeast through Columbia. Most of these people were small farmers of Scottish, German, English, and Welsh stock. Nearly all were Protestants and members of non-Anglican communions. Few had slaves. Much of their farming was subsistence agriculture: corn, peas, hay, hogs, cattle, horses, a few sheep, and poultry of sundry sorts. Their fierce independence and their ancient grudge against the Low Country had not diminished.

The census of 1790 gave the total population of South Carolina as 140,178 whites and 108,895 Negroes. Most of the blacks were in the coastal region, with few in the Up Country. For example, Spartanburg County had 7,907 whites and only 893 Negroes; Greenville, 5,888 whites and 615 Negroes. By 1860, South Carolina had 291,300 whites and 412,320 Negroes. Spartanburg County's population had grown to 18,537 whites and 8,382 Negroes; Greenville, 14,631 whites and 7,261 Negroes.

Cotton accounted for an increase of black slaves in the Up Country, but the preponderance of slaves was still below the fall line.

The cotton gin of Eli Whitney, which made green-seed cotton a profitable crop, altered the agriculture of South Carolina in so short a time that the state almost immediately experienced a labor shortage. After the departure of the British from Charleston with several thousand captured slaves, a few rice planters had been severely handicapped; but they soon acquired additional blacks, and rice production continued to flourish.

Upland farms, however, stagnated for several years. They had been planted in indigo, and the end of British rule also cut off the bounty and the export of the dye to England. Cotton, a plant adapted to the same soil conditions as indigo, proved a Godsend to these planters, who were soon demanding more slaves. Enterprising planters and investors of the Low Country saw that land in the Up Country would produce as good cotton as the alluvial soils below Columbia. These Low Country planters began to buy up large holdings in the Piedmont and to populate them with slaves supervised by overseers. A few planters themselves moved to this area.

Long before 1860, cotton production had become so profitable that South Carolinians were buying rich land in Alabama, Mississippi, Arkansas, Louisiana, and Texas. When I visited the Alamo for the first time, I was struck by the number of South Carolina names listed among the martyrs there. They had gone to Texas with their slaves to get rich by growing cotton— only to meet death at the hands of General Santa Anna. South Carolina, of course, had no monopoly of cotton culture in the early period, for cotton grew well in both Georgia and North Carolina, but South Carolina was by far the heaviest producer and the center from which the greatest number of slaveholders moved to virgin territory in the Southwest.

By the turn of the nineteenth century, the antislavery sentiment in the North was gaining influence, and the United States Congress passed an act banning foreign importation of slaves after 1808. Slaveholders in the South regarded this act as ominous, because cotton had so vastly increased the need for slave labor. Determined to increase the state's labor force, the South Carolina legislature in December 1803 voted to relax a previous prohibition of imports of Africans from overseas. In the four years before the federal ban went into effect, South Carolina planters imported 39,075 blacks from abroad. This number does not include slaves brought in from Virginia and Maryland and elsewhere in the United States.

Not every South Carolinian was pleased with the increase in the number of slaves. Some regarded slavery as an offense against God and man and argued for gradual emancipation, or at least for a ban on further importations of slaves from outside the state. Human greed, however, prevailed over humanitarian instincts or prudential concern over the possibility of slave insurrections.

From early in the colonial period, fear of servile revolt had never been absent from the consciousness of slave holders. A few revolts had occurred, and several plots had been revealed. In 1822, Charlestonians had their blood chilled by the discovery of a plot engineered by a local free Negro named Denmark Vesey. He had been in contact with Negroes on Santo Domingo and was believed to have enlisted more than 6,000 local Negroes in a plan to seize Charleston, pillage and burn it, and take ship for the island. Many refugees had come to Charleston from Santo Domingo at the time of the successful slave insurrection, and Charlestonians were acutely conscious of what had happened there. Vesey and his closest conspirators were given a fair trial and convicted; thirty-five were hanged, and thirty-two were deported.

The facts brought out in the trial were so ominous that they colored thinking about slavery for years to come. The Nat Turner revolt in Virginia in 1831, in which more than fifty whites were slaughtered, added to South Carolina's fears. Unable to get rid of slavery, the state took refuge in stricter surveillance of the black population. Nobody knew a solution. The vituperation of Northern abolitionists and their alleged plotting made South Carolinians stubborn—and robbed local advocates of gradual emancipation of any influence. A number of Quakers and other opponents of slavery moved out of the state. Governor

Thomas Bennett in a message to the legislature after the Vesey plot commented pessimistically: "The institution is established—the evil is entailed and we can do no more than steadily to pursue that course indicated by stern necessity and a not less imperious policy." [1]

Having saddled itself with slavery that brought prosperity to great planters—and to some lesser ones—South Carolina found itself defending an institution that many had earlier believed wicked. Under the lash of self-righteous abolitionists from the North, many of them redolent with unction and intemperate in utterance, South Carolinians reacted as might have been expected of a proud and violent people: they replied in kind and even enlisted the clergy in a defense of slavery, sanctioned, they said, by Holy Writ. Few controversies in American history are so lacking in mutual understanding, reasonableness, and charity as the debate over slavery. The pamphleteering and sermonizing on the question were tedious repetitions of stale polemics. Both the advocates and the opponents of slavery in their writings frequently took leave of logic as well as of truth. Even today, it is infuriating for a South Carolinian to read the sanctimonious diatribes of Wendell Phillips or the violent libels of William Lloyd Garrison. But it is also discouraging and humiliating to contemplate the verbal excesses of that fiery but shallow secessionist, Robert Barnwell Rhett, the assertion by a really profound thinker, John C. Calhoun, that slavery was a "positive good," and the supine concurrence of many of the clergy in this belief. Emotionalism crowded out intelligence, and extremists on both sides drowned with their clamor the voices of reason and moderation. In such an uproar, no peaceful solution was likely to be found.

The potential wealth from cotton raised with slave labor was a temptation that induced unending rationalization of the justice of the system. Recent studies have shown that slave labor was much more efficient and productive than was once believed. An example of a planter's progress from rags to great riches is that of Wade Hampton I, grandfather of South Carolina's great Con-

1. Wallace, *South Carolina*, p. 385.

federate and Reconstruction hero of the same name. Hampton was one of five brothers who escaped when Cherokee warriors in July 1776 murdered their parents on the Middle Tyger River in Spartanburg County. A frontiersman with little education but a habit of hard work in the fields, Wade settled in Richland County near Columbia. He managed to acquire a few slaves and kept adding to this labor force until, by 1799, he could report that he had produced a crop of 600 bales of cotton worth $90,000. He continued to buy land in both South Carolina and Mississippi. When he died in 1835, possessed of many cotton and sugar plantations, he was reputed to be the richest planter in all North America.

If Wade Hampton, an Up-Country frontiersman, could accumulate so much of this world's pelf by the sweat of black slaves, others could hope to succeed in the same way. Increasingly, it became difficult to combat the slaveholding interest. In the years immediately before Secession, Charleston newspapers were declaring that opposition to slavery by free white labor must be eliminated by seeing to it that every white man owned at least one black slave. Self-interest would take care of the future.

Although slavery touched almost every social and political movement in South Carolina, from the end of the Revolution to the outbreak of the Civil War, many significant developments are deserving of notice. Some of these, manufacturing for one example, might have changed the social picture if they had had a chance to evolve.

But in South Carolina tradition has always been a dominant factor, and changes have usually been slow, especially in our earlier history. Agriculture would remain for many years the principal source of the state's income. By the 1830s, in a few of the northern counties, industry had made a faint beginning. For instance, in what is now Cherokee County, iron mines were opened, and foundries produced a little pig iron. A considerable amount of gold was found in Lancaster County, and the Haile Mine was profitable. For the time being, however, the Up Country was more concerned about the improvement of its political lot than about industrial development.

After the Revolution, the Up Country made strenuous efforts to gain more equitable representation in the legislature. A law of 1785, creating thirty-four counties out of seven districts, had given the Up Country increased representation in the legislature, but the old parish system which, since colonial times, had given the Low Country an undue proportion of representatives, remained unchanged, leaving that region politically dominant. In 1786, the legislature moved the capital from Charleston to a new site nearer the middle of the state and named it Columbia. This was a step forward. A state convention held at Columbia in 1790 wrestled with the problem of representation and wrote a new constitution for the state. The counties of the Up Country were permitted more representatives, but the old parishes of the Low Country fought for and succeeded in holding a majority of the legislative body. The constitution of 1790 had to be revised in 1808 to placate unrest in the Up Country, but not until after the Civil War did the region above Columbia succeed in attaining equitable representation in the legislature.

In the antebellum period, efforts were made to broaden the cultural base of the state and improve educational facilities. Here and there, academies provided a modicum of education, frequently classical in emphasis. In 1785, the legislature chartered three colleges: one at Charleston—but not until 1825 did the College of Charleston gain a reputation for higher education; another, Cambridge College near Ninety Six, which soon collapsed; and Winnsboro College (which lapsed into a high school). Military education was supplied by several private academies until 1842, when the Citadel in Charleston and the Arsenal in Columbia became the dominant military schools. In 1801, the legislature created South Carolina College (later the University of South Carolina) to provide higher education for potential leaders who, by getting their learning within the state, could thus escape being contaminated with alien ideas. Furthermore, the Low Country believed that South Carolina College might produce leaders who would share the social ideals of their society. Young men from the barbarous Up Country would come to Columbia, fraternize with their betters from the planter class, and become advocates of that culture. In some cases—but not in all—it did work out that way.

South Carolina College ran into trouble in 1821, when its new president, Dr. Thomas Cooper, antagonized religious folk, especially the Presbyterians, by denying the doctrine of immortality of the soul and the inspired origin of the Bible. Until his resignation in 1833, the evangelicals waged war against Dr. Cooper and the college until the enrollment declined to fewer than 100 students. One of the college's most brilliant teachers in the antebellum period was the political scientist, Dr. Francis Lieber.

Partly to counteract the irreligion of South Carolina College, various denominations founded colleges before 1860. The legislature was sometimes opposed to chartering religious colleges, on the ground that higher education ought to come from the state. Part of this opposition was fear that religious organizations would preach the abolition of slavery. Not until 1850 did Erskine College obtain a charter from the state, though it had been founded by the Associate Reformed Presbyterians in 1839. Furman University, founded by the Baptist denomination, received a charter in 1850. The Baptists had previously operated an academy and a theological school. Wofford College was chartered in 1851 and received its first class in 1854. It was a Methodist institution, endowed with a gift of $100,000 by a Spartanburg preacher named Benjamin Wofford. Newberry College, chartered in 1856, provided education for Lutherans and others. The Lutherans had operated a theological academy at Lexington since 1832.

The education of women was not neglected by religious denominations or by secular agencies. A number of female academies supplied substantial education, not just frills of polite cultivation—a fact that may account for the contributions that women made in the war years and after. One of the most famous of the schools for women was founded by a Baptist preacher, an Englishman, Dr. Thomas Curtis, and his son William, at what is now Gaffney. In 1845, they acquired a health resort, the Limestone Springs Hotel, and turned it into a first-class school providing classical education for girls. In time, it evolved into Limestone College. The Methodists in 1854 founded a college for women in Columbia and another in Spartanburg. The Baptists in the same year began Greenville Woman's College. By 1860, the Associate Reformed Presbyterians had established Due West Woman's College, later merged with Erskine.

Medical education was provided in Charleston from an early date by a brilliant group of physicians. Not until 1833, however, did the state issue a charter to the Medical College of the State of South Carolina, actually supported by private doctors and not by money from the state until 1913.

Perhaps the most famous of all the antebellum educational institutions in the state was an academy opened in 1804 at Willington in what is now McCormick County by a Presbyterian preacher named Moses Waddel. After he became famous, someone asked Waddel why he continued to give his name the homely pronunciation of "Waddle." He replied that he had waddled so far and would continue to waddle as he had begun. The anecdote illustrates the no-nonsense quality of this man who had married the sister of John C. Calhoun and left preaching for school teaching in the Up Country.

The Willington school had the appearance of a pioneer settlement. The main building was a two-room log house. On each side of a long "street" were huts built by the students, a few of brick but most of wood slabs or logs. The fare was Spartan, the comforts few, and the curriculum classical.

In 1819, Waddel left Willington to become president of Franklin College (later the University of Georgia); but in the period from 1804 to 1819, his academy graduated an incredible list of brilliant men. John C. Calhoun went from his brother-in-law's school to enter an advanced class at Yale. Others entered the junior and senior classes at Princeton and Yale. Three graduates became governors of South Carolina: George McDuffie, Patrick Noble, and P. M. Butler; three more were governors of Georgia: George R. Gilmer, Thomas W. Cobb, and George W. Crawford. One, Henry W. Collier, was governor of Alabama. The brilliant antisecessionist James Louis Petigru got his early

training at Waddel's academy, as did a host of other able lawyers, statesmen, and educators.

The legislature made spasmodic but ineffectual efforts to improve elementary education for the state's children. Little was
accomplished, however. Public school teaching was at a low
ebb, and such elementary education as existed in the back
country was provided in what were known as "old-field
schools": neighborhood schools, frequently conducted in log
cabins by ill-prepared, itinerant teachers. Parents among the
poorer whites often preferred for their children to be home
working in the fields instead of wasting their time on "book
larnin'." Illiteracy remained high until long after the Civil War.

If antebellum South Carolina showed little interest in popular
education, it was enthusiastic about what were called "internal
improvements," meaning canals and roads and, in the end,
railroads. Cotton grown in the back country had to be got to
market, and better methods of transportation to the port of
Charleston were essential. The cheapest and easiest means was
by water-borne barge. Below the fall line, rice and other products had floated to Charleston since the earliest colonial times,
but now canals and locks were needed to utilize streams above
the rapids and shoals.

The first important canal, proposed before the Revolution but
constructed later, was designed to connect the Santee River and
the Cooper, shortening the haulage to Charleston. Completed
in 1800, it was never very profitable and was finally abandoned.
The promoters made the mistake of accepting a route proposed
by their engineer, Colonel Christian Senf, a stubborn Swede
captured with Burgoyne's Hessian troops at Saratoga. Senf's
route required an elaborate system of locks, engines to pump
water into the canal during dry spells, and several miles of
trestles to hold the canal trough. Some remains of the canal may
still be seen near the northwest edge of Lake Moultrie.

Meagre profits from the Santee Canal did not discourage
other similar projects, and every community on a stream of any
size dreamed of canals increasing the ease of transportation to
markets. Before 1825, canal building reached a veritable mania,
comparable to the obsession with concrete highway building in

our time. In 1818, the legislature voted $1,000,000 for canals, river dredging, and some road building. For the times, this was a huge amount. Canals were planned, and in some instances completed, to permit barges to float cotton from most of the Up Country to Charleston. As on the Mississippi, crudely constructed cotton barges were often sold for lumber at their destination; this expedient was more attractive than undertaking to pole them back upstream.

The most important canal-and-lock system made possible the shipment of cotton by boat and barge from the upper Catawba River down the Wateree via Camden and on through the Santee Canal to Charleston. Camden was a transfer point, where cotton bales from smaller craft called "mountain boats" were loaded on larger barges for the remainder of the journey. Canals on the Saluda and Broad rivers enabled growers to ship their cotton via Columbia. Elaborate as these canals were, they were never completely satisfactory; they were expensive to keep in repair, and transportation was frequently interrupted by droughts and floods.

Roads were bad, but were usually kept repaired sufficiently to afford passage by loaded wagons, carriages, and buggies. The state had undertaken to open a road, known as the State Road, that ran from Charleston roughly along present U.S. Highway 176 to Columbia, thence up the west side of Broad River, across the Enoree and along its east side past Whitmire to the vicinity of Greenville, and on to the North Carolina line near Saluda. Often virtually impassable in bad weather, the State Road nevertheless offered an overland route for freight both ways and was preferred by many farmers to the canals. It was a toll road, as were most of the bridges and ferries. Travel was not something one undertook for pleasure, although Low Country people did make the tiresome journey to summer resorts in Spartanburg and Greenville counties.

A new form of transportation was soon to make obsolete the whole canal system. Although water transport and wagon roads had made possible the delivery of Up-Country products to Charleston, the fluctuating price of cotton affected the prosperity of that port. No longer did it have a monopoly of Southern exports. Growing competition from Norfolk, Wilmington, North Carolina, Savannah, Mobile, and New Orleans was profoundly felt. In the decade between 1818 and 1828, business was so bad in Charleston that its merchants were ready to take desperate measures. Much of the cotton trade from northwest Carolina was being channeled through Augusta and down the Savannah River to the port of Savannah. If Charleston could deflect this commerce, conditions might improve. Consequently, in 1827, the South Carolina Canal and Railroad Company was chartered with the avowed purpose of building a railroad to Hamburg, on the banks of the Savannah River opposite Augusta, and of obtaining the cotton that was being floated down-river to the Georgia port.

The company employed a shrewd engineer, Horatio Allen, who investigated English railroad projects. It was clear that smooth rails would enable cars to roll more easily than wagons could pull through sand or mud. At first, horse-drawn cars were proposed. One inventor even suggested a wind-propelled train. But Allen placed an order with the West Point Foundry of New York for the construction of a steam locomotive, which was shipped by water to Charleston and assembled there. On Christmas Day of 1830, the engine, named *The Best Friend,* made its first run out of Charleston with passengers. It attained the remarkable speed of twenty-one miles per hour.

Not until October 1833 was the road completed all the way to Hamburg; nine years later, it crossed the river into Augusta and began to make a modest profit. In the meantime, however, in June 1831, the first engine blew up and was replaced by another aptly named *The Phoenix.* Passengers were reassured by the placement of a load of cotton bales between them and the engine as protection against another boiler explosion. This railroad from Charleston by way of Summerville, Branchville, and Aiken to Hamburg, a distance of 136 miles, was the longest in the world when it was completed. By 1860, South Carolina had a network of railroads that made transportation between the Up Country and the coast easy and expeditious.

Ease of shipping further encouraged cotton growing in the back country, despite periods of low prices resulting from over-production in Alabama and Mississippi. Profits from cotton focused so much attention on this one crop that manufacturing was slow to develop. Grist and flour mills, run by water power, were fairly common, especially on the swift streams of the Up Country. It was natural that such power sources would be used for a few early textile mills, but they had begun to decline in the period before the Civil War and would not be revived until later. Significantly, some early textile mills were in Greenville and Spartanburg counties, in time to become centers of a vast textile empire.

The most important manufacturing plant in antebellum South Carolina was established in Graniteville in 1845 by William Gregg, a Pennsylvania jeweler who had come to South Carolina in 1824 and prospered. The Graniteville Manufacturing Company, somewhat like the Lowell Mills in Massachusetts, was paternalistic and insistent upon a strict standard of moral behavior. Gregg personally broke the jugs of sots, on whom he sometimes used his buggy-whip. He also established the first compulsory educational system in the state by requiring parents of children under twelve years of age to send their children to the mill school, for they were not permitted to work until they had reached that age. At this time, children as young as six were working from dawn to dusk in New England mills. Gregg demonstrated that textile manufacturing would prove a benefit to poor white workers who would not be obliged to compete with black slaves.

Manufacturing, however, was discouraged at this time by many South Carolinians, including leading statesmen, who were fighting the imposition of protective tariffs designed to benefit Northern industry. These men feared that succesful manufacturers, if allowed to multiply in the South, would also become protectionists and would weaken the Southern opposition to high tariffs.

The question of protective tariffs had become a burning issue by 1828, when a bill called by the South the "Tariff of Abominations," was passed by the United States Congress. This act brought to a head a long-smoldering controversy over states' rights and the privilege of any state to nullify a law that it did not approve.

Little more than a dozen years earlier, in 1816, two young South Carolina congressmen, William Lowndes and John C. Calhoun, had voted for a protective tariff. At that time, they were nationalists and believers in the loose construction of the national Constitution. Furthermore, for a brief time it looked to them as if the state might develop industry that needed protection. Calhoun, one of the best minds of antebellum South Carolina, had been one of the "War Hawks" in 1812 and had backed "Mr. Madison's war" against England—a war, incidentally, that proved to be one of the most futile and inconclusive in American history. But the Battle of New Orleans made a hero of another South Carolinian, Andrew Jackson, who ironically became the bitter enemy of Calhoun and frustrated his ambition—and opportunity—to become president.

With economic conditions in South Carolina in the 1820s deteriorating, politicians needed a scapegoat. The tariff was both convenient and plausible. For an agricultural region, exporting cotton to and buying manufactured products from England, imposition of high tariffs would increase the cost of imported goods and might even result in retaliatory curtailment of the South's exports. But the tariff was not the only economic calamity facing South Carolina. The fertility of cotton fields in the Up Country was diminishing, for farmers had not yet learned the secrets of fertilizer. Competition from the fresher lands of the Southwest was also reducing profits from cotton.

The slavery question was as troublesome as ever, and Northern abolitionists were growing more numerous and more annoying. South Carolina even had a few home-grown opponents of slavery. Excitement ran high over whether Missouri could enter the Union as a slave or a free state but subsided with the famous Missouri Compromise of 1820, which permitted slavery in the new state but outlawed it in the rest of the Louisiana Purchase north of latitude 36 degrees, 30 minutes. For a brief time, South Carolina did not feel it necessary to agitate over slavery on the national scene.

Before the presidential election of 1828, the South had some hopes of a modification of the tariff. It was believed that Andrew Jackson, if elected, would attempt to reduce it. John C. Calhoun, who occupied second place on the ticket, would certainly work for reductions, for he had now become a strict constructionist in constitutional interpretation and was a vocal advocate of states' rights. For several years before, fiery South Carolinians had talked about nullification and even secession. It remained for Calhoun to become the great apostle of nullification, a doctrine that paved the way for disunion, though Calhoun himself was not in favor of secession. He hoped to find a compromise that would let South Carolina have its cake and eat it, too.

An Up-Countryman born in Abbeville district, Calhoun had married a distant cousin from the Low Country and had become by adoption an aristocrat of the region. His own home, Fort Hill, on what is now the campus of Clemson University, was a gracious establishment, befitting a man who had served in Congress, as Secretary of War in President Monroe's cabinet, and was now vice-president under Andrew Jackson.

Any hope that the South might have entertained, before the election of 1828, that Jackson would oppose the tariff soon vanished. While the vice-president secretly encouraged the nullifiers, the president did nothing about the tariff. Calhoun was the secret author of a resolution, approved by the South Carolina legislature, known as the "Exposition of 1828." This document set forth the doctrine that a sovereign state could determine, in a state convention, whether a federal law was constitutional; and, if the law was unconstitutional, it could then be declared null and void so far as the state was concerned.

While rabid opponents of the tariff were declaring that South Carolina should withdraw from the Union, Calhoun hoped that this "constitutional" device would permit the state to stay in the Union and still avoid being penalized by the tariff of abominations. In 1830 occurred the famous debates in the United States Senate between Robert Y. Hayne of South Carolina and Daniel Webster of Massachusetts, in which Hayne attacked the tariff, defended slavery, and expounded the constitutional right of nullification. Webster's rebuttal was eloquent, but neither convinced the other or the other's respective constituents. Hayne taunted Webster for not opposing disunion at the Hartford Convention in 1814, when New England threatened secession because its vital interests were affected by the war with Great Britain.

Webster's defense of the Union and Hayne's argument for nullification did influence President Jackson. At a Jefferson's birthday dinner in April 1830, the president rose and offered a toast: "Our Federal Union—it must be preserved!" Vice-President Calhoun, feeling that he must respond, replied: "The Union—next to our liberty, the most dear!" The battle was now joined between Calhoun and Jackson.

When the two were nominated as running mates in the campaign of 1828, it had been understood that Calhoun, as Jackson's successor, would be the nominee for president in 1836—with his election a foregone conclusion because of Jackson's promised support. The vice-president's advocacy of nullification, however, was enough to poison his relations with the president. If that had not been sufficient, his aristocratic wife's refusal to call on Peggy Eaton would have finished him. As Peggy O'Neil, daughter of a Washington tavern keeper, Mrs. Eaton had led a scandalous life before marrying Jackson's crony, Senator John H. Eaton of Tennessee, the new Secretary of War. The elite ladies of Washington had persistently snubbed Mrs. Eaton, a discourtesy that aroused Old Hickory's ire. Furthermore, someone dug out an old report that Calhoun, when Secretary of War, during Jackson's foray against the Seminoles in Florida had suggested court-martialing the commander for exceeding his authority. That did it. Henceforth, Jackson was the bitter enemy of Calhoun and all he stood for.

When Henry Clay in 1832 pushed through Congress another tariff act that stirred South Carolina's fury, state leaders called a convention in November 1832, which passed the Ordinance of Nullification. The crisis was so acute that the legislature prepared for war, and President Jackson, on his part, was ready to send troops to coerce the state. On December 28, 1832, Calhoun resigned as vice-president and was elected to the United States Senate in place of Hayne, who had been elected governor.

Not all South Carolinians were nullifiers, nor were all members of the federal government, or even of Jackson's party, in favor of coercion. In South Carolina, men like Joel Poinsett, James Louis Petigru, William Gilmore Simms, David R. Williams, and many other intelligent men opposed nullification and its implications of disunion. But extremists like Robert Barnwell Rhett (born Smith) and scores of other hotheads were ready for open war. In the end, they would bring disaster upon the state and the whole South, but moderates now managed to work out a compromise over nullification, and the crisis passed. Clay put through a tariff act in 1833, reducing some of the import duties, and the South Carolina Convention repealed the Ordinance of Nullification.

The first act of a great tragedy had ended, but the stage was set for grimmer scenes to follow. Although John C. Calhoun himself to the last hoped to avoid breaking up the Union, his logical defense of nullification had convinced many of the constitutional right of a sovereign state to withdraw from the Union. This great but misguided man paved the road to secession and civil war.

9

Triumph of Extremism and
Devastation of War

*T*HE Mexican War (1846–1848) added new territory to the United States and provided further grounds for quarreling over slavery. At the beginning, in 1846, a Pennsylvania Congressman named David Wilmot was the author of an amendment to a money bill which would exclude slavery in the new territories. The Wilmot Proviso immediately raised the hackles of Southerners, and secessionists in South Carolina began to scream louder for separation from the Union.

An uneasy calm was restored in 1850 by a compromise engineered by Henry Clay, in which California was admitted as a free state, with a sop thrown to the South by the inclusion of a more effective fugitive-slave law. Calhoun, old and too ill to speak in the Senate debate, expressed his disapproval through a colleague. Webster, almost as frail as Calhoun, urged upon his Northern colleagues the acceptance of the fugitive-slave provision as a means of placating the South and saving the Union. Clay's compromise, grudgingly enacted, helped keep the peace for a decade, but did not restrain growing talk of violence in South Carolina.

Extremist politicians and newspapers in the state were ready to secede and go it alone. One Carolinian, Edward Bryan, expressed the sentiments of the more irrational element by declaring, "Give us slavery or give us death." [1]

Calhoun died on March 31, 1850, and the state ill-advisedly sent Robert Barnwell Rhett to the Senate in his place. He and other fire-eaters continued to threaten and demand secession, though they made little progress with other slaveholding states.

Inside the state, in the decade before 1860, extremists led by Rhett and Maxcy Gregg continually howled for secession as they attempted to shout down all opposition with their incessant clamor. They went too far and found themselves discredited when, in 1851, a proposed convention of slave states at Montgomery, Alabama, failed to materialize. The extremists had hoped for a mass walk-out from the Union, but the other states all turned down the suggestion. A South Carolina convention called to approve the expected action at Montgomery fizzled.

Only those owning the largest numbers of slaves were eager for an immediate break with the Union. Even the city of Charleston followed the lead of the Up Country in disapproving immediate secession. A Greenville newspaper, the *Southern Patriot* for May 9, 1851, had denounced the efforts of Rhett and his group: "Freemen of the Back Country, your rulers are about to plunge you into the vortex of revolution. . . . Tell the barons of the low country that if they involve the State in war they may defend themselves as well as they can." Meanwhile, however, the state legislature had begun tentative efforts to improve its military stance by voting funds for artillery, arms, and ships capable of war duty.

Slaveholders of the plantation areas realized that they must convince the Up Country that they too had a stake in maintaining slavery, even if they themselves owned no blacks. Abolition of slavery, they cried, would "Africanize" the whole state and turn loose upon the South hordes of ex-slaves who would make another Haiti of the land. Thus the advocates of slavery began a campaign to stir up racial prejudice. Their efforts in the end would succeed and bear bitter fruit for generations to come.

1. Wallace, *South Carolina*, p. 512.

In 1854, Congress passed the Kansas-Nebraska Act, which in effect repealed the Missouri Compromise of 1820 and now permitted the territories to decide for themselves whether they would enter the Union as free or slave states. South Carolina was so concerned over Kansas that she sent several hundred men to Kansas and contributed thousands of dollars to try to win the state for slavery.

Fanatics in both North and South fanned the flames of conflict. In a debate in the Senate in May 1856, Senator Charles Sumner of Massachusetts, one of the most bigoted enemies of the South, heaped so much personal abuse on Senator Pierce Butler of South Carolina that Butler's kinsman, Congressman Preston Brooks of Edgefield district, determined to punish him. After the Senate adjourned for the day, Brooks approached Sumner at his desk, told him he had slandered an old and absent member and deserved the punishment he was about to receive. With that, Brooks nearly beat Sumner to death with a cane. This violence made Sumner a near martyr, heightened tension among the abolitionists against "slave-whipping" Southerners, and made Brooks a hero in his own district. He was showered with silver cups and gold-headed canes, given riotous barbecues, and unanimously re-elected to Congress.

While internal bickering wracked the state, moderates in the national Congress were trying to counsel patience. A South Carolinian, James L. Orr of Anderson district, was elected Speaker of the House early in 1857. He struggled to unite Democrats of the North and South in compromises that would hold the South in the Union. In March 1857, the Supreme Court handed down the Dred Scott decision. Scott, through his lawyers, claimed that he should be given his freedom because his master had taken him from Missouri, a slave state, to Illinois, a free state, later bringing him back to Missouri. The Supreme Court denied his petition. This decision, rendered by Chief Justice Roger B. Taney of Maryland and four other Southern justices, was hailed in the South as evidence of fair play for slaveholders but was denounced in the North by abolitionists, who became more abusive than ever.

An act of John Brown, who may have been the half-crazed

fanatic that many Southerners saw him as, did more than all the oratory of secessionists to convince the South that the slave states stood in real peril from the abolitionists and a hostile North. Brown, with his four sons and three neighbors, in 1856 had murdered five proslavery men in the vicinity of Lawrence, Kansas, but had not been apprehended. There was reason to believe that, in his zeal against proslavery ruffians in "Bleeding Kansas," Brown and his sons would pick an intended victim, call him to the door in the night, and cleave his head open with a homemade sword.

Brown concocted a scheme to establish a fortress in the mountains of Virginia, to encourage runaway slaves to take refuge there, arm them, and gradually to make war on slave territory until all the slaves were freed—or their owners annihilated. He came East, secretly met with abolitionists, received money and some encouragement from them, and on the night of October 16, 1859, he and eighteen followers seized the United States Arsenal at Harper's Ferry, Virginia. (West Virginia, later to include Harper's Ferry, had not yet been created.)

When citizens of the town and local militia failed to take Brown and his men, holed up in the Arsenal, Colonel Robert E. Lee led a file of Marines to Harper's Ferry and captured him and four of his men. Ten others were dead, and four had fled. Tried for treason, Brown was hanged and at once became a martyr to the cause of abolition. Ralph Waldo Emerson declared that his death would "make the gallows glorious like the cross." [2] In recent years a spate of books have sought to canonize Brown. Brown's actions may have seemed to be deeds of a courageous saint to the virtuous of the North, but they inflamed the South to a belief that another Santo Domingo had been narrowly averted, and still another might be in preparation by the friends of slaves above the Mason and Dixon Line.

By election time, 1860, excitement over slavery had become acute. When Abraham Lincoln of Illinois was nominated by the Republicans, Southerners took alarm, for Lincoln, though a moderate, had stated his personal distaste for slavery and his op-

2. Morison and Commager, *Growth of the American Republic,* 1:634.

position to its extension into the western territories. He and the Republicans were willing to promise no interference with slavery in the old slave states, but the South was not willing to believe it. The Democrats had split into factions. The slave states chose as their candidate John C. Breckinridge of Kentucky, who ran on a platform of slavery extension to the territories and the annexation of Cuba. Stephen A. Douglas, who championed popular sovereignty, the idea that new states would be admitted to the Union with or without slavery, according to the decision of the local government, was the candidate of the Northern Democrats. Lincoln was elected, and the secession of South Carolina was assured.

Because of an outbreak of smallpox, a state convention, called in Columbia in December 1860, was moved to Charleston, where, on December 20, in Saint Andrews Hall at 118 Broad Street, the Ordinance of Secession was unanimously approved. It was later signed in Institute Hall at 134 Meeting Street. (Both of these buildings burned in the Great Fire of 1861.) Dr. James H. Carlisle, later the revered president of Wofford College and one of the signers of the ordinance, told a colleague that the ordinance represented "the wild passions of that mad hour." [3] To James Louis Petigru, a Unionist to the last, is attributed the comment: "South Carolina is too small for a republic and too large for an insane asylum." [4] And more seriously Petigru remarked: "They have this day set a blazing torch to the temple of constitutional liberty, and, please God, we shall have no more peace forever." [5] Petigru was more correct than all the bell-ringing, shouting Charlestonians around him.

Many secessionists did not believe that South Carolina's act would precipitate war. They had been convinced by John C. Calhoun's arguments that the Constitution of 1787 had established a confederation of sovereign states and not an indivisible nation. For that reason, in the South's effort to rationalize

3. Wallace, *South Carolina*, p. 529, note.
4. This remark is attributed to Petigru in popular oral legend.
5. Wallace, *South Carolina*, p. 529.

what essentially was an irrational act, it has insisted upon calling the ensuing conflict the "War Between the States." The "Civil War" was a term that states' righters felt implied an effort to dissolve a compact instead of a revolt against a unified nation. It should be pointed out that the South has had no monopoly of the doctrine of states' rights. Others—for example, New England in 1812 and the Republicans in recent years—have invoked the doctrine when it has suited their own expedience.

By early February 1861, even before Lincoln's inauguration in March, Georgia, Alabama, Mississippi, Florida, Louisiana, and Texas had also seceded, although each of these states had strong Unionist minorities who fought against disunion. A Confederate government, organized at Montgomery, Alabama, elected as president Jefferson Davis, a moderate Mississippi planter, and Alexander H. Stephens, a highly intelligent and even more moderate Georgian, as vice-president. Robert Barnwell Rhett of South Carolina, the red-hot secessionist who had done more than any other single individual to bring about the debacle, was so disappointed at not being made president of the Confederate States of America that he spent the next four years criticizing and opposing Davis.

The Confederate States adopted a modified version of the Constitution of 1787; the Confederate Constitution outlawed the importation of slaves from Africa, but allowed the trade within the slave states. Also the Constitution clarified and emphasized the notion of a confederation of states. This theory made difficult effectual operation of the Confederate central government because individual states could—and did—withhold supplies, money, and men within their own borders when it suited them. As during the American Revolution, the weak central government could make requisitions upon the states but had little authority to enforce compliance. Later, after Virginia seceded, the temporary capital at Montgomery was moved to Richmond.

The decision of the border states about secession was critically important. South Carolina brought all the influence it could to bear, but the actual beginning of military hostilities, with the Confederate attack on Fort Sumter on April 12, 1861, did more than oratory and newspaper propaganda to precipitate final action by these states.

Fort Sumter, sitting strategically at the entrance to Charleston harbor, had been taken over by Major Robert Anderson of the United States Army. This fortress, erected on a sand bar, rested on a huge base of granite, some of which had been brought from as far away as Maine. At the time of the attack its brick ramparts were still being strengthened. Other forts in the harbor, Castle Pinckney and Fort Moultrie, had been occupied by the new Confederate government, but Fort Sumter was in the hands of the United States. Anderson's food was running low, and efforts to land reinforcements and supplies had been thwarted on January 9, 1861, when Citadel cadets drove off the supply ship *Star of the West* with artillery fire.

The question of what to do about supplying Sumter, and about secession, fell to President Lincoln upon his inauguration in March. He held the contract of the states binding, but both the Confederate government and Lincoln were playing a waiting game, negotiating and hoping for a compromise that would resolve the problems without resort to war. Major Anderson was under orders not to commence hostilities. But Lincoln, in late March, against the advice of most of his cabinet and his then chief-of-staff, aging General Winfield Scott, ordered an expedition to resupply Fort Sumter. General Pierre Beauregard of Louisiana, Confederate commander of the Charleston district, had orders from Jefferson Davis not to fire on Fort Sumter except to prevent the landing of reinforcements.

Although the relief expedition had not arrived, Beauregard decided on April 11 to demand Anderson's immediate surrender. This Anderson refused, as he still had some supplies, but he promised to surrender with honor when the supplies ran out—within two days at the most. The officers sent by Beauregard would not accept this offer, and one of them ordered the attack, made from Charleston batteries at 4:30 A.M., April 12, 1861, a date fateful in American history. A rabid Virginia secessionist, Edmund Ruffin, is reported to have asked for and received the privilege of firing the first gun.

War had begun, an unnecessary war even though it has been

frequently labelled the "irrepressible conflict." It had been brought about by the emotional irresponsibility of both sides in refusing to respond to intelligent efforts to compromise. Slavery was the emotional motivation and racial animosity the legacy. Even though cotton had made slavery profitable for a few planters, someone has estimated that the federal government could have purchased every slave in the United States and reimbursed the owners for a fraction of the cost of the war that followed, not to mention the loss of life and hatred brought about. "Give us slavery or give us death," Edward Bryan had cried, but little did he foresee the black pall of death that would envelope the land—without preserving the system of slavery that he desired. It is difficult to believe that a solution that would have eliminated the iniquity of slavery and insured racial justice could not have been worked out if reason had prevailed. But when emotions sweep a nation, reason takes wings, and even if rational men are in the majority—as they were in 1861—they cannot be heard.

The fashionable *beau monde* of Charleston hastened to the Battery later that morning, as the firing on Fort Sumter continued. After almost two days, on the afternoon of April 13, Major Anderson ran up the white flag, accepted General Beauregard's honorable terms of surrender, and the first episode of the war was over. It was still a chivalrous war between gentlemen, as some of it would remain—the last chivalrous war in history, if war can ever be really chivalrous.

Three days after the firing on Fort Sumter, President Lincoln called for 75,000 volunteers to suppress disorder beyond the power of judicial proceedings.

That meant armed coercion of the slave states. Virginia faced the dilemma of helping supply troops to fight its sister states or seceding. Already prejudice against Lincoln's action was so great that not to secede would have precipitated civil war within the state. By proclamation of the governor, Virginia went over to the Confederacy. But forty-six northwestern counties, mostly in the mountains, refused to go out, and they became the state of West Virginia.

North Carolina, which had dallied about secession, and Tennessee, which had many Unionists, followed Virginia. Arkansas, which had already seceded, completed the eleven Confederate states. Maryland had many Confederate sympathizers, especially in Baltimore, but, surrounded by Federal forces, did not secede. Kentucky teetered but finally decided to stay in the Union. The territory of New Mexico was pro-Confederate, as was California south of Santa Barbara. A group in New York proposed that the city, which was strongly pro-Confederate, secede. Missouri was almost equally divided between pro-Confederate and Unionist and proved a fertile ground for internecine fighting and bushwhacking throughout the war. The Indians of the Indian Territory (later Oklahoma)—the so-called Five Civilized Tribes, including the Cherokees moved there during Jackson's administration—owned many black slaves and were strong supporters of the Confederacy. Thus the country was divided; in many border families, brother fought against brother.

The trauma of disunion and incipient war was less acute in South Carolina than in most other states, because South Carolina politicians and newspapers had been talking about it for years. In Virginia, the decisions were perhaps hardest. Robert E. Lee, a man of infinite nobility of character, had one of the most difficult decisions to make. Opposed to slavery, he had emancipated the slaves he had inherited. A staunch defender of the Union, he thought secession folly. An honor graduate of West Point and the most highly respected officer on General Winfield Scott's staff, he was offered the command of the Union forces when Lincoln issued his call to arms. But Lee could not go to war against his native Virginia and threw in his lot with the Confederacy. When, early in November 1861, a federal fleet sailed into Port Royal and seized the whole area as a base for blockading the Southern coast, General Lee was sent to take command of the department of South Carolina and Georgia. During the time that he was in the South, he concentrated on the defense of Charleston, a strategy that succeeded.

The story of the Civil War has been so often retold that it needs no reiteration in so brief an account as this; consequently, only a few episodes affecting South Carolina will be mentioned.

If the state had a burden of guilt for its part in precipitating the war, it paid many times over in loss of men and wealth, the sacrifices and contributions of its heroic women, and the privations suffered during four years of conflict. No other state sent such a large proportion of its manpower into action. South Carolina's long tradition of military service by the upper class provided a great reservoir of trained officers, many from West Point, many more from the Citadel and the Arsenal in Columbia. In fact, so many officers were available that a facetious commentator observed that South Carolina would have a pretty good army, once enough officers had been reduced to the ranks to make up a fighting force. Among the most famous of the Carolina leaders was General Wade Hampton, commander of Hampton's Legion. General Joseph Kershaw of Camden made Kershaw's Brigade a noted fighting force. David Duncan Wallace lists thirty-two general officers appointed from South Carolina and notes that several other distinguished generals appointed from other states were natives of South Carolina; these included General James Longstreet, born in Edgefield; General D. H. Hill, York; and General David R. Jones, Orangeburg.[6] For many years after the war, Confederate generals, colonels, and other officers dominated South Carolina politics as hero-worshipping voters returned them to office.

Because the Confederacy critically needed munitions, drugs, and other supplies from overseas, blockade-running into the ports of Charleston and Wilmington, North Carolina, became one of the most daring enterprises of the war. Ships built for speed and easy handling were used by private owners, the majority English, who stood to gain immense profits if they made it—and many of them did. "The list of eighty-eight vessels known to have run in and out of Charleston, some making from six to eighteen voyages, is apparently incomplete," Wallace comments. "Two voyages were sufficient to pay for the craft and net a handsome profit." [7] Without the supplies brought in by these blockade-runners, the Confederacy would have been

---

6. Wallace, *South Carolina*, pp. 554–555.
7. Wallace, *South Carolina*, p. 546.

strangled; hence strenuous efforts were made by federal forces to seize Charleston and Wilmington, the latter defended by Fort Fisher. But the fortifications of the two ports held out, and Yankee attacking forces by land and sea failed.

Samuel Francis du Pont, who had been made a rear admiral for his success in capturing Port Royal in the autumn of 1861, was ordered to attack Charleston in April 1863. His armament consisted of seven monitors (iron gunboats compared to a "cheese box on a raft"), an iron-clad named *New Ironsides,* and another armored gunboat. Monitors had become popular with the federal navy after the duel at Hampton Roads on March 9, 1862, between the first *Monitor* and the Confederate armored vessel, the *Merrimac.* Admiral du Pont was skeptical of using monitors against land-based artillery, because they lacked, he said, "aggression or destructiveness as against forts," [8] a prediction that proved true. His fleet opened fire on Fort Sumter on April 7, but sustained 411 hits from the guns of the fortress and had to withdraw. Five of his monitors were knocked out of action.

The Navy Department relieved du Pont and replaced him with Rear Admiral John A. Dahlgren, who had no better luck in attempting to reduce Fort Sumter. Although he managed to batter down the fort's emplacements and silence its guns after a week's bombardment from Morris Island in September 1863, an attempt to take the fort by assault failed with the loss of 125 of Dahlgren's men. From Morris Island on August 22–23, the Federals threw incendiary shells into Charleston with an eight-inch parrott gun affectionately called by its men "the Swamp Angel." The gun blew up on the thirty-sixth round and did more damage to its battery crews than to Charleston. On October 5, the Confederates frightened the federal fleet by badly damaging the *New Ironsides* with a torpedo launched from a four-man, steam-driven semisubmersible named the *David.* Miraculously, the *David*'s crew managed to back away and get the vessel back to Charleston. Fort Sumter remained in Confederate hands until they evacuated Charleston in February 1865, on the

8. *Dictionary of American Biography,* s.v. "du Pont."

approach of a wing of Sherman's army commanded by a Prussian officer, General Alexander Schimmelfennig. Although gunboats lying offshore became more successful toward the end of the war in keeping out blockade-runners, Charleston was never completely bottled up.

Of many daring enterprises of the courageous Confederate navy, the attempted use at Charleston of an early type of submarine approached a genuine "kamikaze" effort. On February 17, 1864, the *Hunley*, a cigar-shaped submersible driven by a propeller hand-cranked by six men commanded by Lieutenant George E. Dixon, sank the Federal sloop *Housatonic*, on patrol duty off Charleston harbor. The *Hunley* and all her men were lost. This experimental vessel, shipped overland from Mobile, Alabama, was planned as a true submarine to dive under vessels. She was designed to be operated by a normal complement of eight men. Five crews died in experimental diving before the attack on the *Housatonic*. Despite this appalling record of fatalities, volunteers were eager to make up each fresh crew. General Beauregard, in command at Charleston, would not allow another submersible attempt. Instead, the *Hunley* was permitted to use a torpedo attached to a long spar on its prow. It was believed that the crew could ram the *Housatonic* and escape by the time the torpedo exploded. As it turned out, both vessels sank. The full-scale model of the *Hunley* is on exhibition in the Hunley Museum in the basement of the Bank of South Carolina Building, 50 Broad Street, Charleston.

When the blockade-runners could not get through federal gunboats at Charleston, they had a somewhat better chance of evading them on the tricky North Carolina coast. Efforts of the federals to capture Fort Fisher, guarding the entrance to Wilmington, were as unsuccessful as their attempts at Fort Sumter until January 1865. In December 1864, General Ulysses S. Grant ordered the ineffable Benjamin Franklin Butler, a "political" general and an embarrassment to decent men in or out of the army, to take Fort Fisher from the land side. Butler, as incompetent as he was crooked, failed. He was first nicknamed "Spoons," for his alleged proclivity for stealing silverware from unwilling Confederate hostesses, and then "Beast," after his notorious Order No. 28 in New Orleans, which stated: "When any female shall by word or gesture or movement insult or show contempt for any officer or soldier of the United States, she shall be regarded and held liable to be treated as a woman of the town plying her avocation." [9] President Jefferson Davis declared Butler "without the law," deserving of being shot if captured. Butler was almost as despised by many in the North as by Southerners. His political machinations were so wily, however, that Grant could not persuade Lincoln to relieve Butler of his command until after the elections of 1864. At last, in January 1865, Grant sent a competent officer, General A. H. Terry, with a force of 8,000 men to attack Fort Fisher. On January 15, 1865, that fortress fell, and blockade-running into Wilmington was finished. But three months later, so was the war.

Although South Carolina was spared much bloodshed on its own soil, its men gave their lives in most of the important battles of the war. Wade Hampton, who had not wanted secession, organized Hampton's Legion and fitted it out partly at his own expense. A cavalry leader of distinction, he was made second-in-command to the Confederacy's brilliant cavalry leader, General J. E. B. Stuart. When Stuart was mortally wounded at Yellow Tavern, Virginia, on May 11, 1864, Hampton became commander of the cavalry corps. He was wounded in the first battle of Manassas, at Seven Pines, and once more at Gettysburg. He survived these battle wounds, nearly to die in a hunting accident after the war. On Sherman's invasion of South Carolina in 1865, Hampton was ordered to screen the retreat of Joseph E. Johnston's army.

Other South Carolina officers also distinguished themselves in battle, and many died. The death toll of soldiers and officers from the state was appalling. One family near Ninety Six, known to the author of this book, lost every male member, a total of five, but they were not unique in their loss. The exact number killed in battle or all those who died from wounds or disease may never be known, but South Carolina sent to the

9. Robert Werlich, *"Beast" Butler* (Washington, D.C.: Quaker Press, 1962), p. 39.

front some 44,000 fighting men. The loss was about twenty-three percent, or more than 10,000. Like England during World War I, South Carolina lost some of its best blood, leaders who were greatly needed in the decades following the conflict.

In many areas, most of the able-bodied men were in the army, and only women, boys, and old or disabled men were left at home. They had to perform all the labor required to feed themselves and keep the men at the front supplied. In most cases, the black slaves remained loyal and continued to perform their duties. In this period, only in the Port Royal area, where the Yankees were established, did freed Negroes flock to army camps.

Confederate women developed great ingenuity in finding substitutes for both luxuries and necessities. Several recipe books telling how to make do with ersatz materials were published, perhaps the best known being the *Confederate Receipt Book,* printed in Richmond in 1863 and bound in wallpaper. It described methods of making cosmetics, dyes, medicines, and foods. Parthenia Antoinette Hague, an Alabama school teacher, in *A Blockaded Family* (1888), provided a vivid description of some of these substitutes. Dogwood berries were used in lieu of quinine for malaria, as were brews from the bark of wild cherry, dogwood, and poplar trees. Blackberry roots made a brew for dysentery. Castor beans were used for medicine, as well as for lubricating oil. Many women cultivated poppies for homemade opium and laudanum, which Miss Hague tells how to prepare. Coffee substitutes were innumerable, ranging from parched baked sweet potatoes to parched okra seed (the best). Dried raspberry leaves served for tea, as did leaves from blackberry vines and huckleberry bushes. "All in our settlement learned to card, spin, and weave," Miss Hague asserts. And they became adept at reworking old shoes, turning and padding the soles, and fitting them with knitted tops. "We were drawn together in a closer union," Miss Hague comments, "a tenderer feeling of humanity linking us together, both rich and poor; from the princely planter who could scarcely get off his wide domains in a day's ride, and who could count his slaves by the thousand, down to humble tenants of the log cabin on rented or leased land.'' [10]

Dr. Francis Peyre Porcher, a Charleston physician, one of a distinguished group of South Carolina botanists and scientists, was released from active duty with the army to prepare a volume on native remedies, a book entitled *Resources of the Southern Fields and Forests, Medical, Economical, and Agricultural* (1863). An expanded edition was published after the war, in 1869. It provided a vast number of suggestions for herbal remedies, some tried, many untried. Long after the war, Confederate women were still following some of Dr. Porcher's advice. A great-aunt of mine often took me along in her search through the woods for ''cancer weed,'' an herb which, made into a poultice, she believed would cure any boil or other infection.

Not every South Carolinian, patriotic as most of them were, was ready to volunteer for the armed services. A few resisted the draft imposed by the Confederate government in Richmond, some on the issue of states' rights, others because they did not want to go to war. Draft resisters were more abundant in the upper portions of Spartanburg and Greenville counties than elsewhere. Instead of having to go all the way to Canada, as draft dodgers more recently have done, evaders of the Confederate draft could slip up into the mountains and hide with ease. Many did. In what is still known as the ''Dark Corner'' of Spartanburg and Greenville counties, evaders and deserters had a fortified refuge, with lookouts, against capture. They had a similar refuge on an island in Broad River. As in the Revolution, desertion was common in both the Northern and Southern armies. In the Confederate forces, men frequently simply went home without leave to look after their farms or families. Sometimes they returned; sometimes they did not. But out of more than 100,000 Confederate soldiers classified as deserters during the four years, fewer than 4,000 were attributed to South Carolina.

Resistance to the draft in the Confederacy was much less

10. Katherine M. Jones, *Heroines of Dixie* (Indianapolis and New York: Bobbs-Merrill Co., 1955), pp. 261–265.

acute than in the North. In New York City, for example, which was profoundly sympathetic to the South, damaging riots occurred July 13–16, 1863, when the federal government attempted to round up draftees. Before the fighting was over, rioters had destroyed property worth more than $1,500,000, killed at least a dozen people, and injured hundreds, for the most part Negroes. Order was not restored until the Federal Army of the Potomac sent a detachment that killed or wounded more than a thousand rioters. A riot in Boston was less disastrous, but troops had to fire on the draft resisters, killing several.

A bitter war came to a bitter end in South Carolina with the invasion by General William Tecumseh Sherman, which began on January 19, 1865. Sherman intended to reach Goldsboro, North Carolina, by mid-March and then to head north into Virginia to join Grant, who was trying to bottle up Lee's Army of Northern Virginia, then defending Richmond and Petersburg. P. T. Beauregard was again in command of forces opposing Sherman's march through South Carolina, but he was replaced by General Joseph E. Johnston on February 22, 1865.

Sherman tried to give the impression that his army was headed either for Charleston or Augusta, but his real objective was Columbia. His successful "march to the sea" through Georgia, which had left a sixty-mile-wide swath of destruction including the city of Atlanta, was an indication of what South Carolina could expect. Charleston believed that it would suffer destruction like that in Atlanta. Indeed, hints had been given Sherman by high-ranking Union officers that if Charleston were "accidentally" burned, it would be a work of virtue. South Carolina was the particular target for vindictive Yankees, and Charleston especially had aroused their desire for revenge.

But Sherman led his main army northeastward. He had a force of some 60,000 troops, with additional cavalry amounting to about 5,000. His Confederate opponents were greatly outnumbered and could only hope to fight delaying actions. Sherman ordered Brigadier General Judson Kilpatrick to feint with his cavalry unit in the general direction of Aiken and Augusta and sent Brigadier General Alexander Schimmelfennig to occupy Charleston. Sherman, with the main body of the army, moved toward Columbia.

As the armies marched eastward, they proved even more destructive than they had been in Georgia. Without an adequate supply line, Sherman expected to live off the country and did. A believer in the concept of total war, he thought he could break the back of "rebellion" by destroying everything in his path. Consequently, he seized and destroyed all supplies he could not use, burned dwellings and barns, and tore up railroad lines. An effective way of making railway repairs impossible was to remove the rails, build a huge fire, heat the center of the rails, and then twist them around trees. At destruction, Sherman's army had no equal.

But worse than the main army were the "bummers," vagabond soldiers who wandered off in small groups to pillage for themselves without the restraint of discipline by responsible officers. They stole, robbed, and burned at will. To this day, legends throughout upper South Carolina tell of the thievery and burnings of these wretches, and "Sherman" is still a hated name throughout the state. Many a family history records sufferings at the hands of his bummers or of his main army, and gaunt chimneys still stand here and there as monuments of a hated episode in the war. Descriptions in *Gone with the Wind* of the destruction in Atlanta and vicinity were old stories to many South Carolinians. The family home of the writer was burned, and the women were left to shift for themselves as best they could. Every fowl, pig, and cow had been slaughtered or driven away, and not a handful of food or grain was left. The women subsisted for days on parched corn picked up where the bummers had tethered and fed their horse.

As an officer and presumably a gentleman, Sherman had some elements of decency—though few South Carolinians of an older generation would concede it—and he did not permit assaults on women, even though he was content to leave them to starve. Few rapes are recorded. Some of his officers, particularly General Alphaeus S. Williams, tried hard to restrain over-destructive soldiers.

The most vindictive of Sherman's officers was his cavalry

commander, Brigadier General Judson Kilpatrick. A vicious, mean-spirited little man, Kilpatrick expressed pleasure at the opportunity for wreaking vengeance on what he called the "hellhole of secession." About the only good thing that can be said of him is that he cannot be held responsible for the burning of Columbia: at the time he was busy with the torch in Lexington and its environs.

Sherman marched into Columbia on February 17, 1865. The mayor had ridden out of the city in a carriage to meet him and surrender the city in the hope of saving it. Hampton's cavalry, too few to make a defense, had moved out just ahead of the Yankees. Sherman and his officers picked out the best homes for their headquarters, and the troops were left to pillage for themselves. They found supplies of liquor, and soon Yankee soldiers and jubilant Negroes were celebrating in the streets. During the night, most of the town burned. Sherman accused the departing Hampton of setting fire to cotton bales piled in the streets, but his own men confessed that the fires had been started by drunken federal troops and that nothing had been done to stop them. The burning of an "open city," the capital of South Carolina, was greeted with jubilation in the North, but the deed has remained a blot on the commander's memory.

After Columbia, Sherman's army moved across the state, burning and pillaging. Detachments skirmished with Hampton's or General Joe Wheeler's cavalry at Camden, Winnsboro, Hanging Rock, Cheraw, and various other places in the northeastern part of the state. At Monroe's Cross Roads on March 9, Hampton's and Joe Wheeler's troopers surprised and routed Kilpatrick's cavalry. Kilpatrick himself, nearly captured in bed, was reported to have fled without his pants; hence the skirmish was called by Confederate troops the "Battle of Kilpatrick's Pants." But Confederate troops were too outnumbered to do more than harass the Federals and then retreat. In Charlotte, North Carolina, General Joseph E. Johnston had only 20,000 to 25,000 men to oppose several times that number of the enemy converging upon him.

Most of Sherman's troops crossed the border into North Carolina during the second week of March and concentrated at

Fayetteville. After destroying everything of value there, they moved on toward Goldsboro on March 14. South Carolina had been left in ruins.

The end was not far away. General Philip Sheridan had laid waste the Shenandoah Valley, the breadbasket of the Confederacy, so that, as he boasted, a crow would have to carry his rations if he flew over the valley. Grant was slowly enveloping Lee in front of Petersburg. By the first of April, it was evident to Lee that he would have to retreat and that Richmond was lost. His hope was that he could break out, move the Army of Northern Virginia westward, and finally join with Joe Johnston's army. It was a forlorn hope. The retreat began on late Sunday, April 2, as the army moved toward Amelia Court House. President Davis and his cabinet took a train that night for Danville, Virginia, whence they would continue to flee south. By Saturday, April 8, as the remnants of the Army of Northern Virginia camped near Appomattox Court House, it was clear to Lee that he had little chance of marching on to Lynchburg and thence to consolidate his and Johnston's forces. In the meantime, he had written Grant at Farmville to propose negotiations. On Sunday, April 9, the two generals met at Wilmer McLean's farmhouse at Appomattox and terms of surrender were agreed upon. Grant permitted Confederate officers to retain their sidearms and allowed the men to take away horses that they claimed as their own property, which they would need in the spring planting.

In effect, the war was over, but sporadic fighting continued. On April 18, Johnston signed with Sherman at Durham what amounted to an armistice, rather than a surrender, and fighting in North Carolina ended. In the meantime, the South had suffered the irreparable loss of a moderate who wanted to heal the wounds of war when Abraham Lincoln was shot by John Wilkes Booth on April 14 in Ford's Theater in Washington. Ironically, on the morning of the same day in Charleston, South Carolina, the Union flag was again raised over Fort Sumter by the same Major Anderson who had pulled it down in 1861. And that pious parson and alleged adulterer, the Reverend Henry Ward Beecher, delivered an oration on the occasion in which he rebuked South Carolina for her political blindness but had the grace to praise the state's military prowess.

On May 2, President Jefferson Davis, fleeing southward, met with remnants of his cabinet in Abbeville and the next day crossed the Savannah River into Georgia. Eight days later, Davis's party was arrested by federal troops near Irwindale, Georgia. Davis was imprisoned in Fort Monroe until May 13, 1867. For a time, on orders of General H. W. Halleck and Assistant Secretary of War Charles A. Dana, he was kept in irons.

After Appomattox, South Carolina's soldiers began the slow and painful return to their homes and farms. Those who had horses rode; but most trudged the weary way from Virginia to South Carolina. Many were sick or wounded, but nearly all got back, though a few lie buried along the route. They returned to scenes of desolation. Instead of the houses they remembered, they often found only smoke-blackened chimneys. Frequently, not a tool was to be had; not a plow, hoe, or rake was left.

Labor was no longer available. Lincoln's Emancipation Proclamation of September 22, 1862, effective in South Carolina at war's end, freed the slaves that constituted the capital assets of planters in the Low Country. Without money to hire labor, they had difficulty growing rice or cotton. In the euphoria of freedom, Negroes showed no inclination to work so long as they could subsist on rations supplied by federal troops or the Freedmen's Bureau, soon established to look after the black man's welfare.

The state was soon swarming with do-gooders ready to provide guidance to salvation, offer advice, and often to steal what they could. Mrs. Henry Ward Beecher, for example, made off with a piece of the pulpit from St. Michael's Church in Charleston. This sacred souvenir was later returned. Others "liberated" books and manuscripts from libraries or simply scattered them to the winds. Would-be reformers, however, were not all bad. In the first desperate days after the war, they often helped to keep the population, black and white, from starving, and they performed other useful services.

The small farmers of the Up Country fared a little better than the planters in the tidewater region. Few had ever owned slaves, and they were accustomed to heavy labor. But former slaveowners who themselves had never worked in the fields found it necessary to pick up a hoe, or, if lucky enough to find one, to follow a plow. One dignified ex-Confederate soldier who lived near Greenwood was often seen plowing—but not without his small black string tie. Even some professional men, lawyers and bankers, in the first year or two after the war, had to turn to farming because they had no income from the former occupations. No one despised any honest labor that would keep body and soul together. In some fashion, people raised subsistence crops of corn, wheat, sorghum, and vegetables, as they scratched out a living from the soil in the first year or two after Appomattox. The war was over; life had to go on. South Carolina's men and women followed Lee's injunction. They resumed their occupations or adopted new ones and prepared to rebuild a civilization that in time would be vastly different from the one they had defended.

10

From Desolation to
Green Revolution

N the century from 1865 to 1965 and the decade that followed, South Carolina underwent fundamental changes that altered both its social outlook and its physical appearance. Most of these changes were slow in coming; development was hindered by political upheavals, crop failures, periodic depressions, and the natural conservatism of a people suspicious of innovation, social or economic. But out of the ashes of war, a new state has arisen, with a fairer distribution of political power, more liberal social attitudes, and a broader base of economic strength. The way has been hard and, on occasion, devious; at times, many citizens found themselves floundering in the Slough of Despond; often Despair was their companion; frequently they were less than wise in their expedients; but after much travail and error, South Carolinians have erected a commonwealth that is proud, prosperous, and more concerned than most with social justice.

Many South Carolinians have long believed that the darkest, grimmest time in the state's history was the period from 1865 to 1877, called euphemistically the era of Reconstruction. Conditions seemed so bleak and hopeless to some returning soldiers that they did not wait to be "reconstructed," but headed for the western frontier; ex-Confederates could be counted in nearly every cow town in the West; some served as sheriffs; some turned out to be outlaws and bad men. A few planters whose rice fields had been ruined and whose homes were vandalized emigrated to Mexico and Brazil. A considerable colony of Southerners started a colony in Brazil, and their descendants can be found there to this day.

After the surrender and disarming of Confederate troops, civil government in South Carolina also collapsed, and some 7,000 federal soldiers were the main dependence to keep order. Although many of these soldiers were recent German and Irish immigrants recruited at the docks of New York, and some were freed Negroes, their record of behavior as an occupying army is better than one might have expected. For the most part, federal line officers in the army did their job well; in a few instances, faced with insubordination of black militia, they had to call on local whites for assistance.

A provisional civil government was established by President Andrew Johnson, who on June 30, 1865, appointed Benjamin F. Perry of Greenville as governor until an election could be held. Perry had been an antisecessionist, but was generally respected. A month before Perry's appointment, President Johnson had granted amnesty to most ex-Confederates, provided they took an oath of allegiance to the United States. Excepted were former Confederate army officers, Confederate officials, and a few prominent men of wealth. These people had to apply for pardons on an individual basis. Pardoned citizens were permitted to vote for delegates to a Constitutional Convention that formally abolished slavery and reapportioned legislative representation to give the Up Country more power. In an election held in the autumn of 1865, James L. Orr was chosen governor. The Convention of 1865 had considered the question of Negro suffrage but had taken no action to enfranchise blacks; a few leaders, including Wade Hampton, were in favor of giving the ballot to qualified Negroes.

A new and weak elected government, without funds or power of any kind, could do little to rehabilitate a prostrate land. Furthermore, the state was suddenly flooded with agencies appointed by the federal government to enforce federal regulations for the protection of ex-slaves, to confiscate and allot land to the blacks, and to utilize money obtained from a tax on cotton to relieve distress, feed the hungry, and to begin an educational program for Negroes. Some success was achieved, but much of this tax money found its way into the pockets of unscrupulous exploiters.

At the end of the war, South Carolina had some 400,000 ex-slaves, many of whom had been led to believe that the "year of jubilee" had come, and the necessity for work was over. Thousands wandered from locality to locality, rejoicing in their new freedom but wondering where their next meal would come from. Naturally, they clustered around federal army camps and federal agencies, expecting to be fed and cared for. Many contracted diseases and died from exposure and malnutrition. The plight of whites in 1865 was frequently as bad as that of their former slaves. Few had money with which to buy food, had food been readily available. To the credit of federal agencies, they succeeded in providing aid to the destitute, both black and white.

The most active of the federal agencies—and the most detested by whites—was the Freedmen's Bureau, established in March 1865; one of its obligations was to legalize land seizures made by the army. In the previous January, General Sherman in his notorious Field Order No. 15 had set aside for Negroes the sea islands and rice fields extending from the coast for thirty miles inland. It was Sherman's plan to allot to each Negro family forty acres and for the army to protect them in the possession of the property. Throughout the state, much land, forfeited because of failure to pay taxes, was sold at auction, often for less than a dollar an acre, to Negroes and carpetbaggers. The latter were immigrants into the state from the North; sometimes they came to help the downtrodden; more often they came openly to feather their nests as quickly and as profitably as possible. Another group of exploiters were native renegades called scalawags.

Slavery had imposed on the South a fear of servile rebellion, and this fear of black terrorism carried over into the post-Civil War period. Uneasiness over potential domination by an illiterate black population that outnumbered whites resulted in the passage, by the first legislature elected under the Constitution of 1865, of a so-called "Black Code." Although this law guaranteed to Negroes certain rights, it imposed a series of regulations and punishments that did not apply to whites. Other Southern states also passed "Black Codes," interpreted throughout the North as an effort to keep the Negro in de facto slavery.

South Carolina, which had already denied the right to vote to Negroes, now refused to ratify the Fourteenth Amendment, which Radical Republicans had pushed through Congress as a means of coercing the South into granting equal rights to all citizens; the amendment also penalized a state if it denied adult males the right to vote "except for rebellion or other crime," and excluded from office everyone who had held an office under the Confederacy, even such lowly posts as coroner or school official. The passage of the Black Code and the rejection of the Fourteenth Amendment led Congress to enact punitive laws to punish recalcitrant South Carolina, along with other states in the South that had taken similar action.

The most detailed account of the Reconstruction period is that by Francis B. Simkins and Robert H. Woody in *South Carolina during Reconstruction* (1932). Ernest McPherson Lander, Jr., citing Simkins and Woody, explains: "Reconstruction fell into two periods: (1) Presidential Reconstruction, 1865–68, and Radical Reconstruction, 1868–77. All eleven ex-Confederate states went through some form of Reconstruction. But only in South Carolina, Louisiana, and Florida did Reconstruction last until 1877. By contrast, Reconstruction in Virginia, North Carolina, and Tennessee was brief and not nearly so violent and tragic." [1] The worst period for South Carolina was Radical (or Congressional) Reconstruction.

On March 2, 1867, a vindictive Congress passed the first Reconstruction Act and began the era known as "Congressional Reconstruction." The chief architect of the legislation in the House of Representatives was Thaddeus Stevens of Pennsyl-

---

1. Ernest McPherson Lander, Jr., *A History of South Carolina,* 2nd ed. (Columbia, S.C.: University of South Carolina Press, 1970), p. 3.

vania, a bitter old man whose hatred of all things Southern surpassed even that of Senator Charles Sumner. Stevens wanted to treat the Confederate states as conquered provinces. But Stevens was not merely motivated by personal hatred; he had a larger plan. If all ex-Confederates could be disfranchised and all blacks could be enfranchised under the sponsorship of the Republican party, the Republicans could maintain for years to come a solid block of eleven states that had made up the Confederacy. It was a bold, imaginative plan, and it worked for a brief time. But its ruthless vindictiveness eventually turned the South against the Republicans and made it into a "Solid South" for the Democrats.

Congress was controlled by the so-called Radical Republicans, who refused to go along with President Andrew Johnson's relatively moderate treatment of the South. The Radicals preached punishment befitting the crime of rebellion and whipped up emotion by sensational speeches on the mistreatment of Negroes in the South. Rarely has Congress echoed with so much violent oratory to convince the public that strong measures were needed to complete the conquest of the rebellious states. When President Johnson vetoed some of the legislation of the Radicals, they began impeachment proceedings. By a margin of only one vote in the Senate, he retained his office.

Under Congressional Reconstruction, armies of occupation under the command of a general assumed full authority in the conquered states. Johnson had appointed Daniel E. Sickles, one of the less reputable army officers, to govern the two Carolinas, but Sickles was soon succeeded by General E. R. S. Canby. The army could contermand civil laws, try anyone before a military tribunal, and otherwise interfere with civil government. Actually, army officers in the upper echelon were superior to the carpetbaggers who ran the Freedmen's Bureau and other federal agencies, and these officers often served as a moderating influence during a period of misrule.

Scandalous as was the corruption and thievery during the period of Reconstruction, some good results can be credited to the "reformers." For instance, a new Constitution of 1868, created by a convention of forty-eight whites and seventy-six

Negroes, marked an advance in democratic government in South Carolina. Representation in the legislature for the first time was based entirely on population, and each county was allowed one state senator. Better provisions were made for secondary education than the state had ever known. Imprisonment for debt was abolished. Married women were guaranteed the right to control their own property; before this time, South Carolina had followed the English legal tradition of giving the husband control of his wife's possessions. Although the Constitution of 1868 contained some unfavorable provisions, the state did not get around to revising it until 1895.

The older histories of Reconstruction painted a dismal picture of complete corruption in the government of South Carolina. Disfranchisement of whites, the elevation of illiterate Negroes to high office, bribery, theft of public funds, illegal favoritism to railroads and other corporations, and almost every form of unethical practice known to politicians disgraced the state. But it was an age of corruption throughout the land. In New York, the Tweed Ring was plundering that city, and Congress was almost as susceptible to bribery as the black and white-carpetbagger legislatures in South Carolina.

Not every Negro was illiterate. "Numbers of the Negro leaders were the moral superiors of the average carpetbagger or scalawag, and some were of high ability," comments David Duncan Wallace.[2] F. L. Cardozo, a mulatto who could claim descent from an intellectual Jewish family of Charleston, was a graduate of Edinburgh University. He served as South Carolina's secretary of state and as treasurer. The Reverend R. H. Cain and Martin Delany were men of courage and integrity in a period when both qualities were rare.

The story of Reconstruction has been so often told that it need not be repeated in detail here. If the older histories stressed only sensational stories of corruption and depravity, a newer generation of revisionist historians has sometimes gone to the opposite extreme and pictured the era as a time of emerging democracy. Equipped with a fund of idealism and sloshing buckets of white-

2. Wallace, *South Carolina,* p. 576.

wash, a few of these revisionists have prettied up Reconstruction and given many phases of it virtues that not even the most sanctimonious carpetbagger would have claimed. Although some beneficial advances in democratic participation in state government and some improvement in education occurred during Reconstruction, the legacy of racial strife and the intensity of political animosity toward the Republican party fastened upon South Carolina a "lily-white," one-party system that lasted until the present decade.

By 1876, the carpetbaggers and scalawags had overreached themselves, and internal friction among the exploiters split the Republicans. Taking advantage of "confusion among thieves," the Democrats made a determined effort to wrest control from the opposition by nominating a ticket headed by their most popular hero, General Wade Hampton. Unlike some of his more fiery supporters, such as General Martin W. Gary of Edgefield, Hampton was a moderate who promised to be "governor of the whole people . . . holding the scales of justice with firm and impartial hand." [3]

Although the Republicans, with a solid bloc of Negro voters, had a potential majority, the Democrats were determined to win the election. Taking a cue from Garibaldi, the contemporary hero of Italy, they organized bands of "Red Shirts" who rode through the countryside enlisting every white man to vote and intimidating Negroes when they could. The Red Shirts exerted important political influence, unlike the Ku Klux Klan, which had slight impact in South Carolina. Bands of grim-faced white men dressed in their red shirts roamed the countryside and appeared at Republican rallies to let the assembled blacks know that a new force was abroad in the land. Although Hampton himself tried to woo black voters into the Democratic ranks, "Mart" Gary, head of the militant wing of the resurgent Democrats, believed in threats of violence to keep the blacks from the polls. Some violence occurred during the campaign, and neither party was innocent. Riots at Ellenton and Cainhow resulted in casualties among both whites and Negroes. The miracle was that so few riots occurred.

3. *Dictionary of American Biography,* s.v. "Hampton."

The results of the election in November showed that Hampton had won over the incumbent Republican governor, Daniel H. Chamberlain. Undoubtedly, there had been fraud on both sides, and many Democrats later admitted to voting more than once on election day. The Republicans would not concede the election and inaugurated Chamberlain, but when federal troops were withdrawn from South Carolina in April 1877 by newly elected President Rutherford B. Hayes, Chamberlain and his party gave up and allowed Hampton to move into the Statehouse. The dread of black dominance in South Carolina during Reconstruction helps to explain the long history of white supremacy as the battle cry of every demagogic politician from that day to our own time.

Despite the virulent racism of Mart Gary and many others of like opinion, Hampton pursued a policy of justice and fair play toward all classes, black and white. A political realist, as well as a man of great humanity, Hampton realized that South Carolina could not afford to give the federal government an excuse to send an army back to prevent widespread disfranchisement of Negroes. Furthermore, he hoped to win a permanent majority of them for the Democratic party. To show fair play, he appointed a number of blacks to state offices.

It is not generally remembered that, for a long time after Hampton's election as governor, blacks also won elective offices. Although, in spite of Hampton's influence, whites utilized various subterfuges to keep Negroes from voting, blacks were never completely eliminated from politics. "Probably 10,000 to 15,000 Negroes continued to vote," Ernest M. Lander points out, "and until 1900 Negroes were elected to the legislature (mainly from Georgetown, Berkeley, and Beaufort counties). Also, one Congressional district in lower South Carolina elected a Negro to Congress nearly every two years until 1896. In no state-wide election, however, did a Negro win office after 1876." [4] For many years after 1876, politicians found that the issue of white supremacy was a potent factor with the South Carolina electorate, and many a violent demagogue rode into office on this issue alone.

4. Lander, *History of South Carolina*, pp. 28–29.

Hampton's conciliatory policy won him a sweeping victory as governor again in 1878, but the legislature soon after elected him to the United States Senate. He was succeeded as governor by another conservative aristocrat, General Johnson Hagood. Moderate conservative aristocrats held a monopoly of the principal state offices until 1890, when Benjamin Ryan Tillman, known as "Pitchfork Ben," won election to the governorship as the friend of the poor man of the Up Country. He inaugurated an era of demagogic politics characterized by violent opposition to the "Charleston ring."

Struggling to regain her political soul after 1865, South Carolina was also striving to survive economically. Cotton was still king, and nobody could think of a better money crop. Rice fields in the coastal region had been ruined, and although some rice was raised until the early years of the present century, rice never again brought great wealth to the state. The ruin of war, a succession of devastating storms, and the competition of Louisiana and Texas eventually wiped out the cultivation of rice in South Carolina. Today, not a grain is grown commercially in the state. After the Civil War, cotton seemed to be the only hope.

But cotton required labor, and few planters had money to hire freedmen. At length, the Freedmen's Bureau diminished its support of idle blacks, and they had to look for employment. The best the landowners could do was to work out a system of sharecropping, or tenant farming, a plan that persisted until recent years. In his first administration, President Franklin Roosevelt declared that the South represented the nation's No. 1 economic problem, a problem intensified by the plight of the sharecroppers. But for a decade after the Civil War, the almost total bankruptcy of landowners left no other expedient. The landowner would furnish the land, livestock, seed, and fertilizer, and the sharecropper would furnish his labor. At the end of the year, they would divide the proceeds. The landowner himself had to obtain supplies on credit from local merchants. Some landless farmers became tenants instead of sharecroppers. That is, they rented land and obtained credit from merchants until they could make a crop and liquidate their debts.

This was the origin of the "lien" system by which the merchant took out a lien or mortgage on the crop. Since the merchant assumed heavy risks, he charged a high interest rate as a protection against losses. The local merchant himself was usually "carried" by a bank or a mercantile house in the larger cities. At the end of the year, the farmer who had grown the crop was lucky if he had any surplus cash after he had settled his debts. The local storekeeper was in part responsible for keeping cotton enthroned, because he had to insist upon a marketable asset. The farmers themselves had no knowledge of any other crop that could be turned into ready money.

Bondage to the cotton field left the sharecropper and tenant little time for subsistence farming, but sweet potatoes, a little corn, a garden with a few collards and other truck helped him to eke out his food supply. Not everyone owned a cow, but some did. Nearly all kept a few chickens; most raised a hog or two. Many added to their larders in the winter by hunting rabbits and possums. At best, however, the sharecropper and the tenant, white or black, had a Spartan existence and knew no luxuries.

By shrewd management, planters of some larger tracts contrived to prosper, and by 1900, despite periods of depression, South Carolina from the seacoast to the mountains was dotted with substantial homes, comfortable wooden houses of no architectural pretensions, usually painted white, though some owners let the natural wood weather to a soft gray. Although a few of the more prosperous cotton planters attained moderate wealth, most were lucky if they could boast a servant or two and keep their debts paid. In many respects, South Carolina's economy was virtually cashless. Not many citizens had money to throw around.

The never-ending grind of the cotton economy left little time or inclination in many areas of the Up Country for improving the land. Neglect during the Civil War and immediately afterward resulted in soil erosion that continued for years until the rolling red hills were cut by gullies that sometimes looked like small ravines. Worse still was the diminishing return from the exhausted soil. Land planted year after year in cotton gradually wore out. Unless heavily fertilized, the cotton stalks hardly grew knee-high, looked spindly and stunted, and produced only a hatful of bolls. World War I, however, brought an enormous increase in the price of cotton, which reached an unprecedented forty cents per pound. The total value of the state's agricultural products nearly trebled, and many a farmer managed to get out of debt.

He was fortunate if he did, because the boll weevil picked this period to invade the state, and by 1921 cotton production had been cut in half. Gradually, farmers learned to cope with the weevil by using vast quantities of arsenic poison, which added to cost and introduced a new hazard to health generally unrecognized at the time. The boll weevil was followed by two depressions that left many a cotton farmer bankrupt.

But intelligent men had been trying to salvage South Carolina's agriculture. Clemson College (now Clemson University), which started as a state agricultural college, received its first class in 1893 and exerted a powerful influence on the state's economy. It trained county agents who taught soil improvement and the value of diversification. Beginning in 1914, an ingenious seedsman of Hartsville, David R. Coker, introduced new and better varieties of cotton, better methods of fighting the boll weevil, and encouraged the growing of the best types of corn, sweet potatoes, soybeans, and small grains such as wheat and oats.

The cultivation of tobacco, tried in colonial times, was stimulated in 1890 by the introduction of a bright-leaf variety. By the end of the century, the tobacco crop brought in a million dollars each year. Most of it was grown in the Low Country. Truck farming gradually brought prosperity to some areas that once had depended upon rice as the sole crop. But despite improvements in agriculture, so long as cotton remained the principal money crop, South Carolina could not hope to compete with agricultural states with better soil. The rejuvenation of its farmlands would have to wait for new developments a bit later.

The salvation of the poor tenant farmer and sharecropper came with increased development of industry, especially textiles. Although William Gregg at Graniteville had been a pioneer builder of cotton factories before the Civil War, by 1860 the state had only seventeen mills, employing a total of 891 workers. By 1900, the number of mills had increased to 115, with 30,201 workers; and by 1930, the mills numbered 239, with 94,756 workers. The great development took place in Greenville, Spartanburg, and Anderson counties, though other areas made notable progress.

The building of mills was often a community enterprise with local citizens buying stock, sometimes more than they could afford, because it was a patriotic endeavor. Mills would bring prosperity, it was believed, to any town able to build them. Some capital was sought in the North but, wherever possible, South Carolinians tried to retain control.

The greatest asset of the textile factories in South Carolina was what seemed an inexhaustible supply of labor. Farmers with their families deserted their rented shacks on the land and flocked to the mill villages, where all of them could find work and better houses than they had ever known. For all the mills, there were villages built of simple, substantial cottages within walking distance of the workers' jobs. Before the automobile or the development of mass transportation, the village was essential, because workers had no way of getting to work from their country farms. The village in time revolutionized the social condition of the workers, for the management provided schools for their children, built churches and supplied preachers, and set aside land for gardens as well as for recreation. Many of the mill villages organized baseball teams that challenged neighboring mills. The schools and churches became centers of social activities previously unknown in the country. Although later generations of social thinkers have condemned the mill villages as paternalistic, they were essential at the time they were created, and they served a highly useful social purpose in educating a generation of poor whites, many of them illiterate, to a better way of life.

As time went on, some mill villages showed a concern for aesthetics and genuine town planning. Examples were the villages of the Greenwood Cotton Mills, the creation of a local citizen of that town, James C. Self. Neat brick houses, well-kept lawns, handsome schools and churches characterized these villages. When corporate villages were no longer necessary, the houses were sold to the workers. Self illustrated the best type of South Carolina capitalist. Born in Greenwood County, he began as a clerk in a country store in the hamlet of Kirksey, moved to a bank job in Greenwood, and ultimately became an official in a struggling cotton mill in the town. At his death, he had succeeded in developing one of the most impressive textile empires in the state and had become a generous philanthropist. A hospital that he built and presented to the town of Greenwood is one of the most modern and best equipped in the state.

From 1930 onward, the textile industry has continued to grow throughout the Up Country. With the invention of synthetic fibers, factories to make the synthetics and to manufacture them into fabrics rapidly developed. Capital from the North and from foreign countries poured into the state, along with skilled technicians from this country and abroad. Today, German and Japanese businessmen and specialists of various sorts can be met any day on the streets of Greenville and Spartanburg.

The development of the textile industry helped the Negro population only peripherally. A few mills at first hired black workers, but the experiment did not work out. The mill owners claimed that blacks were unreliable and inept; the white workers objected to their company and their competition. So black workers were relegated to unskilled, outside jobs.

For many years after the Civil War, the Negro's economic lot was bleak. Ill-educated and untrained, he had to be content as a farm laborer or a sharecropper. An effort had been made by the Freedmen's Bureau to allot plots of land to black owners, but most of them soon lost their land and drifted away. A few, however, retained their holdings and became independent farmers. In Greenwood County, a region still known as Promised Land consists of farms owned by Negroes whose ancestors received them from the Freedmen's Bureau. But the owners of Promised Land are in the minority. Most of the recipients of the largesse of the Freedmen's Bureau quickly ceased to be independent farmers, and most became day laborers or sharecroppers. The legend long persisted that the Freedmen's Bureau planned to give every black forty acres and a mule, but few Negroes ever received any land or even a mule. The industrial development in South Carolina before World War I provided more jobs, but the blacks remained at the bottom of the labor totem pole.

Labor scarcity in the North during World War I had profound repercussions upon the black population of South Carolina. A few who first ventured to New York, Philadelphia, and Washington sent word back to their relatives, and soon a constant stream of migrants headed North. For South Carolina Negroes, Philadelphia was the most popular haven, but all the eastern industrial centers drew a quota. Farms were deserted, sometimes with crops still growing. Small towns lost most of their "help." South Carolinians had to learn to do without cheap black labor.

The black ghettos of the North did not always prove the heavens that had been pictured. During the depression of the 'thirties, many blacks drifted back to the South. With the improvement in race relations in recent years and a fairer wage scale, a reverse migration has begun, and Negroes are returning to better jobs, better homes, and more satisfactory living conditions than they previously had known in the South or found in the North.

From colonial times, transportation in South Carolina had been a problem, the result of unnavigable rivers, streams, and swamps. By 1860, the state had already developed a network of railroads, but these were virtually all destroyed or impaired by Sherman's raiders. After the Civil War, the state embarked on a feverish railway development. By the end of the nineteenth century, nearly every town of any size had some sort of railway connection. The shortest and most distinctive was the Due West Railway, connecting that little college town with the junction point at Donalds, a distance of five miles. Owned by Associated Reformed Presbyterians, the Due West did not run on Sunday and would not haul liquor.

After World War I, the state embarked on a highway construction program that ultimately resulted in numerous throughways between the principal cities connecting with the interstate highway system. The building of concrete highways and the development of interstate trucking companies vastly curtailed rail traffic. Many small feeder lines were abandoned, and passenger trains gave way to buses and private automobiles. Smooth highways and the almost universal ownership of automobiles spelled the ruin of small towns. No longer were they self-contained entities; they became dormitory towns for industrial centers. Shoppers no longer depended upon the local drygoods merchant, milliner, or even grocer, but journeyed to the nearest chain store or shopping plaza for both routine supplies and luxuries.

Ironically, wars in our generation have helped to restore some of the prosperity destroyed during the Civil War. The two World Wars saw thousands of soldiers, sailors, and marines trained in South Carolina. Camp Wadsworth, in Spartanburg, one of the first training centers for troops in 1917, brought the Twenty-Seventh Division from New York to South Carolina, the first "invasion" of Yankee troops since Reconstruction. Some friction between soldiers and townspeople developed, but on the whole the experience was beneficial, both economically and socially. Greenville had another training center, Camp Sevier. After the war, a number of soldiers returned to settle in South Carolina. Camp Jackson (now Fort Jackson) at Columbia proved an even larger and more permanent army establishment. It has brought to Columbia vastly more wealth than Sherman destroyed. In similar fashion, the Charleston Navy Yard in two wars has released in Charleston enormous payrolls and provided thousands of jobs to civilians, an economic asset that has brought renewed prosperity to that proud coastal city. An unexpected dividend for Charleston has been the large number of retired men from the armed services who have chosen that city for permanent homes. Parris Island, site of early French and Spanish forts, has become the largest marine training base in the United States.

The demands of industry for electric energy helped to change the face of South Carolina's landscape. Streams that in colonial times had provided water power for a few gristmills were harnessed to turn electric turbines. In 1930, a great dam across the Saluda River ten miles west of Columbia created Lake Murray, at the time of its completion the largest power reservoir in the United States. Twelve years later, dams across the Santee and Cooper rivers impounded water that drowned former rice fields and swamps and made the huge Lake Marion and Lake Moultrie. Designed principally for power, these lakes have also become pleasure resorts for boating and fishing. Earlier, a dam farther up the Saluda had made another important power source by creating Lake Greenwood. In the extreme northwest portion of the state, Lake Jocassee and Lake Keowee occupy land once claimed by the Cherokees and provide water for a nuclear plant as well as power for conventional hydroelectric turbines.

On the Savannah River, a complex of dams impounds water in the Hartwell and the Clark reservoirs. These lakes extend their fingers deep into Pickens, Anderson, Abbeville, and McCormick counties. Below Augusta on the South Carolina side, the Atomic Energy Commission occupies land that was once the site of Ellenton and other small towns. The vast plant built here for the U.S. government by the Du Pont Company during World War II remains an important resource of the Atomic Energy Commission.

Elsewhere in the state, especially on the Catawba and Wateree rivers, dams have made lakes that provide hydroelectric power and fishing for sportsmen. Where, in the period before World War I, a fisherman could only hope to catch a few mudcats in the murky red rivers of the Up Country, he can now land bass, bream, and other varieties of edible scale fish from clear lakes.

A discovery by a Georgia chemist, Dr. Charles Herty, during the depression of the 'thirties had a tremendous impact upon South Carolina agriculture. Dr. Herty invented a process for making paper out of loblolly pines, the commonest, quickest-growing pines in the Up Country. Profits from wild stands of pines induced farmers to plant worn-out cotton land in seedlings supplied by nurseries established by the State Commission on Forestry. During the next two decades, millions of pines were planted, and the work still goes on. South Carolina from the air now looks like a green carpet. Few red hills are any longer visible, and soil erosion cutting the land into gullied scars is no longer a problem.

The flight of cheap black labor from the farms necessitated a shift from labor-intensity crops to cattle raising. Cotton land was turned into thousands of acres of pastures, where black Angus or white-faced Herefords now graze contentedly while the landowners are even more contented at forgetting the worry of trying to find labor for row crops.

This is not to say that diversified farming and the production of a variety of crops have ceased, but farming has become a far more scientific enterprise than it was in the old days. Most tenant farmers have left the land for industrial jobs, and the sharecropper is extinct. South Carolina farms are larger, more mechanized, and more productive. "Frequently South Carolina ranks second to California in the production of peaches, and third to North Carolina and Kentucky in tobacco," Lander comments. "In truck crops for fresh markets, the state usually ranks from fourth to tenth in such crops as lima beans, snap beans, green peas, cucumbers, and watermelons." [5]

The growth in population of the Up Country from 1880 onward, and the drift of the poorer white population to industrial centers had a significant influence upon the political destiny of the state. Henceforth nonaristocratic farmers and industrial workers of the Up Country would have a majority of the votes, and they only needed a leader to help them shake off the dominance of the Low Country conservatives who had kept control of the whole region since colonial times.

That leader was found in Benjamin Ryan Tillman, a one-eyed Edgefield farmer with a vitriolic tongue who was elected governor and took office in 1890. Tillman's manners were coarse, his speech abusive, and his attacks on the Charleston and Columbia "establishment" bitter and effective. He made no bones about setting class against class and stirring up racial friction. His campaigns set precedents for demagogues for a generation to come. His violence and vituperation earned the scorn of the editor of the *Columbia State,* Narciso G. Gonzales, the aristocratic son of a Cuban revolutionary general. Gonzales was dedicated to Tillman's political destruction. In 1902, after Ben Tillman had been elected to the United States Senate, his nephew James H. Tillman, then serving as Lieutenant Governor, was running

5. Lander, *History of South Carolina,* p. 228.

for governor. Gonzales wrote in his paper that Jim Tillman was a "proven liar, defaulter, gambler, and drunkard." [6] Whereupon Jim Tillman shot him down on the streets of Columbia on January 15, 1903. The Tillman era was one of violence.

When Ben Tillman was governor, he helped push through the legislature a bill for establishing Winthrop College at Rock Hill for the education of women, and he encouraged the development of Clemson College. His Dispensary Law establishing state liquor stores was unpopular and led to corruption and even to a bloody riot at Darlington. His efforts to rewrite the state constitution led to the Constitution of 1895, which included a literacy test designed to curtail the Negro vote.

In the United States Senate, Tillman was a stormy petrel, often using the floor of the Senate for a demagogic speech to curry favor with his followers back home. He habitually fought the incumbent in the White House, whether Democrat or Republican. He got his sobriquet of "Pitchfork Ben" by declaring that he intended to take a pitchfork to Washington and poke it in the fat ribs of President Grover Cleveland. Yet, as he grew older, Tillman became more conservative and fostered constructive legislation, especially laws in aid of agriculture. His influence was responsible for breaking the tight hold of the Low Country upon the state and of giving the Up Country electorate power commensurate with its population. He remained in the Senate until his death in 1918 and was succeeded by a conservative moderate, N. G. Dial of Laurens.

Tillman's political tactics provided instruction for demagogues more cynical than he, the worst being Coleman L. Blease of Newberry who, after three tries, won election in 1910 as governor. Blease served as governor for three terms and defeated Senator Dial in the 1924 race for the United States Senate, where he served for one term. Blease was an unmitigated demagogue, who shouted about white supremacy, appealed to the cotton mill operatives by playing on their racial and other prejudices, and succeeded in creating a voting bloc of the most ignorant and most easily influenced of the poor whites in the

6. Wallace, *South Carolina*, p. 651.

state. His period as governor was characterized by corruption, and his term in the United States Senate by blustering rhetoric and ranting, especially when he chose to filibuster against some bill he disliked. In 1930, James F. Byrnes, who became one of South Carolina's ablest statesmen, defeated Blease for a second term in the Senate.

In spite of his bloc of what he himself was pleased to call his "wool-hat boys," Blease never again was able to win a public office. He tried to unseat veteran Senator Ellison D. Smith in 1932 and failed. Smith, known as "Cotton Ed" for his consistent efforts over many years to promote legislation that would benefit cotton farmers, was no novice at campaigning and knew how to appeal to the poor whites as well as to the better element. So successful was he that he stayed in the Senate longer than any other South Carolinian.

Increasing literacy, an influx of intelligent citizens from outside the state, the gradual decrease of semiliterate poor whites, and the improvement of social and economic conditions throughout the state have produced an electorate no longer susceptible to the kind of rhetoric used by Ben Tillman and Cole Blease. At last, South Carolina has the beginning of a two-party system. At the moment, one of its United States senators is a Republican. The friction between Up Country and Low Country has gradually diminished, largely because of a greater homogeneity of interest in all regions as a result of the diversity of industrialization.

The race question remains a problem, but South Carolina after much bluster has settled down to an acceptance of the essentials of civil rights legislation. The schools are desegregated; Negroes are accepted without question as workers in the textile and other industries alongside whites; and there has been far less racial disturbance than in many a northern metropolitan area. All is not perfect, of course, but the state has come a long way since the enactment of the "Black Code" in 1865.

With the prosperity that industrial development and diversified agriculture have brought, the state has made immense strides in education and in cultural affairs of all sorts. In the 1920s, H. L. Mencken could sneer at the South as the "desert of the Bozart,'' and he could point to South Carolina as particularly backward. But that is past history. The older colleges—Wofford, Furman, Erskine, Presbyterian College, Newberry, and others—have expanded and have made important contributions to the state and nation through their graduates. The University of South Carolina has made phenomenal strides and has branches throughout the state. Clemson, once merely an agricultural and mechanical college, is now a university with an excellent record, especially in the sciences.

The principal cities have centers for the promotion of music and the arts. No town of any size is without a good library. Some of these libraries have set about collecting local historical material and have become useful historical resources. Greenwood, for example, has a remarkable collection dealing with the history of that region.

Historians have reason to thank the South Caroliniana Library at the University of South Carolina in Columbia and the Charleston Library Society for their efforts in finding, preserving, and making available historical source material from colonial times to the present. The University of South Carolina Press has performed an important service to the state by publishing such landmark works as the papers of Henry Laurens and John C. Calhoun, and the writings of William Gilmore Simms.

We cannot afford to be complacent, however, for many states still surpass South Carolina in educational facilities, in cultural opportunities, and in the average annual income of their citizens. We are still capable of producing loud-mouthed demagogues in politics, though their dominance is far less marked than in the days of Tillman and Blease. Indeed, we have been luckier in our leaders at times than we deserved. While Tillman was fulminating in 1902, for instance, the state managed to elect as governor Duncan Clinch Heyward of Colleton County. Heyward, descendant of an ancient and honorable family of rice planters, was a gentleman and a wise and intelligent governor. Later, with Cole Blease making the most blatant appeal to the prejudices of the electorate, the state came to its senses and in 1930 elected James F. Byrnes of Spartanburg to the Senate. Byrnes went on to become a justice of the United States Supreme Court, Secretary of State, Director of War Mobilization during World War II, and virtually "assistant president" under Franklin D. Roosevelt.

Like Scotland, South Carolina has produced a surplus of competent men and women for export. Throughout the country, South Carolinians can be found in colleges and universities, in positions of trust in many great corporations, and on the staffs of publishing houses and newspapers. The state need not preen itself too much on this fact: many of these men and women left home because the opportunities were so much greater elsewhere.

Although we have come a long way since the state lay prostrate in 1865–1876, we still have far to go. No longer do we moan over the "lost cause," because most of us realize that the cause was a mistaken one. Although we revere the memories of our ancestors who fought heroically for that cause, we are not willing to accept at face value the fictions generated about the glory of antebellum culture. We may wish for a greater degree of states' rights, but we no longer believe that the states ought to be supreme over the national government. Our political thinking has become more realistic than it was when we were hypnotized by the sophistries of John C. Calhoun.

Yet we are still an obstinate and stubborn people, slow to accept change and suspicious of social innovations. We once fought compulsory education, child labor laws, and the expansion of the suffrage. Only in 1948 did South Carolina legalize divorce, the last state in the Union to do so. We are willing to criticize ourselves, but we resent the unfavorable comment of outlanders. The surest way to arouse a South Carolinian to defend a dubious cause is for a supercilious Yankee to ridicule it. We do not like to be called to repentance or reform unless it is by one of our own kind.

In spite of our faults and an innate contentiousness, South Carolina has astonished itself and others by its progress in our time. We have achieved a reasonable peace among ourselves. We have improved our natural environment: from the mountains to the coast, the green revolution has brought us profit and pleasure, and our land, clothed in green trees or pasture grass, lies inviting before us. Great lakes dotted with pleasure boats have blotted out miasmic swamps. It is a pleasant land in which the populace, white and black, can take pride and find satisfaction.

Epilogue

$\mathcal{W}$E South Carolinians are proud of our state. Although we have often quarreled among ourselves and still oftener thumbed our noses at other folk, we are at heart a kind and generous people. We Up-Countrymen can even be forgiving and simply shrug when Charlestonians maintain that only they, who have weathered quietly in salt air, have any genuine patina of culture. Likely as not, such Charlestonians are recent emigrants from New Jersey or Indiana, for there is no zeal like that of a convert. And South Carolina, both in the Low Country and the Piedmont, now can count many emigrants from all over the United States—and even from foreign countries. A retired army colonel, after looking the country over, decided to retire in the pleasant suburbs of Spartanburg. He liked the climate, and he liked the people. We welcomed him, as we have welcomed countless others, not ostentatiously, with a "Welcome Wagon," but with the kindly handshake of a neighbor who is pleased to have him sit on his porch of an evening and swap yarns of other days and other places.

The colonel is right about the climate. It is temperate and rarely violently extreme. But occasionally, lest we take the weather for granted, a tornado cuts a destructive path across the state in spring, and every few years a hurricane blows up out of the Caribbean to devastate the coastal region. These, however, are abnormal aberrations. In general, South Carolina enjoys long springs with gorgeous flowers, wild and cultivated: flaming azaleas, camellias of every color, hillsides of snowy dogwood, and meadows of wild iris and violets. The summers are long and lazy, sometimes sizzling hot but usually moderate with

210

cooling breezes. This is the season of peaches ripe from the tree, dripping juice as sweet as honey. Outlanders who have never picked a dead-ripe peach from the tree don't know what a gourmet delicacy they have missed. Summer is also the time of luscious watermelons, of barbecues and picnics and fish-fries, a time for lazing in the sun on creek bank or lake shore, waiting for the fish to bite.

Autumn—or the fall, as we say—is the best time of all, in the opinion of many. Like summer, it too is a fruitful season, with red apples hanging from the trees and sparkling cider sold on roadside stands. In the memory of men still living, covered wagons from the mountains used to bring down, each fall, apples, cabbages, cider, and chestnuts—and perhaps a drop of moonshine for the knowing and the thirsty. But chestnut trees are long since dead of blight, covered wagons have gone the way of prairie schooners, and moonshining isn't what it used to be. Fall is also the time when South Carolina sportsmen get out their guns, call their bird dogs, and beat broomsedge and pea fields in search of partridges. Northern sportsmen come down to their lodges in the old rice fields looking for quail. Later in the season, they will go hunting for deer and wild turkey.

Game is now more plentiful than it was a century ago. During colonial times, deer were so numerous that their skins were one of the region's principal exports. They never died out, but they got mighty scarce in the nineteenth century. With reforestation, they have made a tremendous comeback. Controlled hunting in the state and national forests is necessary to keep the deer population within the limits of the food supply. Wild turkeys are now once more abundant in these forests.

Winter is the time that attracts most hunters of deer and turkeys. The winters are rarely severe. During the first century of South Carolina's development, when experiments were being made with all kinds of exotic plants and fruits, oranges were grown on the coast until a few destructive—and unusual—cold spells discouraged further attempts to produce tropical fruits.

A generation ago, the crisp early days of fall saw the harvesting of sorghum cane. Nearly every farm had a cane mill, where a mule hitched to a sweep turned the grinders that pressed out the cane juice, caught in wooden tubs. The juice was heated in a nearby evaporator that boiled it into syrup—"long sweetening," the field hands called it. Sorghum is still grown for cattle feed, but few any longer bother to make syrup. This is a pity, because "sorghum molasses" had a piquant taste and body different from other syrups. Many a South Carolinian would prefer sorghum to maple syrup—if he could get it.

Chambers of Commerce and garden clubs advertise the glory of South Carolina in the spring—and well they may—but someone should speak up for the fall. Only sufferers from hayfever will regret nature's abundance then, for one must admit that ragweeds grow with vigor throughout the state. But that plague aside, few times are more satisfactory. From late September until the end of November, the countryside glows with a mixed palate of color.

Already, in September, in the hill country of Oconee, Pickens, Greenville, Spartanburg, Cherokee, and York counties, the sumac is turning red. Pokeberry bushes along the roadside hang heavy with purple berries. Just a little color is beginning to show in the forest trees: yellow in hickory and maples, red in sweetgums and blackgums; in another month, all the hillsides will be a blend of variegated colors in every shade and hue of yellow and red. The last leaves to fall will be the oaks and sweetgums. Some oak leaves will slowly turn brown and hang on the limbs until spring. Small boys will hurry to the woods to pick up hickory nuts and, here and there, black walnuts.

The hill country has no monopoly of fall coloring; it just begins there first and slowly trickles south, like colored ink spreading on a blotter. By November, gum trees in the swamps of the Low Country will blaze with color against the green of pine and cypress. The limbs of persimmon trees will bend under their burden of fruit, astringent when just beginning to ripen, but sweet as sugar after frost falls. During the Civil War, persimmons were eaten in place of raisins and dates, and they are still regarded as a highly edible fruit. A tasty beer is often made by fermenting persimmons in a keg on a bed of clean wheat straw to filter it. The drink is amber-colored, sparkling, and potent.

So South Carolinians can still revel in external nature and the good things it supplies to the eye and the taste. Although industry has transformed the economy and even the appearance of much of the state, the population can still get out into the country. We remain a rural land. The newer incoming industries, particularly chemical and drug plants, have taken care to landscape their premises to make them look almost like parks.

Although we have retained the appearance of a rural state, industrialization has had a profound effect upon both the economics and the culture of the whole region. Although we remain politically volatile, with strong prejudices against outside interference in our affairs, we are much more tolerant than we were even a generation ago. Low Country and Up Country continue to be aware of their differences, but the spread of industry throughout the state and the multiplication of industrial workers from Charleston to Oconee County have tended to blur the social differences of the two regions. No longer are planters in the coastal area great magnates influencing the political life of the whole state. The rich plantations have disappeared: some to become industrial "parks," others to become real estate developments and playgrounds for tourists. The landed magnate of an earlier age is now likely to be president of a fertilizer factory or of a chemical plant. He shares an economic and political affinity with his managerial brethren in the textile industries of the Up Country.

This is not to say that we have suddenly become a benign and blessed land free of contention, economic and political. We can still work up a great head of steam in an election year. But conditions have been changing. South Carolina in 1974 elected a Republican governor, the first since Reconstruction, and its senior United States senator is also a Republican. These changes represent a new sophistication in the electorate, a refusal to be stampeded by old clichés, like "white supremacy."

The new tolerance has made racial tensions less acute. Black South Carolinians who emigrated to the North in previous years have been coming home in increasing number. The state offers better opportunities and greater freedom than the ghettoes of New York, Detroit, and Chicago. Southern industry at all levels is absorbing larger numbers of black workers.

The most obvious difference between the present generation

and earlier periods is the relief from widespread poverty. The sheer struggle to survive is no longer acute, as it was during the Great Depression of the early 1930s and a generation before. The relative ease with which most people nowadays can procure basic needs and even luxuries has made the population more tolerant and less contentious. Nearly everybody has a motor car of sorts, and we, like other Americans, have become a people in constant motion. Only an acute energy crisis will curb our appetite for speed over South Carolina's vast network of concrete highways. The ability of the populace to visit all parts of the state has helped to break down insularity. This is not to say that we have eliminated provincialisms: backcountrymen in the mountain regions or in isolated pockets in the Low Country retain many of their old ways, but there are fewer regional prejudices than existed in an earlier period. The Up Country can now smile with tolerance over Charleston's air of superiority, especially when expressed by some neo-Charlestonian from Indiana or New Jersey.

If we have not yet made our region blossom into the paradise that Sir Walter Raleigh believed might exist along the 35th parallel of north latitude, we have made a beginning. Natives of the state, long absent, come back and view the changes with astonishment and approval. A few may be nostalgic for the good old days that never were, but the realists know that South Carolina is now a better place to live for both rich and poor, black and white.

Suggestions for Further Reading

The history of South Carolina is well recorded, and good bibliographies appear in the recent histories. The most comprehensive reading list for nonspecialists is Lewis P. Jones, *Books and Articles on South Carolina History,* Tricentennial Booklet no. 8 (Columbia: University of South Carolina Press, 1970). A more detailed bibliography is J. H. Easterby, *A Guide to the Study and Reading of South Carolina History: A General Classified Bibliography* (Columbia: University of South Carolina Press, 1950). Lewis P. Jones's *South Carolina: A Synoptic History for Laymen* (Columbia: University of South Carolina Press, 1971) is readable, accurate, and succinct, the best available history of South Carolina for readers who do not want to become bogged down in too much detail.

The wisest, most comprehensive general history is David Duncan Wallace, *History of South Carolina,* 4 volumes (New York: American Historical Society, 1934). The fourth volume, not compiled by Wallace, contains biographical sketches of South Carolinians, many of them obscure. A condensed version of Wallace, *South Carolina: A Short History* (Chapel Hill: University of North Carolina Press, 1951) is almost as inclusive as the longer work.

A readable book supplying folklore and human interest is Henry Savage, *River of the Carolinas: The Santee* (Chapel Hill: University of North Carolina Press, 1968); and a good account of aboriginal inhabitants will be found in Chapman J. Milling, *Red Carolinians* (Chapel Hill: University of North Carolina Press, 1940).

Writing on the colonial period, theme of countless books, centers in Charleston and the Low Country. Verner W. Crane, *The Southern Frontier, 1670–1732* (Durham: Duke University Press, 1928) is a pioneer work, useful and readable. Paul Quattlebaum, *The Land Called Chicora: The Carolinas under Spanish Rule* (Gainesville: University of Florida Press, 1956) gives an account of early European competition for the Carolinas. M. Eugene Sirmans, *Colonial South Carolina:*

215

A Political History, 1663–1763 (Chapel Hill: University of North Carolina Press, 1966) brings much controversial material in earlier works into proper perspective. An excellent book on the intellectual life of Charleston in the colonial period is Frederick P. Bowes, *The Culture of Early Charleston* (Chapel Hill: University of North Carolina Press, 1942). A readable account of rice culture in South Carolina, written from the experiences and records of the author's own family, is Duncan C. Heyward, *Seed from Madagascar* (Chapel Hill: University of North Carolina Press, 1937).

One of the most useful books on the War of Independence in South Carolina is John R. Alden, *The South in the Revolution, 1763–1789* (Baton Rouge: Louisiana State University Press, 1957). An old work, filled with detail of war in the Up Country, is Lyman C. Draper, *King's Mountain and Its Heroes* (1881; reprint ed., Baltimore: Genealogical Publishing Co., 1967).

Literature on slavery is voluminous and controversial. A good account is Peter H. Wood, *Black Majority: Negroes in Colonial South Carolina from 1670 through the Stono Rebellion* (New York: Knopf, 1974). U. B. Phillips, *Life and Labor in the Old South* (Boston: Little, Brown, 1929) is a classic on the subject, but is now out of favor because of its old-fashioned concepts. A highly controversial work, Robert W. Fogel and Stanley L. Engerman, *Time on the Cross,* 2 volumes (Boston: Little, Brown, 1974), seems certain to alter many clichés about the condition of slaves and their place in the economic picture.

From the Revolution to the Civil War, books on the state are numerous. Considerable attention to South Carolina is given in Thomas P. Abernethy, *The South in the New Nation, 1789–1819* (Baton Rouge: Louisiana State University Press, 1961). Rosser H. Taylor, *Ante-Bellum South Carolina: A Social and Cultural History* (Chapel Hill: University of North Carolina Press, 1942) is a useful survey.

The story of the Civil War has been told and retold. Some books of particular relevance for South Carolina are: Charles E. Cauthen, *South Carolina Goes to War, 1860–65* (Chapel Hill: University of North Carolina Press, 1950); John Barrett, *Sherman's March Through the Carolinas* (Chapel Hill: University of North Carolina Press, 1956); and James G. Randall and David Donald, *Civil War and Reconstruction,* 2nd edition (Boston: Heath, 1961).

Much has been written recently to revise the story of Reconstruction in the South, especially in South Carolina. A concise treatment of the subject, with a brief appraisal of recent works, is Ernest M. Lander's *A History of South Carolina, 1865–1960* (Columbia: University of South Carolina Press, 1970). Francis B. Simkins and Robert H. Woody, *South Carolina during Reconstruction* (Chapel Hill: University of North Carolina Press, 1932) remains a standard, reliable treatment of the subject. Wallace's observations on Reconstruction, although written long before the flood of revisionist books, reveal farsighted wisdom and accuracy. Lewis Jones's *South Carolina: A Synoptic History* also gives a good account of Reconstruction.

The development of industry in South Carolina is traced in Broadus Mitchell, *The Rise of the Cotton Mills in the South* (Baltimore: Johns Hopkins Press, 1921). The story of the political independence of the Up Country is told in Francis B. Simkins, *The Tillman Movement in South Carolina* (Durham: Duke University Press, 1921). Ben Robertson, *Red Hills and Cotton: An Upcountry Memory* (New York: Knopf, 1942) is a poetic but shrewd appraisal of Up-Country life. In somewhat similar vein is Louis B. Wright, *Barefoot in Arcadia: Memories of a More Innocent Era* (Columbia: University of South Carolina Press, 1974), which deals with the first two decades of the twentieth century.

Index